*I was aware once more of the
continuity of life, as if I were a
part of events past, present,
and to come, and I could choose
my way among them*

Alison Uttley, *A Traveller in Time*

Travelers in Time

Past, Present, and to Come

CLNE/Green Bay

The Publishers wish to thank the following for permission to reproduce copyright material:
Hans Siegal and Greenwillow Books for permission to use the cover and titlepage logo, from *The Windeye* by Robert Westall;
Shirley Hughes and Victor Gollancz Ltd. for illustrations from *The Secret Garden,* and for a sketch of 'Alfie'; Viking/Penguin Ltd.,
for the illustration from *Thy Friend, Obadiah* by Brinton Turkle; Julia Macrae for the illustration from *Hansel and Gretel* by
Anthony Browne; Jonathan Cape Ltd. for the illustration from *Come Away from the Water, Shirley,* by John Burningham; Peter
Dickinson for permission to quote stanzas from Merlin Dreams.
Illustration from *My Noah's Ark* by M.B. Goffstein, Copyright (C) 1978 By M.B. Goffstein and illustration from *Come Away from
the Water, Shirley,* (Thomas Y. Crowell)Copyright (C) 1977 by John Burningham. Both illustrations reprinted by permission of
Harper & Rowe, Publishers inc. Illustration from *Sylvester and the Magic Pebble* by William Steig (C) 1969 reprinted by permission
of the publisher, Simon & Schuster Inc, New York, NY.

Cover design by Pat Craddock

British Library Cataloguing in Publication Data
Travelers in time

1. Children's literature — critical studies
I. Children's Literature New England
   809.89282

ISBN 0 948845 02 3

First published 1990 by Green Bay Publications
72, Water Lane, Histon, Cambridge CB4 4LR

Printed in Great Britain by Antony Rowe Ltd.
Bumper's Farm, Chippenham
Wiltshire SN14 6QA

CONTENTS

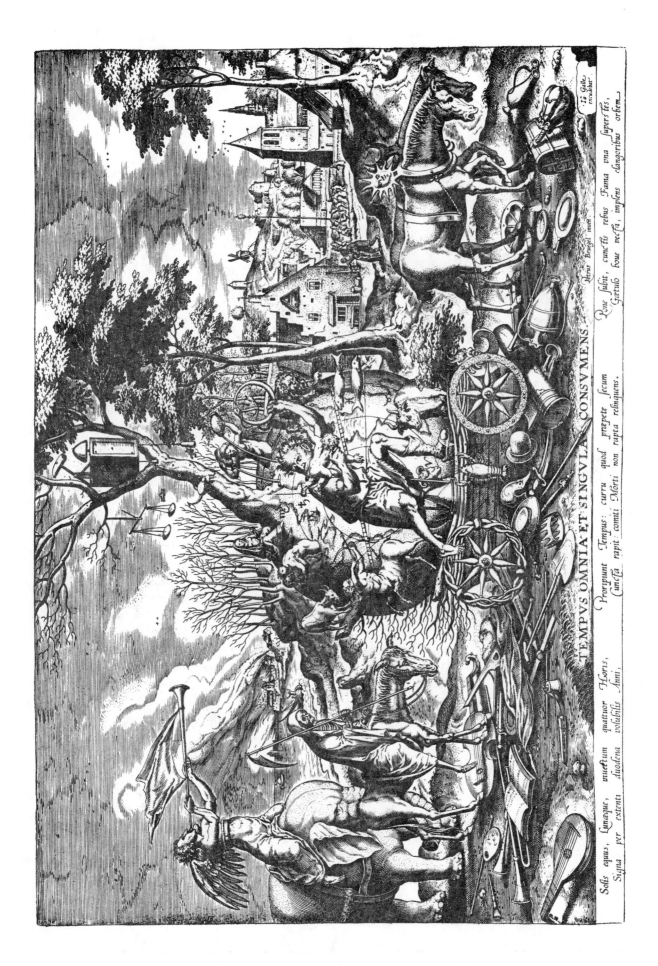

TEMPVS OMNIA ET SINGVLA CONSVMENS.

Petrus Bruegel inuen.

Ioã Galle
excudebat

Solis equus, Lunæque, innectum quattuor Horis,   Prorumpunt Tempus: curru quod præpete secum   Pone subit, cunctis rebus Fama vna superstes,
Signa per extenti diuodena volubilis Anni,   Cuncta rapit comiti comiti Morti non rapta relinquens.   Gætulo boue vecta, implens clangoribus orbem.

PREFACE

AT THE SOUND of the words *Once upon a time*, people are brought to rapt attention. They move forward in their chairs and lean in the direction of the teller. They sense that the story they are about to hear has been singled out from infinite possibilities, that it is a story worth passing on, gleaned from all the rest — the one that is apt to create coherence in their too-often random and incoherent lives. The words are pure magic, an arousing call. At Newnham College in the context of the institute's challenging title, "Once upon a time" was a recurring motif keeping participants at the edge of their seats.

"Once upon a time" might mean a long, long time ago but, then again, as Helen Cresswell writes in the opening sentence of her book *The Secret World of Polly Flint*, it might mean last week or last year. Indeed, it might mean August 1989, when participants gathered their belongings and set out for Cambridge, England; or it might even mean this very second as you embark on these proceedings. For readers who attended the institute and who clamored for the proceedings, this material will seem familiar. Once upon a time, and twice upon a time, and a very good time it was — an exhilarating time.

In August 1989 two hundred intrepid travelers gathered at Newnham College, Cambridge University, Cambridge, England, to examine children's books in which time plays a central and animating role. The institute brought together a rare assemblage of talent

---

THE TRIUMPH OF TIME

The illustration on the facing page — an engraving by an unknown hand from an original by Pieter Bruegel the Elder — is extensively discussed in Barbara Harrison's introduction, pages 7 — 9

---

from both sides of the Atlantic. Speakers from England included such authors as Rosemary Sutcliff, Peter Dickinson, Philippa Pearce and from the United States, Virginia Hamilton, Katherine Paterson, Susan Cooper. This volume — *Travelers in Time: Past, Present and to Come* — constitutes the proceedings of the conference. It is the first book of proceedings to be published by Children's Literature New England.

Children's Literature New England, Inc., is a nonprofit educational organization incorporated under the laws of the Commonwealth of Massachusetts, to further children's literature studies. With the generous support of many friends, it was launched in 1987. Its board members were formerly associated with the Simmons College Center for the Study of Children's Literature in Boston, where for over a decade they developed and taught graduate courses and created programs in children's literature.

In 1987 Children's Literature New England presented an institute at Harvard University entitled *Robinson Crusoe and His Heirs: Survival and Conquest in Children's Books*. In 1988 at Massachusetts Institute of Technology, Children's Literature New England presented *The Heroic Ideal In Children's Books: Legacy and Promise*.

In addition to providing a forum for examining topics in children's literature, Children's Literature New England offers an opportunity for people to reaffirm the value of their work and to develop ways of transmitting their knowledge and love of children's books. The conviction of CLNE — its approach to studying the books — is that children's literature has integrity as art and as literature and should be considered critically in literary and artistic terms. CLNE organizes its programs around expansive themes, believing that the literature is a reflection of life and has something to teach us about ourselves and our times.

The institutes attract an extraordinary number of teachers, college professors, librarians, editors and aspiring and accomplished authors and illustrators, both as speakers and as conferees. At Newnham College individuals constituted a cross-section of the United States, England, Ireland, Scotland, Wales, Australia, Canada and Japan, all brought together by their love of children and books. Because of the limits of space, at least one hundred people were turned away.

For one week participants devoted themselves to the business of unraveling time in an effort to comprehend its texture, its meaning, its profound hold on the imagination. In the introduction to the institute, questions central to the inquiry were raised: What is the definition of time? What are the contours and shapes of time in children's fiction? How do children — in reality — perceive time? What imaginative possibilities of time are experienced by child protagonists in their fictive worlds? Months before the institute began, participants received a recommended list of contemporary children's books of remarkable imaginative power; these people had done substantial reading in preparation for the program.

Susan Cooper commented in her talk, "I daresay a lot of piles of books had Eliot's *Four Quartets* at one end and Stephen Hawking's *A Brief History of Time* at the other." Among the wealth of books between Eliot and Hawking were Cooper's own *The Dark is Rising*, Virginia Hamilton's *Arilla Sun Down*, Natalie Babbitt's *Tuck Everlasting*, Alan Garner's *Red Shift*, Philippa Pearce's *Tom's Midnight Garden*, and Alison Uttley's *A Traveler in Time*. For many participants *The Dark is Rising* was the quintessential time novel; for others, such as Susan Cooper, it was Alan Garner's *Red Shift*. For still others it was Virginia Hamilton's *Arilla Sun Down*. Several held John Burningham's *Come Away from the Water, Shirley* to be the emblematic picture book.

The talks represent a range and multiplicity of themes within the larger context of time in children's fiction. Given from the perspectives of the historian, psychologist, literary critic, author and illustrator, the talks contain some curious observations and some intriguing revelations.

Seminar leaders — Jill Paton Walsh, Paul Heins, Gregory Maguire, John Rowe Townsend, Betty Levin and Ethel Heins — formed the teaching base of the institute. Each of them was charged with the task of examining five or more books in the context of a particular time shape or category, including narrative time, memory, slippery time, past and future time and picture book time.

In discussing the books, seminar leaders considered such topics as the influence of art and technology on the language of memory and on Martin Heidegger's "presencing" — the observation that the past is present in the future; instructors provided images such as that suggested by Paul Heins of an accordion to reveal the dynamics of narrative time; at least one seminar leader outlined a concise history of time, while another explained the origin of the phrase *Once upon a time*.

Except for copy-editing, the talks are published as they were delivered. It has not been possible entirely to standardize British and American punctuation or spelling. The word *traveler* in the title is a case in point; the American spelling contains one *l*, and the British spelling contains two, causing no end of amusing consternation. Unfortunately, talks that were given off the cuff with few written notes are not represented in this collection. Although several lectures incorporated slides, constraints of space forced us to include only a few representative illustrations.

Conference proceedings — valuable though they are — cannot record the spirited exchanges among members of the small group discussions that were essential correlations to the plenary sessions. We would like to thank the discussion leaders not only for mediating discussions but for acting as house leaders, each discussion group a microcommunity within the Newnham College community. We are grateful to Therese Bigelow, Eleanor Cameron, Wendy Davis, Bert Porter, Ginny

Golodetz, Ginny Moore Kruse, Dorothy Powdermaker, Barbara Scotto, Frances Sedney, Ann Thwaite and Tony Watkins.

In proceedings it is difficult to recapture ambiance and tone — the informal chatter in the early morning hours among groups of joggers, the talk about the creative process among writers and aspiring writers clustered at breakfast, or the excitement among teachers talking about transforming time into a unit for classroom study. Or the journey taken by an appreciative group of pilgrims to Lucy Boston's ancient home in Hemingford Grey, the setting for her *Green Knowe* books, where in thanks for her hospitality, they gathered round her, singing "Wild Mountain Thyme" as a hymn of love. Or another group conversing with Philippa Pearce at her childhood home in Great Shelford, the setting for *Tom's Midnight Garden*. Or traveling with Ann Thwaite to her house in Norfolk while exploring the British countryside.

It is impossible to communicate in print the quality of beehive activity — in lectures, dialogues, panels, book discussions, receptions and common meals, during which old friendships were renewed and new ones were made. And of course it is impossible to re-create the sound of two hundred children's bibliophiles led by Ashley Bryan in a choral speaking of poems or conducted in song by John Langstaff — confirming the primacy of poetry and music in drawing people together in community. Or the feeling on being greeted on arrival in dorm rooms with a beautiful copy of Rupert Brooke's *The Old Vicarage, Grantchester,* which our indefatigable British organizers Jill Paton Walsh and John Rowe Townsend designed, typeset and printed as a gift to participants. And at week's end extended an invitation to all to join them for lunch in their home.

The amount of work, done by many people, in organizing a program such as *Travelers in*

Time is prodigious. CLNE would especially like to extend thanks to several individuals who contributed crucially to the success of the program: to Marilyn Butler, King Edward VII Professor of English in the University of Cambridge, whose speech of welcome, and whose presence in our midst on our opening night, signalled clearly the long-hoped-for end to the banishment of children's books from the field of serious academic literary studies; to Carolyn Gavett, institute registrar; to Martha Walke, who assisted in countless ways and helped Rosemary Davidson, who enthusiastically planned and led a coach tour of England following the institute; to Lindsey Fraser of Heffers Bookshop for her invaluable assistance in making books by institute speakers available for sale; to the unfailingly helpful Sharon Flint, of Newnham College; and to Hugh Surridge, Custodian of the Sidgwick site, — where the Lady Mitchell Hall, our home for the week's presentations is situated — an expert, willing media specialist.

For financial assistance and support we would like to thank the British Arts Council, the Welsh Arts Council, Children's Literature New England, Inc., the Foundation for Children's Books, Inc., Penguin Books Ltd, Heffers Booksellers Ltd, Victor Gollancz Ltd and the Glebe House Trust. These organizations provided assistance in underwriting many of the costs of the program and in providing bursaries and tuition assistance for American and British participants.

Finally a special thank you to Ethel Heins for her discreet copy-editing and to John Rowe Townsend and Jill Paton Walsh for the typesetting, design and production of this volume.

BARBARA HARRISON,
Cambridge, Massachusetts,
April, 1990

BARBARA HARRISON

Introduction

ON BEHALF of Children's Literature New England I would like to welcome you and to sound the gavel announcing the official opening of *Travelers in Time: Past, Present, and to Come*. My task this morning is to introduce the topic, to talk briefly about the nature of our investigation, and to raise questions central to its inquiry.

During the week, in formal and informal talks, panels, and discussions, we will examine the nature of time in children's books. Not time as it is merely measured by clock or calendar but time as a quality — a flavor, an atmosphere, a psychological phenomenon. Time in all its myriad configurations will be explored — time continuous and disjointed, logical and illogical, ordered and disordered.

So let it be recorded that at 9 o'clock am, on August 7, 1989, in Lady Mitchell Hall at Cambridge University, Cambridge, England, at an august gathering of speakers and conferees, it was roundly declared:

"The time has come," the Walrus said,
"To talk of many things:
    Of shoes — and ships — and sealing-wax —
    Of cabbages — and kings -
    And why the sea is boiling hot -
    And whether pigs have wings."[1]

Several years ago on an airplane I had the good fortune to sit next to a six-year-old child traveling alone. And in the course of talking of many things, she told me what she wanted to be when she grew up. She said that on Monday she wanted to be a doctor, on Tuesday, a lawyer, on Wednesday, a teacher, on Thursday, a ballet dancer, and so on. This young child had an amazingly fluent and agreeable relationship to time. As a citizen of the republic of childhood, she commanded time in enviable ways. Children "stand in a different relationship to the flow of time," Jill Paton Walsh reminds us. "They are nearer the beginning...They are the Lords of Time."[2]

The little girl also asked me if I wanted to hear a story she had written. She began, "Once upon a time near a great forest there lived a poor woodcutter and his wife and his two children; the boy's name was Hansel, and the girl's name was Gretel." She told me the story of Hansel and Gretel as if it were her own. My first reaction was that she had heard it told so many times that she had made it her own. But then it occurred to me that this child, in fact, could have written this story. Indeed, it was her story — once upon a time, in the great flux of time, the theme of every story ever told.[3]

For all of us the conference is indeed high adventure. We have come from many places near and far, brought together by our love of children and books. *Yo-Ko-So*. One hundred thousand welcomes. I arrived on Thursday, among my books, my dog-eared copy of John Rowe Townsend's children's novel and wonderful guide to Cambridge, *The Visitors*. This impressive gathering lends credibility to John's statement in the book that at this time of year lots of unusual things take place in Cambridge, England.

For Children's Literature New England this is a landmark event. We've coaxed Jill Paton Walsh and John Rowe Townsend to the New World many times, but this is the first time that we — in such great numbers — have come to the Old. We are excited about being here, grateful to both of them for the opportunity and grateful to them for their generous hospitality. We are delighted that so many accomplished people in the world of children's books could join us. The program represents a coalescing of two Cambridges, two Englands, both of which have come a long way from John Cotton's seventeenth-century *Spiritual Milk for Boston Babes in either England, Drawn out of the Breasts of Both Testaments.*

There is a particular kind of heroism that we herald every year at our institutes, and I would like to champion it this morning — the heroism that brings us all here in early August 1989. For there is a heroism implicit not only in being a poet, writer, or author but in upholding the arts and humanities in societies in which the arts and humanities are not valued highly enough. Your presence at this institute speaks to that heroism — the patience it takes as a teacher, librarian, writer, or parent to make a persuasive case for children's books, for the intelligence of the books, for their inextricable connection with language, with the imagination, with memory, and with our very freedom as human beings.

For over a decade, under the direction of the individuals sponsoring this program, many British and American authors, illustrators, publishers, educators and librarians have met in summer institutes to examine questions related to childhood, literature and society. In *The Child in Literature: Songs of Innocence, Songs of Experience* the visionary William Blake was the benevolent spirit at work. Lines from Blake's poems served as the organizing framework of the seminars.

In *Ithaka and other Journeys* we traveled figuratively to Odysseus' island. With us were the spirits of Homer and of the modern Greek poet C P Cavafy, whose lines provided the resonating challenge. Cavafy's challenge echoes here in this room at this embarkation, as it echoes in all our work —

> As we set out on the voyage to Ithaka
> Pray that the journey be long,
> Filled with adventures, filled with wisdom.

Recently, at Harvard University, we explored fictional heroes who like Robinson Crusoe are "divided from mankind ... solitaire ... banished from humane society." The program was entitled *Robinson Crusoe and His Heirs: Survival and Conquest in Children's Books.*

Last year at Massachusetts Institute of Technology we investigated heroism in contemporary life and literature at *The Heroic Ideal in Children's Books: Legacy and Promise.* And we also celebrated the heroism implicit in the creative process — which we do each year that we come together — the courage it takes to wage the lonely battle of putting words on paper.

Each institute is an extension of the other — all stories, in some way, one story. Each institute is not a beginning but a continuation.

Between last year and this year — from August 1988 to August 1989 — the sun rose and set 365 times as our own personal lives played themselves out against a backdrop of world events — individual time lines moving forward alongside the time line of history.

It was a year in which a book was denounced as blasphemous and the denunciation sent shivers of fear through the world; the price of more than five million dollars was placed on the author's head. In seclusion one frail and vulnerable man, born in Bombay, educated at Rugby and here at Cambridge University, has been trembling for his life. Salman Rushdie's personal time line and the world's public time line merge, coalescing, touching many of us in this room, and raising questions of censorship and freedom of expression. Human beings everywhere were affected by the edict from Iran.

It was a year in which a remarkable exhibit, *Goya and the Spirit of Enlightenment,* made its way from the Prado in Madrid to the Museum of Fine Arts in Boston, revealing Goya's preoccupation with the eternal conflict between light and dark and his relentless battle against forces of greed, bigotry and brutality. Francisco Goya, who was born in 1746 and died in 1828, talks to us today through the legacy of his art, giving testimony to the timelessness of art.

It was a year in which a researcher spent four months in a cave in Carlsbad, New Mexico, without clocks, sunlight, or any form of measuring time. During this period, her perception of time became completely awry. Just about the time the researcher emerged from her cave, Gregory Maguire's *I Feel Like the Morning Star* was published, and Greg's pilgrims emerged from their dark world and saw the light of day.

> This is the shape of the leaf, and this of the flower.
> And this the pale bole of the tree
> Which watches its bough in a pool of unwavering water
> In a land we never shall see...
> This is the shape of the tree,
> And the flower, and the leaf, and the three pale
>   beautiful pilgrims.

Gregory includes these lines from Conrad Aiken's *Priapus and the Pool, IV* as an endpiece in the book. Priapus is, among other things, a friend and protector of travelers.

And last night, August 6, 1989, as we celebrated the opening of our institute with poem and song, in ceremonies around the world and here in Cambridge, England, as well, the bombing of Hiroshima on August 6, 1945, was commemorated. From that day forty-four years ago, our perspective of time has never been the same.

Each of us is a traveler in time, a single current in the great river of time, participants and witnesses in an ongoing saga that began before we were born and will continue after we are gone.

The institute bookmark is a valuable source of recommended readings, including books carefully selected that will be discussed formally and informally throughout the week. We hope, as the week progresses, that the bookmark will also serve as a source of comic relief. On the bookmark, Harold Lloyd, Chaplinesque actor and mime, hangs by his fingertips from the hands of a clock, in what appears to be an effort to stop the flow of time. In juxtaposition, imagine Shakespeare's famous lines from *Henry the Sixth*:

> So many hours must I take my rest;
> So many hours must I contemplate;
> So many hours must I sport myself;
> So many days my ewes have been with young;
> So many weeks ere the poor fools will yean;
> So many years ere we shall shear the fleece;
> So minutes, hours, days, months, and years.

This week, as we examine one of the great mysteries, we will need to remind ourselves that yes, so many hours must we take our rest and contemplate and sport ourselves.

During the week, in studying the books, we will use two major measurements of time; one is public, or clock time, and the other is private, or individuated time — the one that prompts Josh Plowman in Ivan Southall's *Josh* to say on his first day at Aunt Clara's, "Yesterday's breakfast! How many thousand years ago was it?" Josh lives a week of time as if it were an eternity.

Southall is in familiar territory as he describes the eccentricities of the "timepiece of the mind." One of the important motifs in *Josh* is a disjuncture in time. Time is out of joint — a certain inexactness in the context of Josh's expectancy of exactness. Aunt Clara's house has a profusion of clocks, "a frantic confusion of nervous clocks all ticking against each other."

Through his use of language, Southall reveals his preoccupation with time. The language is spontaneous and fresh, swift, and energetic, with few syntactical boundaries. A long sentence is often followed by one word and a period. Repetition is not uncommon, often as a turn of the same phrase or the same thing said again and again in a different way. Southall's use of language conveys his perception of the passage of both clock time and psychological time. His obsession with time dramatically affects the treatment of his subject and provides us with a splendid example as we embark on our journey.

In a fascinating discussion, Frank Kermode, former professor of English at Cambridge University, explains time as that which takes place between *tick* and *tock* — "kairos ('the fate of time') poised between beginning and end." We humanize time, Kermode says, by providing the fictional difference between the two sounds. "Tick is a humble genesis, tock a feeble apocalypse."[4]

Plato describes time as "a moving image of eternity." In his recent article on our program in *The Times Educational Supplement*, John Townsend reminds us of St Augustine's declaration, "I know what time is, but if someone asks me, I cannot tell him." When I asked a few friends for a definition, one said, "Time is that quality that is running out."

In *The Court of the Stone Children* Eleanor Cameron defines time as Marc Chagall's river without banks — "Time is a river without banks," Nina says, "yes, immeasurable and indefinable." And in Philippa Pearce's *Tom's Midnight Garden*, Uncle Alan tries to explain time to Tom. "Imagine," he says, "a painter standing in a landscape and painting it, and a second painter coming behind him and painting the same landscape with the first painter's picture of the landscape in it, and yet a third painter coming up and painting the same landscape with the first painter's picture of the landscape and with the second painter's picture of the first painter's picture of the landscape, and then a fourth painter."

In addition to the quest for definition, there are other questions central to our inquiry: how is the growing societal consciousness of time — a preoccupation that has become increasingly articulated — reflected in children's books? Can Stephen Spender's statement that modern literature is obsessed with problems of time also be made about modern children's literature? What is the attitude of children's authors toward time? Is time viewed as enemy or friend?

In Helen Cresswell's *Winter of the Birds*, Mr Rudge lives without clocks and mirrors "because a clock is merely an anchor for time, and a looking glass an anchor for space." Mr Rudge says that most people "need to cage time, or rather to parcel it out in hours and minutes, or he might find that time was slipping free like sand through his fingers, and then he would be afraid."

How do children — in reality — perceive time? How could my young traveling companion believe that on Monday she could be a doctor, on Tuesday, a lawyer, on Wednesday, a teacher, on Thursday, a ballet dancer? Are children, as Penelope Lively suggests in *Moon Tiger*, traveling around in their own time capsules "inhabiting not our world but a world we have lost and can never recover?" Are they, as Jill described them, "Lords of Time?" And then, what are the elements of time in children's books — its

contours and shapes? In novels and picture books, what are the recurring motifs? What techniques are used for time slips and shifts? Our fundamental concern is the infinite imaginative possibilities of time experienced by child protagonists in their fictive worlds.

As I was thinking about ways of introducing our topic, I came across J T Fraser's book *The Voices of Time*. As a frontispiece, there is a reproduction of Pieter Bruegel's engraving "The Triumph of Time," and it provides a springboard as we make a quantum leap into a very complex subject.

In the picture Pieter Bruegel, the Elder, the sixteenth-century Flemish painter, working deliberately in the manner of Hieronymus Bosch, portrays countless symbols that the human imagination has brought to bear on the conception of time. Many of these motifs exist in the children's books we are considering. It might enlarge our understanding of the books to take a close look at the engraving, to identify the motifs, and this week to relate the motifs to the books under discussion.

In the center of the engraving, Bruegel depicts Father Time sitting on an hourglass. Bruegel portrays Father Time as the Greek god Cronus consuming his child, suggesting that Time devours all things. Francisco Goya and Peter Paul Rubens have rendered dramatic portrayals of the Titan Cronus devouring his child. In art there are many depictions of time, its meaning and symbolism, including those by Tiepolo and Salvador Dali.

The origin of the notion of time devouring all things is rooted in the Greek creation myth. When it is prophesied that one of his own children will overthrow him, Cronus swallows his children as they are born. But when Zeus is born, his mother, distraught by the loss of her children, substitutes a stone wrapped in swaddling clothes, and sends her son to Crete. Zeus grows to manhood among the shepherds on Mount Ida and eventually overthrows Cronus.

In his uplifted left hand, Father Time holds a serpent biting its tail. In many early cultures the serpent with the tail in its mouth symbolizes the ongoing cycle of time. In some depictions, instead of a serpent, a dragon is portrayed biting its tail. In at least one book on our list, the motif of a serpent swallowing its tail exists. Trivia question of the week: in which book does this motif appear? [5]

The Tree of Life representing the sustaining aspects of time — evergreen, ever-bearing — is being nourished by the spherical earth, and the globe itself is encircled by signs of the zodiac. The tree is a recurring symbol in our books — copper beeches in *The Visitors*, the fir tree in Philippa Pearce's *Tom's Midnight Garden*. In the branches of the Tree, in stark contrast to the hourglass, we see a clock suggesting the human being's increasing consciousness of time passing as well as the human desire to measure time.

Pulling the chariot are two horses, one light horse wearing the sun ornament suggesting daylight and the other, a darker horse, wearing the moon ornament suggesting night, both horses revealing the relationship of the rhythm of life to the rhythm of the natural world. The archetypal Hindu symbol of completeness — the mandala — is the wheels of Time's chariot. One wheel is woven of vines, the other displays a decorative pattern.

Like the wheel, our institute has, at best, a circular form. James Joyce's

"riverun, past Eve and Adam's, from swerve of shore to bend of bay, brings us by a commodius vicus of recirculation back to Howth ('Newnham') Castle and Environs."

From Natalie Babbitt's *Tuck Everlasting*:

"Everything's a wheel, turning and turning, never stopping. The frogs is part of it, and the bugs, and the fish, and the wood thrush, too. And people. But never the same ones. Always coming in new, always growing and changing, and always moving on. That's the way it's supposed to be. That's the way it *is*."

From Virginia Hamilton's *Arilla Sun Down*:

"'Life goes round and round, he saying. I am drawn within the circle ... On and on in a circle for all time.'"

To return to the picture: in the background on the right, Bruegel depicts spring. Notice the people dancing around the maypole in the spring festival commemorating new life and fertility for crops and cattle in a celebration of the return of spring. Spring is a jubilee time.

From E. B. White's *Charlotte's Web*:

The early summer days on a farm are the happiest and fairest days of the year. Lilacs bloom and make the air sweet, and then fade. Apple blossoms come with the lilacs, and the bees visit around among the apple trees. The days grow warm and soft.

In the left background Bruegel depicts autumn; the trees are barren and leafless, and with spring in the right background, we have a suggestion of the rhythm of the seasons, the grand procession of the seasons. Again, from *Charlotte's Web*:

The crickets sang in the grasses. They sang the song of summer's ending, a sad, monotonous song. "Summer is over and gone," they sang. "Over and gone, over and gone. Summer is dying, dying." The crickets felt it was their duty to warn everybody that summertime cannot last forever. Even on the most beautiful days in the whole year — the days when summer is changing into fall — the crickets spread the rumor of sadness and change.

The zodiac itself symbolizes the wheel of life — the familiar symbol of cyclical and seasonal transformation. Bruegel depicts the signs of the zodiac of the globe defining the plane of the earth's orbit and of the sun's: Taurus, the bull, just above the right wheel, symbol of property and wealth; Cancer, the crab, between the two wheels, symbol for the home; Leo, the Lion, behind Cronus' uplifted arm, a sign of love, a sign of children; Libra, the scales, in the branches of the tree, sign of justice and balance; Sagittarius, the great archer, to the left, sign of great philosophies and religion.

Time is seen as friend and time is also seen as tyrant, a devourer; time is depicted as an immense brevity, the transitoriness of our lives reflected in Death following Time and holding the inexorable scythe; the human being, haunted by time, is a tenant of time plagued by Odysseus; question — What in the long run will befall me?

The approach of death also prompts the return of the romantic dreamer Quixote to a few basic realities. At the end of his life Quixote insists that provision be made for twenty ducats to provide a new dress for his housekeeper. At the end of his life Socrates exclaims to his friends, "I owe a cock to Asclepias; see that it is paid." Queen Elizabeth I, with her dying breath, pleads, "All my possessions for a moment of time."[6]

Under the wheels of the Bruegel's chariot — at Death's feet as well — are all the items made by the human being turned to nothing by time:

And nothing 'gainst Time's scythe can make defence
Save breed, to brave him when he takes thee hence.[7]

From Mollie Hunter's *A Sound of Chariots*: Andrew Marvell and Bridie McShane:

But at my back I always hear
Time's winged chariot hurrying near..

It had all started with her father dying, after all, and it was thinking about him, missing him so much that kept the fear of Time catching up with her, of dying, always active in her mind.

And as Gran tells Peter in Jill Paton Walsh's *Unleaving* —

"Well, we all die, but first we all live. Don't worry about what's the point. Just take your share. Take it two-handed and in full measure. You have to clap your hands and sing."

You must seize the day.

Behind Death an angel riding an elephant heralds something. From Philippa Pearce's *Tom's Midnight Garden*:

"'Time no longer...' murmured Tom, and thought of all the clocks in the world stopping ticking, and their striking stopped too, drowned and stopped for ever by the sound of a great Trumpet. "Time no longer ..." repeated Tom; and the three words began to seem full of enormous possibilities."

Another important subject in our investigation is the time experienced by readers as they travel in fictive worlds. Another is time experienced by the writer creating a work, as in Rilke's "For the Sake of a Single Verse"; and yet another is the notion of timelessness and, in particular, the timelessness of art. Only art is a fit competitor for time; an exhibition of Goya's paintings has meaning today, and a sixteenth-century Bruegel engraving places our twentieth-century institute in context. Sophocles is still read today, 2500 years after his death, and so are the works of the blind bard Homer and of Goethe and Shakespeare. And the works of other giants hovering around this room — Wordsworth, Byron, Milton.

And which of the books we examine will survive the test of time? The timelessness of

art is one way for us to deal with the darker implication of time moving toward death.

In André Malraux's words, in the "victory" of any masterpiece of art, time-ridden man somehow rises into grandeur and timelessness. For Malraux — and perhaps for Bruegel — Art is "at once the conqueror and the destroyer of time."[8]

The Bruegel engraving, so busy with allegories and symbolism, reveals the multilayered dimensions of our topic and provides us with many important motifs we will encounter in the literature.

In *The Rise of the Novel* Ian Watts states that the novel in general has interested itself much more than any other literary form in the development of its characters in the course of time. In novels of youth the time frame is usually no more than a few years in the life of the individual. By and large, the novels do not take the youth from childhood to maturity but from one stage of childhood to another, higher stage on the journey to autonomy. The individual, in other words, does not, at the end of the novel, attain "a definitive life-form." In few of the novels under discussion could words of graduation be pronounced over the hero as they are over Goethe's Wilhelm Meister: "Hail to thee, young man. The apprenticeship is done." Only one phase or stage of the apprenticeship has been surmounted.

Still, many of the novels signal the end of childhood. The haunting sound of the bullroarer — the instrument sounded in initiation rites since Paleolithic times — echoes in the background; it makes a sacred sound, a booming sound, heralding a rebirth, a movement forward, one miraculous unfolding, myriad unfoldings.

Narrative, like life itself, can be seen as movement through time. In *Christ and Apollo*, William Lynch portrays the movement as a horizontal line with arrows on the line suggesting points of illumination, each point progressing toward the next and yet dependent on the one before it — as much a march of the soul as a march of time. The line is reproduced on the institute bookmark. "Time in fiction is amazingly malleable and elastic," says David Higden, and "authors pursue it forwards, trace it backwards, fragment it into slivers of varying duration, or arc it gracefully in circles, ellipses and even spirals."[9] For purposes of discussion, the institute seminars are roughly organized around time shapes — narrative time, memory, slippery time, past and future time, and picture book time; these are rather crude counterparts of Higdon's four categories — process time, retrospection, barrier and polytemporal time.

Although each book displays a dominant shape, each book could contain elements of the four shapes. Our rough schematic provides an organizational framework, a way for us to discuss the books. Other frameworks could be developed, but we agree "that time, public time, functions as one of the primary structural elements in fiction, and that the shape time takes significantly affects the nature of the telling."[10] In *Tom's Midnight Garden*, "Uncle Alan ... had taken for granted that there were twenty-four hours in a day — twice twelve hours. But suppose, instead, there were twice thirteen?"

Process time can best be understood by a straight line moving from point to point, a process forward and its underlying causality. Time as process, each event contributing to the next in the development of the story and the development of the protagonist. Higdon signals the word *becoming* as the central word in narrative time. Each day, month, season and year moves forward steadily, emphasizing the progression of the actions. In our program, process time is most similar to our seminar entitled Narrative Time to be led by Paul Heins and Jill Paton Walsh.

Retrospective time takes to heart Kierkegaard's statement that "life can only be lived forward and understood backward" — a person proceeding through life trying to make sense of his past. Three time blocks comprise retrospective time — then, now, and in-between. Confessions, spiritual autobiographies, Saint Augustine's *Confessions*, for example. Retrospective time is most like the Memory that Gregory Maguire's seminar is concerned with.

In the polytemporal time shape the clock hands go berserk, bearing little, if any, relation to private and public time — no barriers, no connections; several time lines run simultaneously. Polytemporal time is comparable to Slippery Time, the seminar to be taught by John Rowe Townsend.

Barrier time. In a prescribed period of time something must be done; the miller's daughter in "Rumpelstiltskin" must spin the straw into gold before dawn, or she will die; Cinderella must be home by the stroke of twelve. In Vladimir Nabokov's *Invitation to a Beheading*, the first sentence is "In accordance with the law the death sentence was announced to Cincinnatus C in a whisper." Betty Levin's seminar Past and Future takes barrier time into consideration along with the other time shapes. And Ethel Heins's seminar on Picture Book Time encompasses all of the time shapes defined by David Higdon.

Every book we have so carefully selected speaks to our topic in its own particular way. As we began to think about this topic many months ago, one of the first books that occurred to us, in addition to Southall's *Josh*, was Virginia Hamilton's *Arilla Sun Down*.

Arilla Adams, the twelve-year-old protagonist, was born into two traditions rich in myth and story. Her father is part-black, part-American Indian; her mother is black. Told in the first person, the novel intersperses chapters written in a colloquial, contemporary idiom with what Hamilton calls "rememories," chapters written in surrealistic, impressionistic language out of Arilla's self and out of the collective unconscious — recollections of Arilla's early childhood and of the childhood of the Indian race, told in the old way from a long-ago dream time, when "the people were the only ones."

In *Arilla Sun Down* Hamilton reveals a cosmic order inspired by Indian myth and story. Life is an endless circle without beginning and without end; Arilla's dad says to Arilla, "Your mind may forget the past. But it always remains inside." The world is an "Eternal Circling." Time is not linear but cyclical — birth, death, rebirth; James False Face and The People are alive in Arilla as

Great-grandfather Plowman is alive in *Josh*.
As "Wordkeeper" Arilla must put down on paper what she sees, record it for others, and interpret the world; to talk "stories to the tribe," she must save and protect the words "in a memory pouch" and "now and then, take out the words and cause us to be strong and not afraid."

For Hamilton memory is empowering; truth is empowering; although childhood must end, the memory of childhood — and the hope associated with childhood — must never end.

George Orwell provides a fictive account of the loss of memory in his prophetic novel *1984*, and Jan Mark provides a fable in her fine work of science fiction for children, *The Ennead*, in which Moshe tells a story that could save their lives to a group of people who can't comprehend it because they have forgotten what a story is. Unlike Hamilton's Arilla Adams these people have no memory pouch. Somewhere along the way the whole notion of memory has faded away.

For Hamilton the trumpeter's message in the Bruegel drawing would most likely be that only through the word — through poem and story — will the memory of childhood, and thus the memory of hope, survive. The trumpeter is the Wordkeeper, defender of the word and of the imagination.

As Hamilton and other authors go about the work of writing, they perform the role of the ancient Greek *moirae*, or fates. Each author is Clotho, the spinner who spins the thread of life; Lachesis, the Disposer of Lots, the Measurer, who assigns destinies; and Atropos, who at death, cuts the thread.

As we explore the varied ways in which time is defined, and as we examine the recurring motifs and the time shapes in children's books, our concerns are the techniques of the spinner — the author's skill with spindle, rod and shears — and the true nature of the tale spun.

Our investigation of time promises to be an immense journey of the heart and the soul, our voyage is by its very nature a deeply humane quest.

So let our circle begin.

1. Lewis Carroll *Through the Looking Glass*
2. *The Openhearted Audience*
3. Meyerhoff, *Time in Literature*
4. *The Sense of an Ending*
5. *Unleaving* Jill Paton Walsh
6. *Christ and Apollo* William Lynch
7. Shakespeare, Sonnet 12
8. Lynch op.cit.
9. David Higdon *Time and English Fiction*.
10. Higden, op.cit

PAUL HEINS AND JILL PATON WALSH: SEMINAR

Narrative time

Remembering the Dimensions
Of Possibility
— Emily Dickinson

JPW: Let's try to begin simply, in a subject which is a quagmire of complexity. The most commonplace way to travel in time, to move through a shift of time, to go backwards or sideways in time, to enter a different space-time continuum is to open a book. The events in a work of fiction take place in a created time which is not that of reality. Even if the author is not interested in Time, and thinks of the story as taking place in a realistic time, the imaginary and elastic nature of the medium of fiction moderates everything. Playing games with time when writing a novel is inescapable. But, as the Chinese proverb has it, the fish is the last to discover the water, and transparently obvious things can have escaped notice!

Let's look at two childishly simple compulsory time games played by a novelist. Shall we call them skipping and shuffling? Anyone who has looked at an amateur attempt at novel writing will be familiar with skipping; or, rather, the need for it. "Peter descended the stairs," the typescript reads, "reached out for the doorknob, turned it, and opened the sitting room door. He walked across the room to the bureau, turned the key in the bureau lock, lowered the lid of the writing desk and stared at the bank of drawers. Opening the third drawer down on the right-hand side, he felt inside the drawer and brought out a bundle of letters. With shaking fingers he undid the ribbon that bound the bundle, and spread out the many sheets of paper ... "
Unless we are very lucky we shall next be given extracts from the letters Peter is *not*

BOOKS FOR DISCUSSION:
Peter Dickinson: *Merlin Dreams*
Leon Garfield: *Footsteps* (U.K. title
   John Diamond)
Betty Levin: *The Keeping Room*
Katherine Paterson: *Jacob Have I Loved.*
Jill Paton Walsh: *Unleaving*

looking for ... then, "At last! Peter seized the sheet of paper, reached for his reading glasses, put them on, and read the dreaded words — 'I, Bertrand, being of sound mind, leave every penny to cousin Neville ...'" Or whatever. A more experienced writer might show us the bureau drawers being opened; ransacking someone else's desk having the charm of the illicit, but would never bother with the doorknob on the sitting room door, let alone troubling to tell us that our hero, having reached for his reading glasses, puts them on. "Moments later he was looking at the letter ..." would be more likely.

It is easy to laugh at the amateur writer, struggling to get characters through doors, in and out of rooms and gardens, in a storm of circumstance. and nobody suggests it is possible to open doors without reaching out hands, trembling or otherwise, for doorknobs. It is even possible — have some of you spotted the source of my example? — to use the act of reaching for a doorknob as the fulcrum of some dramatic element in a fictional schema. But the principle remains the same; which is that fiction works by skipping the insignificant, the endless dust-storm of tiny detail with which real life bombards our attention, and moving from significant moment to next significant moment, in pursuit of some kind of pattern, some revelation of structure in events. If too much is included, the pattern is destroyed. You cut away masses of undiffer-entiated white marble to reveal the David in the block; you work like a child artist using one of those little books in which a picture can be drawn by connecting numbered dots in the right order. Both the selection of the dots, and the connection of them involve massive skipping across the surface of time, for time is the whole page; but the whole page is not a picture, just a blank.

We cannot live in this selective way, existing as we do on the whole page, but we can think in it. And we are so used to storytelling in it that attempts like those of Robbe-Grillet to put everything in, partial though such an experiment necessarily is, leave us baffled, or even enraged with frustration. If he's telling us a story, he ought to get on with it — he ought to skip to the next meaningful dot — if that means sixteen years later in Bohemia, so be it.

Once we have discovered the water, and understand the game of skipping, the game of shuffling is an obvious variation. I don't mean shuffling as in dragging ones feet, but as with a pack of cards. Why not connect the dots in the wrong order and see if a different picture emerges? Any sort of disordered sequence in narration tends to seem slightly experimental and unreal, though its hard to see why when our memories shuffle all the time. But perhaps it is only in our own century that people have noticed how thoroughly shuffling memory is. And there is one extremely important difference between skipping and shuffling; when an author skips something, it really has gone for good. There simply is no answer to the question how many children had Lady Macbeth, it can neither be discovered nor deduced. But when an author shuffles, the new order of events is in counterpoint to an actual sequence, which is always implicitly present, even for imaginary events. The tricks of memory, the tricks of ordering and reordering the

sequence in which events are unfolded to the reader, overlie and counterpoint a real order, which the reader can deduce. And though for the getting of effects the shuffled order may be very potent, for the *meaning* of events the real order has an insuperably important part to play.

For the true order of events can be read causally. If father died three days before the road accident, then the road accident did not cause his death, tell it or remember it how you will. And causes and effects are interesting to us because they condition our sense of responsibility as well as our understanding of the world. For the moment I am making only a far less grand point, which is that any work of fiction which uses a shuffled sequence — flash-back, flash-forward, interpolated memories — also contains the sequence in which it all really happened.

There are, of course, wonderfully more elaborate games that can be played with time and sequence in novels. But there may be good reasons why children's literature is not in the van of experiment on this axis, profounder than the weary old idea that children need things easy. For when it comes to playing across acres of the space-time continuum, children have only as yet a garden plot of their own, much of their short span of memory is forgotten as they grow, and their first experience of time-games may well be in the books they read, as they watch the author as conjurer shuffle and skip.

PH: Early in her discussion Jill made two very important points in considering the nature of narrative time: "Fiction works by skipping the insignificant" and "The events in a work of fiction take place in a created time which is not that of reality."

Skipping the insignificant — or, to put it another way, stressing the significant — applies, of course, to all of the elements of fiction, whether they are temporal or not. In Shakespeare's *Othello*, it is a mere handkerchief which is important. Actually, in the example that Jill gave of the listing of unimportant actions, which concomitantly seem to overload and devour narrative time, she was drawn in to heaping up undifferentiated specific details: doorknob, door, bureau, key, lock.

But when this principle of avoiding the insignificant and emphasizing the significant is applied to the created time of fiction, we can observe a particular kind of dynamic pattern that seems to rule the ebb and flow of fictive time. If one tries to visualize this pattern created by the time implicit in a narrative plot, or even in a dramatic plot, one can see that the movement of events and the movement of the sentences in which they are recorded take on an accordion-like motion. With a squeeze of the accordion the author can say "ten minutes later," "ten hours later" "ten days later," and even invoke larger chronological units. In the story of *The Sleeping Beauty* a hundred years are conveniently compressed.

In presenting dialogue, however, the author makes use of a more leisurely tempo. It is obvious that the time taken to read dialogue orally would coincide with what we consider to be real time. Incidentally, it was once said that the dramatizations of one of Dostoyevsky's novels simply required lifting the dialogue from the page to the stage. Loosely, then, the writer of narrative can alternate between a compressed indication of time and an actual measuring of time, and also make use of more or less relaxed units filled with essential details not necessarily elongated.

It is worth noticing that this accordion principle can be found in the tersest of narratives, particularly in biblical accounts. In the Second Book of Samuel there is a famous passage, which — interestingly — has given rise to a number of sensitive musical settings.

And the King was much moved, and went up to the chamber over the gate, and wept: and as he went thus he said, "O, my son Absalom, my son, my son Absalom. Would God I had died for thee, O Absalom, my son, my son."

Comparing the fictitious time of this biblical selection with real time one observes the following. "And the King was much moved" can be said as quickly as it took the king to be moved. "Went up to the chamber over the gate" eliminates any picturization of the staircase (was it a spiral staircase?) or of the

number of treads and risers, and encapsulates the motion and pace of the distraught king by using the operative word *up*. However, in what David said so poignantly one finds a measurable correspondence between narrative time and the time we call reality.

The accordion method can also lead to a drawing out of thought or emotion as in a stream-of-consciousness novel, one of the best examples being Molly Bloom's fifty-page soliloquy at the end of James Joyce's *Ulysses*. And a text set to music can be elongated by the introduction of another temporal art, so that various settings of "Absalom my son" exceed in time performance the actual duration of David's agonized words.

Of course, Jill spoke about shuffling time as well as about skipping details. And at this point we can well believe with Jill that a consideration of narrative time creates a quagmire of complexity. If the accordion principle is worth anything, it would have to apply to shuffled narratives as well as to straightforward — that is chronologically ordered — narratives. And in the discussion of the specific books both of us have chosen to consider from the point of view of time patterns, we may actually come upon one kind of accordion motion being played against another kind. But we shall have to leave that possibility to further consideration.

JPW: I am far from complete agreement with Paul over the relationship between the spoken word written down and the real time in which words are spoken.

It seems to me that the lyrical repetitions and inversions of "Absalom my son" are intended to indicate — indeed *do* indicate — the King's grieving going on and on for many hours; surely we are not to suppose that he said these words just exactly once through as they are written, and that it all took roughly twenty seconds? The actual duration of David's agonized words, I would have said, is not knowable, and does not in the least matter — but I think I risk taking a branch line of the subject ...

I would like to accept and annotate Paul's image of the accordion, which brilliantly embodies the nature of the speeding up, and slowing down, the slippery relationship between time in a narrative and the time of the world of reality. It gives us precisely what we need to consider the treatment of time in Paterson's *Jacob Have I Loved.*

But I would first like to apologize for discussing the structure of this work. It is not a work that invites discussion in terms of structure. A richly textured, touching and convincing evocation of the changing relationships of the children and the adults in a remote community, it asks rather to be considered in terms of human insight into the wells of self-pity, self-respect, happiness and kindness and misery.

Nothing so theoretical as structure is in the foreground of the author's attention, or the reader's; yet the structure serves the purposes of the book. Nine tenths of the length of the book is a slow-moving, intensely detailed account of childhood on Rass Island. Paul's accordion is being played stretched out very far. Perhaps we should notice that even when stretched out far, the narrative accordion abbreviates immensely; otherwise reading about a childhood would take fifteen years! Still, relatively speaking, we are moving slowly, seeing in depth.

When Louise leaves Rass Island, suddenly the accordion is squeezed very tight; it takes fewer than eight pages to recount Louise's graduation, training as a midwife, settling and working in a remote Appalachian valley — several fewer than it takes in the body of the book to recount just the incident with Aunt Trudie's cats. It takes only six pages, fewer than it takes to cover any other element in the book that I can find, to tell us the incident which brings the ultimate meaning of the story into focus — the laying aside of a healthy twin baby while the endangered one engrosses all the available care and love.

Such syncopation is a very important part of the rhetoric by which Paterson achieves her effects. Counting pages may be a crude measure, but the time taken by the reader to encompass the ground is a subtle element in the effect of books, and is perhaps the only real intersection between narrative time and real time — the reader's time is real!

One might compare the sudden acceleration of the narrative to the "Twenty years later in Bohemia" sort of stage direction; or back to those number-joining pictures, where the next dot may be all the way over to the other margin of the page. But the effectiveness of the device is terrific. The relative slowness of life on Rass Island, and its relative reality; the hallucinatory clarity of detail that characterizes childhood in memory, and the relative slipperiness and speed of adult life is conveyed as much by the manipulation of the accordion as by any other of the author's impressive rhetorical skills. And there is also the measure of time implied by change in the narrator — that hardest of all aspects for a young reader to grasp — that with time the self changes and becomes another; so strong has our sympathy for Louise been during her bitterly unfair childhood, that only when she becomes someone else do we realize what was wrong with her before. The passage of time is always part of the subject of a written text; in this book structure and subject are inseparable.

PH: It may be ironical that I, as a reader, feel it is not necessary for Jill, an author, to apologize for discussing the structure of *Jacob have I Loved.* While time, or any other element of narrative was probably not in the forefront of Katherine Paterson's attention when she wrote the book, I tend to believe that she either consciously or instinctively made use of, or, better still, incorporated time or any other storytelling element as a necessary portion of the narrative. After all, Jill and I are discussing narrative time, which could conceivably be a dry or forbidding subject, but we are trying to show that the art of a book serves its purpose — serves its spirit. The better the art, the better the spirit has been served. And Jill's illuminating discussion of *Jacob Have I Loved* surely demonstrates the symbiosis between the art and the meaning of a text.

The image of the accordion may serve the purpose of encapsulating the dynamics of narrative time, but there are, in addition, other aspects or elements of narrative time that should be considered. The opening sentence of *Jacob* strikes a simple, solemn chord: "As soon as the snow melts I will go to Rass and fetch my mother." The first-person narrative creates a layering of time — and in a sense, Louise has become a traveler in time, returning to an earlier, crucial period of her existence, revealing its meaning. In this instance, moreover, as Jill has explained so well, the first-person point of view reinforces the meaning and the emotional intensities of Louise's adolescent years. In Leon Garfield's *John Diamond* (American title *Footsteps*) we shall find that a first person perspective may be used for a different kind of narrative purpose.

Another familiar aspect of narrative time in *Jacob* is the casual use of historical references to anchor the story to a particular time as well as to a particular place. The news of the bombing of Pearl Harbor, skillfully inserted to show Louise breaking the taboo of listening to the radio on Sunday and Louise's preoccupation with the idea of German spies serve to set the chronology for the story of an isolated evangelical community.

John Diamond is essentially an adventure story, even though the plot springs from the haunting guilt of William Jones's father and William's attempt to justify the truthful but undiplomatic statement he had made about his father's wrongdoing. And even, at the end, the rather abstract competition between the notions of evil and hope serves to bind loose ends rather than having a life of its own. *John Diamond* is a different kind of story and intended to be a different kind of story from that of *Jacob Have I Loved*.

From the very beginning, the kind of narrative is made manifest. "I ought to begin with the footsteps, but first of all I must tell you that my name is William Jones, and that I was twelve years old when I began to hear them." The story bears many time references to the months between September and April, but William is still essentially the same kind of boy at the end of it all — still, like many boy heroes of traditional fiction, fascinated by the idea of hidden treasure. Of course, it is true that his adventures were frequently accom-

panied by terrific stampedes and footsteps, and finally he realized that he was himself responsible for having inaugurated the weird, yet often humorous, experiences that made up his story. In terms of the accordion image, William's story consists of one quick squeeze after the other, as it should in any third person, briskly episodic narrative.

William's story, also, follows the form of a quest — to find John Diamond and make atonement for Mr. Jones's guilt — and moves to a conclusion by means of another kind of temporal pattern. In *Time and English Fiction* (Macmillan, London, 1977) David Higden uses the term "Barrier time" and describes it thus: — "Numerous fairy tales and folk tales prescribe a precise time span during which certain tasks must be performed. Dire consequences await if the prescribed time span is not heeded." At the beginning of chapter 20 of *John Diamond*, William tells of racing home from London to prevent Jack Diamond's doing harm to the Jones family and makes the following comment: "If only the journey had been as quick as it is to say it."

The statement includes both the tension of the situation and the difference between real time and narrative time. Thus it can be seen that if time in *John Diamond* is not as morally crucial as in *Jacob Have I Loved*, it has the merit of giving an air of reality to the bizarre adventures of William Jones. For the fictitious London of Garfield is redolent of Georgian London, ranging from the period after the building of the dome of St. Paul's Cathedral, through the era of horse-drawn stage coaches. It is not the fictitiously nostalgic medieval London of William Morris, who called it "small and white and clean." Rather it is a murky, drab, and labyrinthine city, dominated by Sir Christopher Wren's masterpiece, bathed in shadows and fog. It is a London of the author's imagination, springing eerily from his richly metaphorical and humorous style, and kept in check by the passing of recognizable days and hours. "A wind came in gusts driving the fine rain straight across the bridge leaving it swept cold, gleaming and empty. There was a moon of sorts, rolling through the muddy air like an old drowned eye."

JPW : Isn't Garfield marvelous — a continuous firework display of verbal illuminations! But what interests me about *John Diamond* — as Paul says an adventure story, is the position of the past in it — positioned in the present. It is among other things a dazzling exposition of a theory of the past — that it is *not* past, that it dictates and shapes the present; perhaps even that only in so far as it does so shape and govern the present does it exist. Certainly in a brilliant double plot the events of the book's present unfold and reveal the past, and gradually establish a resonant contrast between the protagonists, the two sons; William Jones, ignorant of the past, and innocent, untouched by his father's guilt, for all that he shoulders its consequences; John Diamond, enslaved by the past, burning in hatred, corrupted by his innocent father's suffering. Though the drama of events is leading us to a message about forgiveness and reconciliation, which is always a note sounded by Garfield, there is also in this book a clearly discernable warning; the past may be lethal, and human souls can only grow and flower if they face away from it.

The web of connections between past and present, however, is, in *John Diamond* entirely real — not a whiff of fantasy about it, though, perhaps, one should stress that it is the *connections* that are all real; for in Garfield's world the present also is fantastic, and largely psychological, without objectivity; a moving panorama of fantastic shadows cast by the hopes, fears, illusions and misunderstandings of the characters.

When we turn to Betty Levin's *The Keeping Room*, the connections of past and present are immediately problematical. Here again there are two stories unwinding, one in the past, one in the present; but if the story in the past is influencing events in the present, as Hal, the increasingly obsessed hero of the book comes to believe, the author withholds certainty about it; coincidence is always a possibility. The imperfect synchronization of the two tellings increases the uncertainty we feel — the abduction of Emily, the present-day child, does not begin until halfway through; the unfolding of what really happened to Hannah, the lost child of the past, extends past the accounts of how each story ended — Hannah's story in tragic death, Emily's in the comic scene of a naked child in an airport lavatory, yelling for the police.

The spectacular skills of Garfield as a plotter are not available here; instead, we experience a sense of struggle to contain and understand a shifting and elusive meaning, as changeable as the weather of the New England winter, which enlists *us* in the work of comprehending. Because one of the engines of the story is a school history project, Levin can easily and naturally employ the opinions of characters in the drama on the subject in hand:

> Later on in Social studies class ... Hal whispered to Josh, "They don't believe Hannah has anything to do with Emily calling," Josh answers, "Thought they loved the past and all," "In its place," Hal responded. "I think they want it to stay put."

Or later, when Hal eventually has to write up his project:

> "Can't get started?" His father was in the doorway.
> "I keep starting with the end."

However, this story does not really continue beyond its end, because the true protagonist is a parcel of land in New England, and a large part of the true subject is the way in which the landscape contains the past. Hannah reminds us of Wordsworth's Lucy:

> No motion has she now, no force;
> She neither hears nor sees;
> Rolled round in earth's diurnal course
> With rocks, and stones, and trees.

The land contains whatever has happened on it, inerasably. Did you notice Hannah finding and using the Indian arrow-heads that surface when she cultivates the ground? To understand the past, Levin would have us see, we need to look at the land with the aid of a chain of human memory — here stretched almost to breaking point. Miss Titmarsh remembers her grandmother's inconsolable grief for the vanished sister — and because she remembers it, it is still present. And surely we are to understand that the true links of present and past are not supernatural; the creatures that wander on the hillside of the Candlewood lot are not really the ghosts of the farm animals of the long ago deserted farm — they are their descendants. Against the changes that unroll while the school project is being pursued — the cutting of a new road, the arrival of new neighbors, the fading competence of an old woman — the book counterpoises continuity and recurrence; together, a complicated vision of the nature of the timestream in which we all swim. To this pattern the breed of a new family of ducklings is — I nearly said a good ending, but of course I mean a good narrative stopping-point.

PH: I should like to list a number of statements from Jill's views of the narrative time problems, and of their solutions, in *The Keeping Room,* and see whether they can be fitted, as well, into another kind of time pattern. Jill speaks of "the imperfect synchronization of the two tellings," of the fact that a school history project is "one of the engines of the story," and of the books counterpoising "continuity and recurrence." She said "any work of fiction which uses a shuffled sequence — flash back, flash forward, interpolated memories ... also contains the sequence in which it all really happened."

Now, Betty Levin overcame "the imperfect synchronization of the two tellings" by the use of a simple natural device — the calendar. Both Hal's experiences and Hannah's journal are specifically based on events which start in September, reaching through Thanksgiving, Christmas and New Year's day to March, and what is more, the school history project is a long-term assignment contemporaneous with a similar span of calendar time as is the Thoreau-like evocation of natural fruition and springtime revival that binds Hannah's environment to Hal's. In Betty's landscape, despite many material changes the present and the past touch each other.

Moreover, in reconstructing the past, Hal has to relive it as well as to rebuild it. Impelled on his way by an academic assignment, he not only applies an archaeological approach to what he considers historically important in a dump, but becoming acquainted with the Titcombs, and delving into their

sparse written mementoes, Hal is eagerly ready for the discovery of Hannah's journal. And in the last chapter of the book, which is surely an apotheosis as well as an epilogue, he is ready to write — as Hanna might have written — "This morning the ducklings came."

Unlike the previous books we have been considering, *Merlin Dreams* by Peter Dickinson is not a novel, but a series of narratives rising from a psychological ambience, the subconscious awareness of Merlin, the ancient magician familiar to us from the stories of King Arthur.

A quotation from Sir Thomas Malory tells how:

"a damsel named Nenyve ... persuaded Merlin to go under a rock to let her know of the marvels there, but then she worked a spell so that he could never come out, for all his skill."

At this point Dickinson takes over, and assumes that the magician continued to sleep and dream and wake from time to time, remembering his past experiences in the form of mythic patterns or archetypes rising and falling in his memory: ancient rites of human sacrifice; structures of standing stone; the courts of kings; heroes, magicians, and goddesses. The narrative accordion is stretched out to the end of the book where a poem entitled "Dreams" captures the symbol of human creativity that pervades the concept of Merlin and his dreams.

Times into Time ... in this Time, this Place
  A boy lies watching the raven's flight
Not outside, but filling the self-same space
    As the dying knight ...

And others whose times are still to be
  Here in this instant, layer within layer,
Mind within mind, like the rings of a tree
    Grown fresh each year

Till it holds the centuries, age within age ...
  The last knight dies in the evening dew
Knowing the tale of the sleeping mage
    Was a lie, but true.

Nowhere, ever, for him to find
  Under any boulder on moor or hill
But buried in minds fresh born that mind
    Dreams on, dreams still.

The nine stories interpolated among

Merlin's dreams follow the simple sequential pattern of traditional oral storytelling, save for an occasional flashback; and Dickinson uses knight errantry, unicorn, mermaid, and dragon to serve his own purposes, which are often sardonically revisionist in nature. The stories are given brief titles — "Sword" "Stone" "Enchantress" and stem from a key word at the end of one of Merlin's dreams. Thus "He holds the horse in his mind" generates the springboard for "Damsel." But in the economy of the whole book, it is Merlin who dreams and becomes the source of creative memories. The brisk pace of Dickinson's invented narratives is rounded out by the slow legato of Merlin's dreams.

JPW: Peter Dickinson is an ideas man; his fiction is often driven by a metaphysical concept of some kind, often very sophisticated. Surely he is the only person to have based a children's book on a meditation on the ontological argument, which he did in *The Blue Hawk*. *Merlin Dreams* contains a beautiful imaginative structure — a hypothesis that the stories are the dreams of Merlin, as we have sometimes been thought to be "in the mind of God." Are dreams real? If something is a dream dreamed by Merlin, or by God, then what seems like reality on one level, is fantasy on another. And in a dream, of course, Time is dissolved. Does a dream have duration? If so, we cannot measure it or relate it coherently to waking time. These are flights of fancy which everyone makes; even children, inexperienced in time, experience dreams, and the shuffling movements of memory, the invisible duration of thought; far from finding such devices in literature more difficult than adult readers, they are likely instead to be less aware of the primacy of public, measured time; less compliant with the adult conspiracy to discount the reality of everything which does not progress along a measurable and one-way linear dimension. The poem which Paul quoted to you — do read it in full when you have a moment — proposes a subtle and cunning image of time; Merlin is a lie, but true. The sleeping magician is not lying under some as yet undiscovered mound of earth,

somewhere — but is lying in the minds of people as yet unborn, at the center of an inner reality which puts on rings like a growing tree.

In my experience children like ideas and cotton on to them quickly; in spite of which the conscious playing with ideas by authors carries danger with it. Designing a book to embody an idea is too intellectual and too authoritarian an activity to be capable of success, unless on the margins — in an overarching frame-work, perhaps, which is where Peter puts it in this book — or in any corner where it will not dominate.

I think I can no longer avoid discussing my own book. But before I do so I would like to enter a warning against believing what I say about it. Writing is not a fully conscious activity, conducted in a rational way like the writing of a lecture. An author's intention and his or her achievement are not at all the same thing. An author's opinion as to whether the intended effects have been achieved is worthless — she has not read her book. Authors can never read their books, only read them over, which is not the same thing, not at all like the experience of a true reader — anyone who has not written the book, who reads it and does not know what it will say ahead of reading it. I have come to believe that what the author did not intend is the most valuable part of many books — thank heaven that it is possible so to abdicate control as to allow the radiance of what one knows, unknowing, and feels, unfeeling, to shine through. It happens that a sleight of hand with time was part of my deliberate intention in writing *Unleaving*; but in general I think that a view of the nature of time is likely to form part of the unconscious message of fiction; to be something about which the authors' opinions emerge unexamined, as something on which they intended no comment, though they necessarily made one, because storytelling compels them to.

So now to the confessional. I thought I would try to trick young readers into so strong an identification with a character, that they would find themselves imaginatively in the skin of a very old person. The conventional wisdom

was, and is, that young readers need young eyes at the center of the story, need a young character to identify with. I thought that understanding that the old were once young — a thing known but not felt as true by young people very often, together with the associated truth that the young will themselves be old — was an important understanding. By narrative trickery I would defeat the protective ageism which locks the young in, or out, depending on how you look at it. The presence in the story of Madge young, under the influence of her own grandmother, whose death at the opening of the story foreshadows and substitutes for her own at the end; and of Madge old was contrived for this "trick." It involves the shuffling together of episodes from two time horizons, which is why *Unleaving* fits the theme this week so perfectly that neither my natural embarrassment, nor the later books I have written have kept me from having to talk about it now. I had another conscious intention, which was, while I was at it, to invert the usual two-time motif, and celebrate time as a healer, and a restorer of loss.

The large majority of books in which one is looking back at a former time are elegiac; how good it used to be, how happy we were, how great the destruction time has wrought. I think it is almost a consensus that the world is getting worse, and that children now have missed the better things that held sway when we were young; on the other hand they'd better make the most of it, because things will go on getting worse, and childhood is the happiest days of one's life. *Unleaving*, instead, looks back at suffering of an acute nature in youth from a perspective in which that suffering has been surmounted, and survived, and replaced by happiness. It is Patrick's grandchildren who scamper through the book, laughing and playing and talking philosophy. Times have got better, not worse. Though I am convinced that time does indeed have a direction, as Stephen Hawking says it does, it does not, I think have that particular grain, later does not always mean worse, and it is particularly necessary not to burden young readers with gloom on that account.

But you see the rhetorical trickery in

Unleaving does not work for many readers. They guess the double identity of Madge in the two layers of episodes far too soon for any kind of tension, or they do not notice it at all. I cannot say I am surprised when ambitious enterprises like *Unleaving* fail to work perfectly in my hands, but I am surprised that readers for whom the central design of the book has failed to work should nevertheless enjoy and admire it. But it is while talking to people who are telling me how much they enjoyed it that I have learned that they did not catch on as I hoped.

Any potency *Unleaving* may have is something I did not intend, arising while I worked somewhere on one side from the places where my intention was bent. It feels to me as though it were an autonomous thing, and any merits it has are its own, not mine. I will take responsibility for its shortcomings.

PH: Jill, when you spoke of readers for whom the central design of *Unleaving* had failed to work, I was at first uncertain whether you meant the shuffling together of episodes to form two time horizons, or the theme of "Suffering surmounted" or perhaps a combination of the two. On second thoughts I now perceive that the two concepts are intimately related, and realize how well your intention was accomplished. As a reader I like to perceive, or at least discover an author's intention, for I feel that such a perception on the part of the reader is an attempt at securing and granting a kind of justice — aesthetic justice. At the same time I like to reserve the right to decide whether the author has achieved his or her goal, or not.

One cannot fail to notice the immanence of time in *Unleaving* by Jill's use of the present tense, making moments and memories one, so that Madge and the book can both end their course by exultantly stating, "What shall we sing? The beauty of the world."

I should also like to stress another temporal element — or rather temporal pattern — in *Unleaving*. I have read *Unleaving* a number of times, and at my last reading I was especially taken by the recurrent rhythmic patterning and surging of the restless multitudinous seas on the shores of Cornwall and was led to think of how Hokusai caught a wave in a moment, and how Debussy caught the shifting of the sea in a symphonic poem. Jill, too, has sung the beauty of the world in its variousness.

By now it must be obvious that the nature of narrative time is not to be stated simply. A storyteller must honor the old grammatical categories of time, past, present and future; the events may be sequential in nature or shuffled — as Jill has suggested — flashback or overlay; the accordion suggests images of compression, identity with clock time, or the drawn out elasticities of memory and emotion. And, yet, we must remember that all of these patterns are created by words and sentences. I find it especially cogent for our purposes that Rudolph Arnheim in an essay entitled "A New Laocoon: Artistic Composites and the talking Film" (1938) [included in *Film as Art*, Univ. of California Press.1957] wrote:

'As far as content goes, the word has the range of all the other media together; it can describe the things of this world as immobile or as constantly changing; with inimitable ease it can leap from one place to another from one moment to the next; it presents not only the world of our outer senses but also the entire realm of the soul, the imagination, the emotion, the will.'

And since I think it is good to correlate what we have said about time and narrative time with what others have said, I beg your indulgence for one final quotation.

In *Swann's Way* there is a lengthy fragment which comments on time and stretches the accordion to embody Proust's particular variety of narrative flow:

All things made the church for me something entirely different from the rest of the town; a building which occupied, so to speak, four dimensions of space — the name of the fourth being time — which has sailed the centuries with that old nave where bay after bay, chapel after chapel, seemed to stretch across and hold down and conquer not merely a few yards of soil, but each successive epoch from which the whole had emerged triumphant....

JPW: I would like to draw one deduction from all this. The process of writing fiction is a learning process, a deeply enlightening one, like the process of reading fiction. I think the world is so complicated, and some aspects of it, like Time itself, so mysterious, that the rational, conscious part of our selves cannot contain, and hold within one steady gaze, all that we have perceived. La Rochefoucauld said neither the sun nor death could be stared at fixedly; surely he should have added time to death and the sun.

Somewhere at the edges of our awareness we catch a radiance of things partly seen; and as though writing conferred a power of squinting from the corners of our vision, when it works, we say far more than we intended. In every narrative we read, we see how time has struck the writer, either in the conscious plan at the center of the story, or catching the light glancingly, in seemingly chance illumination, diffracting the colors of the world. The chance illumination may be the more enlightening. For chance is the first consequence of Time.

LEON GARFIELD

Historians and storytellers

NOT VERY LONG ago I was asked for a story that would have some reference to one or other of the properties administered by the National Trust. As it was to be the first of a series, it was suggested that I turn my attention to the Blewcoat School in Westminster, which is the headquarters of the organization. Accordingly, I went to look at it and obtained such documents as were available relating to its foundation and administration. I found, to my relief, that it fitted in quite well with an idea I had had some time previously, which had been flickering at the back of my mind like a moth in search of a candle; and it required very little adjustment to shift my idea from a chateau in Revolutionary France to a slum dwelling near Westminster Cathedral, in the 1850s. I make no apology for this. Such is the way of historical fiction. Even Procrustes would have been awed by the rigorous lopping and stretching of ideas indulged in by an author to make them fit the bed on which they must lie.

Naturally, I did a great deal of research into the chosen setting, and mainly of a topographical nature. The story required a time after the introduction of a uniformed police force and before the majority of the slum area had been swept away by the construction of Victoria Street. In addition, I preferred to avoid the time between 1840 and 1857, when the new Houses of Parliament were being built, as the undoubted disruption of the streets during that large undertaking would certainly have come to the attention of my characters. I did not want to be bothered with the building of Parliament; and sometimes when I look at it, I wish other people hadn't, too. Therefore, the story had to take place

between 1857 and 1864, when Victoria Street was completed. I did not give a date, partly because to mention a particular year would arouse expectation of its being significant and related to some important historical event, and partly because I did not want to annoy the reader with wholly unnecessary detail. However, all the information for anyone meticulously inclined was present.

The book was published and, in due course, was noticed. Mostly, the reviews were not unfavorable. Perhaps none was ecstatic; none was of the kind that arouses a warm glow of pleasure in the bosom of the author and promotes feelings of undying friendship and a wholehearted admiration for the reviewer's perspicacity; but none was bad. Except for one. It appeared in a respectable journal, which made it worse. I have forgotten the gentleman's name; and my feelings of outrage have long since subsided, together with my fixed intention of hiring an assassin to put an end to his wretched career. I remember I used to think of him at night. I could see him quite clearly: a pin-striped monster with two heads, both of them empty.

Perhaps you think my response to an unfavorable review a little intemperate and that I would have been better advised to have followed Somerset Maugham's practice of never reading his reviews but just measuring them. But even as you lay a ruler along the printed column, you cannot avoid catching sight of such expressions as: "trite," "ill-written," "badly conceived" or "worthless trash." They fly out at you like wasps, and sting. Not that this particular reviewer went in for such plain dealing. He contented himself, in such terms as a schoolmaster might employ when correcting a third form essay, with dismissing both the characters and the tale as being tediously predictable. Then he went on to say that "surely Mr. Garfield is an experienced enough author to have given us, without straining the patience of his young readers, something about eighteenth-century education, which would have been interesting."

Well, no doubt it would have been, had my story been set in the eighteenth century and had my hero been a schoolmaster puzzling over his curriculum. But as the story was plainly set in the nineteenth century and its hero was an illiterate ten-year-old, I felt it not unreasonable to spare my readers the occasional chapter on the educational system in force a hundred years before my story began. But even supposing he had said "nineteenth century," I would still disagree with him. However, he was right in saying that I am an experienced author; and my experience has taught me, sometimes painfully, that it is often better to suppress knowledge than to display it over-zealously.

In the writing of fiction or, at least, in the variety of fiction that I practice, which is to attempt to evoke the feelings and atmosphere of a past time, there are certain proprieties to be observed. First and foremost, the author should keep his nose out of it. The story is in the hands of the characters. Whatever is seen is what they see. They look about them. They take for granted what is commonplace and remark only on what is unusual. Thus, although I, the author, know quite well that to light a candle or a fire in the days before safety matches might well have taken a good five minutes of fumbling with flint and tinder, I would not expect my characters to find this to be something worth mentioning unless the delay in obtaining a light had a dramatic significance. Similarly, I did not think that my illiterate ten-year-old, who had only become enrolled in the Blewcoat School as he felt that a little learning would turn his nine-year-old sister into a marriageable article, would be well enough acquainted with the English educational system to provide my hostile reviewer with much more than an ill-informed and highly derogatory sentence. So I spared

him the dissertation that might have won his approval and incurred his disgust by confining myself to feelings rather than facts. This is not to say that I ignored the educational aspect of the story altogether. It was, after all, partly to do with a school. So, if you will bear with me, I will read you the way that I dealt with it. The boy's name is Young Nick, his sister is Jubilee, the schoolmaster and his wife are Mr and Mrs Rummer. Mr Owen or, as the children refer to him, Old Parrot-face, is their newly-acquired father, and Smudgeon is a pupil of the Blewcoat School. Their home, prior to their elevation to Mr Owen's slum dwelling, was on the wild side of St. James's Park, among beetles and earwigs in a cave of ivy and hawthorn.

You will notice that I elected to deal with the first day at school in retrospect, rather than directly. That was because I did not want to impede the progress of the narrative with events which could have no bearing on it and because, had I gone into the school with them, I would have been encumbered with some forty extra characters, which my slender story could not possible have accommodated.

She opened the door and a powerful smell of stale boys came out. 'Into school with you!' she cried, and Young Nick and Jubilee, clutching each other tightly by the hand, crept fearfully into their strange new life.

'Well, now!' cried Mr. Owen, welcoming Young Nick and Jubilee back to his lodging at the end of the day. 'How was it, eh? Your first day at school!' 'We done alphabets,' muttered Young Nick, not wanting to say that it had been the worst day in all his life.

... It had been a day of misery and bewilderment, of drowning in rivers of words he couldn't understand, and of being pushed off his bench by the boy sitting next to him, who never got caught. It had been a day of loneliness and fright, and of living in terror for the safety of his ears, which, he found out, had been given to boys not just to hear with, but to be used as handles, like cups, when the Rummers wanted to wake a boy up. Even the fine new clothes hadn't been much comfort. They'd itched and prickled like they was full of ants and bees, and Jubilee's bonnet had made her look like one of them mushrooms you couldn't eat.

In short, it had been a bad day, and if Jubilee hadn't been sitting a hundred miles away, at the other end of the huge wooden schoolroom, and in the middle of twenty great bony, grinning girls, him and her would have made a bolt for it, back to their ivy and hawthorn home. There, at least, though they'd always been hungry, and had often been wet and cold, they'd belonged to themselves. Now they belonged to the Rummers and the Blewcoat School, just like they was sacks of potatoes or coal! Earwigs and beetles were better off!

'We done singing!' said Jubilee, forgetting that she'd cried her eyes out every time she'd gone to the bog, and skipping round old Parrot Face's room, happy as a flea. 'And we had a pie with Smudgeon at dinnertime, on the corner of Horseferry Road!'

'We had a story,' said Young Nick.

'So did we!' said Jubilee. 'Right out of a book!'

'We done adding up and taking away,' said Young Nick. 'Money and things!'

'We done sewing,' said Jubilee, sucking her pincushion fingers. 'Look what I made!' She fished down inside the neck of her petticoat and pulled out a bit of cloth, edged with stitches as black and wobbly as a spider's legs, and speckled all over with her blood. 'It's a handkerchief! I made it for you, Mr. Owen,' she said. 'Our dad!'

Old Parrot Face stared at it and blinked — as well he might, for it weren't even big enough to wipe a butterfly's nose, let alone his great beak.

That, I still feel, although perhaps not as interesting as a dissertation on eighteenth century education, is more in keeping with the propriety of my storytelling, which, in this instance, is maintained almost entirely through the consciousness of Young Nick. After that brief scholastic excursion, I kept as far away from the school as possible. The account of the boy's sensations was not, I admit, the result of research. I relied on my own memory of my own feelings on my first day in a new school. I did not think that a boy a hundred years ago, or even a thousand years ago, would feel any differently. Just because a man might have worn a triangular hat, it does not mean that he had a triangular head. It was the same shape as yours and mine, and, doubtless, contained much the same mixture of hopes and fears, envy and affection, anger and joy. The trappings may change, but the trapped do not. That is why, when I write, I tend to superimpose the present on the past and make, as it were, a corridor of time.

Generally, in my attempted recreations of past time, I avoid well-known historical events, partly because to use them would imply a historical purpose in my narrative (which it never has) and partly because it would anchor my story too firmly in the past. However, on occasion I have ventured into that dangerous area with, perhaps, mixed success. I remember when I first decided to set a story during the early years of the French Revolution, I did an enormous amount of research. I read omni-

vorously. My history master at school would have been amazed by the industry I displayed, once out of his clutches, in my single-minded pursuit of knowledge. I read biographies, diaries, newspaper accounts, and the works of the very latest historians. In fact, I knew enough about the Revolution to have conducted the whole turbulent affair single-handed. I knew exactly how and why the Bastille was stormed, the numbers involved, and even the trades followed by those who stormed it. I knew a great deal more about it than anyone could possibly have known at the time. At first, I was inclined to put it all in, with the laudable intention of passing on knowledge. But then, little by little, I came to understand that the whole truth must give way to the partial, in the interests of the novelist's higher truth of being true to people. I will read you now an extract from that book, in which a Sussex schoolmaster, who nowadays would have been called left-wing — the term, incidentally, deriving from the seating arrangements in the National Assembly, with the Jacobins on the left and the Girondists on the right — first learns of the events of July the Fourteenth. The information at his disposal was wildly garbled; but I felt it proper to refrain from pointing it out. Far from adding to the verisimilitude of my story, I felt that scholarly interpolations would have subtracted from, rather than added to the truth I was trying to convey. Here, then, is the passage. The setting is Lancing, a small town in Sussex, and the Mortimers referred to are an aristocratic family in the neighbourhood.

Mr Archer had once had a cold - a bad, heavy, thick cold that had lain on his chest like a wet blanket. Then fever had stalked into his monastic rooms and laid him even lower. He'd summoned Dr Stump, who, setting aside political differences, had dosed him and arranged for Mrs Coker — Mrs Mortimer's attendant nurse — to visit twice a week and maintain the feeble flicker of life.

Mr Archer recovered from the cold — but not from Mrs Coker. She kept up her visits, on Fridays and Mondays, and enriched Mr Archer's mind with details of life in a high-class establishment like the Mortimers'.

Reluctantly he paid her a small stipend for her offices, which she always received with the glassy discretion of an official taking a bribe. If, for any reason, he forgot, or was absorbed in a book, she came and stood at his elbow and stared at the back of his head until he became aware of her. She never asked.

As Mr Archer was unmarried and Mrs Coker a seasoned widow, it was commonly supposed that she had designs on his liberty as well as her meagre wage. Now, towards the end of July, Mr Archer fell victim to another cold, and Mrs Coker brought him, on her Friday visit, a copy of the *London Chronicle* she had 'tidied away' from the Mortimers' parlour. She knew that gentlemen liked to read the newspaper and she watched red-nosed, red-eyed, chesty Mr Archer with maternal indulgence as he endeavoured to hide himself behind her thoughtful gift. Suddenly he put it down. His eyes were bright.

'At last!' he exclaimed. 'At last — at last!' (His actual expression had been 'Add last!' — his nose being totally obstructed.)

Mrs Coker folded her arrns and put her head on one side. There was a gentle smile on her broad, fleshy face.

'Something cheerful in the newspaper, Mr Archer?'

'Subthig wudderful, Bissus Coker!'

'That's nice.'

'Great dews frob Paris!'

'Have you got relations there, then?'

Mrs Coker was one of those souls whose interest in foreign parts was confined to the affairs of relatives and the nuptials of royalty. Beyond these two areas of interest existed a curious limbo that, for all Mrs Coker knew, might have been the place people went to when they died.

'They've risedd at last, Bissus Coker!' spluttered Mr Archer, banging his fist on the newspaper. 'The people have risedd! They've storbed the Bastille! This is trebeddus dews! My fred Bister Tom Paine will be over-joyed! Here — listedd to it, Bissus Coker! Listedd and rejoice!'

He sat bolt upright in his bed and, with intense excitement, read aloud to Mrs Coker the brief account in the *London Chronicle* of the great event. Breathlessly (in every sense), he read how, on the evening of July 14th, a crowd of armed citizens had demanded the surrender of the Bastille — the ancient royal fortress and symbol of tyranny and oppression. Under a flag of truce a party of forty citizens had been admitted to parley with the governor, Marquis de Launay. Once within, the drawbridge had been raised and the whole party treacherously massacred by the guards. Whereupon the crowd, incensed beyond all endurance, had stormed and taken the fortress, executed the luckless de Launay and carried his severed head round the city, fixed on a pike.

'Mr Mortimer's been to Paris, of course,' said Mrs Coker; 'and I rather think Mrs Mortimer has a married cousin living somewhere in France.' She said this with some complacency, as if bestowing on Mr Archer a piece of news quite overshadowing the rowdiness of the French capital.

'Good God, Bissus Coker!' cried Mr Archer. 'Do you doh what this beans? It's the fall of the Bastille! Do you doh what it sigdifies?'

'Oh, I expect it will blow over, Mr Archer,' said Mrs Coker comfortably.

Speechless, the one-time friend of Tom Paine sat in his ruthlessly tidied sick-bed and glared at this woman of the people with savage contempt. She exasperated him. He felt a ridiculous desire to awaken her, to shock her, to make her cow-like eyes start from her head at the violence that was erupting on behalf of penurious souls like herself. He wanted to make her scream.

'They cut off the goverdor's head!' he exploded. 'Cut it off with add axe . . . or a dife — it doh't say which! Thed they stuck it, pourig blood, odd a pike! Id the street, Bissus Coker!'

He gestured frantically to the window as if inviting Mrs Coker to go and witness, if not a severed head, at least a street.

'Now I come to think of it, Mrs Mortimer's married cousin lives in the south,' said Mrs Coker uneasily. 'I expect it's all right down there.'

Mrs Coker, by the way, was no creation of mine. I cannot take the credit for her. She was the creation of a higher power — Nature herself. She was, in point of fact, a cleaning lady whom we had the honour to share with a far more affluent family in the neighborhood. She came to us on Tuesdays and Fridays. She had been widowed three times and was, as I remember her, something between Mistress Quickly and the Wife of Bath. She was a novelist's godsend. All one had to do was to listen. To improve on her dialogue would have been to paint the lily and gild refined gold. I remember we once had a puppy. After some months of growing up, it performed an action that excited and fascinated our small daughter. At last, it had raised its leg against a tree. Proudly, our daughter informed Mrs. Coker — for so I always think of her. Mrs Coker fixed our daughter with her solemn brown gaze, and said, wisely:

"Ah! He's a man, now!"

After a moment of awed contemplation, one could not but wonder what criteria she had employed in the selection of her husbands.

Yes, indeed! Mrs. Coker was a treasure in every sense of the word; and although she has long since left us for more opulent pastures, she remains with me in spirit. She has been my companion on many a journey. She was with me in Würzburg in 1764, in Lancing in 1789, and in Labour-in-Vain Court, at a date unspecifed but probably around 1820. She has, in short, been a great traveler in time. Nor was she alone. Uncles, aunts, parents, friends and enemies have likewise accompanied me on my travels. The truth of the matter is I like to surround myself with familiar faces: that way, I never feel strange or alone. Even the streets and houses and, particularly, the shadows, are part of the luggage I carry with me back into the past. Like many of my generation, my early imagination was enriched by the cinema of the 1930s, that wonderful, explosive period with such great artists as Fritz Lang. My debt to such films as *M, Dr Jekyll and Mr Hyde,* (the Mamoulian version), *Frankenstein* and *King Kong* is incalculable. I still regard *King Kong* as a masterpiece of storytelling, from which it would be foolish not to learn. In my imagination, Ancient Rome still trails clouds of *Ben-Hur* and *The Sign of the Cross* and not even the Almighty could have parted the Red Sea with the distinction of a Cecil B. de Mille.

Not very long ago, I watched with great pleasure that wonderful old film, *Captain Blood.* I had not seen it for many years and when the slave auction scene appeared, I became acutely aware of how recklessly I had plundered it in the writing of my first publish-ed book, *Jack Holborn.* I am amazed that no one noticed and accused me of it.

But then reviewers — and I think back to the gentleman who so hankered after eighteenth-century education — in my exper-ience, are far more astute in noticing what isn't there than what is. But that is the common fate of books: what the writer laboriously puts in is not at all what the reader takes out. I have, in my time, with delicious malice, ridiculed my enemies; but they have never seen it. And that is a great sadness. I once wrote a piece about my own family. I misrepresented them, for dramatic effect, quite shamelessly. An elderly aunt read it and found it true. I felt guilty. But then I came to think that the past only lives in our minds. Historians are the custodians of the past; we, the storytellers, are its physicians, who strive to keep it alive.

VIRGINIA HAMILTON

Take your time

MY PURPOSE as a novelist, biographer and compiler of stories has been to entertain myself and others, to write well, to tell good stories and to introduce readers to the joys of literate language. A further purpose is to portray the essence of a people who are a parallel cultural community in America. I've attempted to mark the history and traditions of African Americans through the writing, to bring to readers strong stories and memorable characters who live near to the best that they know how. I rarely plan a book in note or outline form, unless it is one in which the material is not wholly created by me. I write, usually, from a simple and limited thought or idea. But each day thereafter I am involved in expressing through fiction and nonfiction the qualities that created characters and historical individuals bring in empathetic experience to today's children and young adults. In the nonfiction work which I find is as important to me as my fiction, I've documented the deeds, the defeats and successes of talented and significant individuals, relating their lives and works to the times in which they lived. The young readers may then comprehend rather painlessly the idea that society can be of their own making, expressing their needs which are fundamental to their existence as citizens. By doing, they themselves can effect change. The reader as a responsible being is never far from my thoughts as I write.

In nonfiction writing, the singular truths — truths as facts — are placed within a literary system through time-as-history in which an historical period is then transformed through the experience of an historical personage into a form of art. In fiction writing, one starts with artistic forms that portray a created character within a time frame and a place, and the literary purpose is directed toward the possibility of truths. The heart of any book is the making of its time, place and story. One begins a story with character, but all characters are shaped by their movement through time shared in one special place. There is the reality of the author's true existence in real time and there is the fictional time and place that is a limitless frontier. The reality place, the civilized place, lies next to the fertile, unexplored frontier. The author criss-crosses the border between the two. Hearing the call of the imagination from the frontier, she deciphers the urgent message, as it were.

A story I write often relates to my historical past time. I make the mind-and-time leap back to my ancestral continent and oral narration; forward to America and folk-telling; on to my hometown time and place and storytelling. From there, the work I do and the way that I do it becomes more abstract, involved with education, critical analysis, research, experience, and imagination. The reader assumes that the subject and its artistic form have not before been presented, that the reader is having an overwhelmingly new experience, something she or he couldn't have imagined. Then, it is the stuff of life, this story telling. It combines all of the elements of fact and memory, feeling and imagination to evolve finally into something greater than the sum of these parts.

Place and time are at the heart of the story. Place has much to do with the manner in which I create character and plot. I am a product of Mid-West America. The mighty Ohio River, some sixty miles from my home, forms great loops in my imagination as it does actually on its snake and wind through rich borderland. Time, in such rural places of America, does move slower than in other, larger places. No huge shopping mall has descended upon the populace overnight, forever changing the rural landscape. No McDonalds or Burger King to mar the rural north entrance into the village. The one Kentucky Fried Chicken franchise, located to the south out of town and on the highway to Xenia, the county seat, took years to pass stringent rules of the zoning, planning and priority boards. My mother, now ninety-six years old, was born in Yellow Springs. Her father came there as a fugitive from injustice. The story of Grandpa Perry's sojourn from the slave state of Virginia to Ohio defines the parameters of my creative writing. That I am named Virginia can be no accident. I am the only one out of generations named from a state. Serendipity. If I have the aptitude for making desirable discoveries by accident, and I do, time and time again, so too did my mother, at least once. By naming me Virginia she made me ever aware of my legacy and my responsibility to history as it relates to my historical past. Ancestry. I am of two minds within my writing, to say nothing of the female force of gender.

There is tension in the cross purposes that allows me to use a technique of opposition in my writing. The fabric of my fiction becomes a force against itself.

I begin a book with a character. I find I write against that character. There is often the stability of tradition and traditional life — timelessness — which is the character's background in opposition with the transient and unstable modern urban life — and time — usually represented by another more worldly character. The power of these opposites is dealt with in separate ideas — past and present, light and dark, staying and leaving, natural and supernatural, tradition, superstition and enlightenment. Somewhere between the opposites is a synthesis or balance.

My characters have contradictory desires, as I do. Tradition and at least the slowing down of time is likely to win out in my books, but with a profound feeling of sadness and loss.

At the end of the novel *M.C. Higgins the Great*, there is finality to the fact that M.C. uses his great-grandmother Sarah's gravestone in order to strengthen the land against the tearing loose of the spoil heap from strip mining, swollen by rain and poised precariously above his home:

He (M.C.) made a rectangle large enough and Ben (his friend) fitted the stone in. M.C. shoveled dirt over it and all of them helped Ben pack it in.
"Sarah, good-bye."
All of this time, the day stayed gray. Sarah's (mountain) was gray. But as the afternoon wore on, the mist rose into gathering clouds from mountain to river. They hung low, crowding above the high steel of M.C.'s pole. M.C. never looked up, but he sensed the clouds massing. He knew his work was urgent.
"Lurhetta, good-bye.
"Good-bye, M.C., the Great."
There began to take shape a long, firm kind of mound. The children fed it. M.C. shoveled and Ben packed it. In the immense quiet of Sarah's Mountain late in the day, they formed a wall. And it was rising.

This passage suggests a world wheeling through time and quiet. We sense the immediacy and urgency of time and experience.

In his thoughts, M.C. says goodbye to Lurhetta Outlaw, who has wandered into the hills of his home to change him forever. And in his mind, she says goodbye to him. It is to say that whatever is to be M.C.'s fate will continue to be shaped by the mountain, by his father's and mother's regard for past and time and place. Tradition wins M.C.'s heart, but with a new wisdom, with a longing for risk, modernity, other places, Lurhetta, all (at the moment) beyond his reach and will to know.

My being part of a parallel culture, of a minority group in a sense in opposition spiritually and societally to the empowered American culture adds, I think, to this sense of opposition in my characters. They want to be American; they are black. They are uncertain of their position in society. They move through life and time with dis-ease. They seek some relief from the conflict. They know that any moment of time and in any place the American dream can become a bad dream and may well become their nightmare. This then is their reality. My grandfather fled slavery toward freedom. But did he find it? My characters search for happiness; does this search cause them to move, to run? Two separate thoughts give them strength and unity of definition when at last, they do define themselves. Jane Langton wrote in *The Horn Book* in December 1974 ("Virginia Hamilton The Great") that in all of my books

a succession of solemn children — each one grasped by a mystic sense of significance and purpose — moves through space and time, passing among tall columnar presences of immense dignity (Zeely, Mr. Pluto, Mr. Pool, Banina, Jones), intent on strange random errands or journeys in which peculiar events are part of the circumscribing dailiness.

It's quite true, the protagonists I create are indeed loners but they are also leaders. They have their own minds; things happen to them and around them. I think of Teresa Pratt, Arilla Adams, Sheema Guidama Hadley, Talley Barbour, Pretty Pearl. Junior Brown and Buddy Clark in the novel, *The Planet of Junior Brown* might be two sides of the same coin. Or mirror images in which one reflection is oddly distorted. But all of these characters define themselves through their own actions. Characters come to me unbidden. They somehow create themselves out of the needs I have to define the conflicts of my own nature and imagination. They often present themselves with names, dressed a certain way, in motion. And they are born into my consciousness with conflicting emotions and desires. Once they are visible to me, I execute conscious choice to establish them within a plot structure, time-frame and place.

Everything I write can be thought of as a quest I have for relief from conflicts in order to discover a balance in my mental and physical environment. I play out this creative process again and again through book after book while devising plot and character development that will express with new insight things in opposition.

There is a deeply organic way of writing. It feeds upon itself, creating all of the elements of itself. In this sense I am a born writer. Making stories and problem-solving is the way

I think. Characters are thought and action personified within time and place.

Time is of quality. Remember the time? A grand time was had by all. Once upon a time. In the beginning. My time is your time. Time to leave. Time to be born. Time to live. Time to die. There is no time.

Time is of quantity. I spent all day. Time hangs heavily. I have time on my hands. His shoulders were bent, were weighted by time. She let time dribble away.

What does happen to time in a book? Whose time is there in a book? What happens to the writer's time; what is its significance, its definition? In a fiction, several kinds of time seem to be at work simultaneously. The real time of the author ceases to exist as she becomes immersed in the time and place of a fiction or nonfiction and within the intensity and time-beat of characters. What begins then is the time of the novel, and the march in time of characters, within which, time expands and contracts as if it were a living entity.

The prime tool of a novel is narration. By placing events before us, narration tells the story. The movement of an event within narration is by means of time, going from one point to another. We are speaking here of units of time, not segments of time, but units in which one or more processes can be fulfilled. The emphasis is therefore on something moving from its beginning to its end. We start a story or even a unit of a story when something is ready to begin. A condition is set but it is alterable, therefore, unstable, and we end when something has happened and the condition is now unalterable.

In my most experimental work entitled *Arilla Sun Down*, I use all manner of literary devices to expand, bend and contract time. My main idea for the book was my observation that we all carry our pasts around with us. Some of that past is conscious, but a good deal of it remains steeped in childhood or the layers of the unconscious. Nevertheless, we respond to that past as though we remembered it, through mannerisms, tone of voice. We reflect the looks of mothers, grandparents, and so forth. We have character propensities that sometimes are unfathomable to us but may seem perfectly reasonable to a relative who observes biological evolution in action. "Son, you walk just like your grandaddy. You never knew him but you walk and sound just like him," a relative might say.

My thought was to give the past and present in *Arilla Sun Down* a feeling of simultaneousness by alternating different time frames and focusing as though both were there in the present before the readers' eyes. The protagonist is a teenager but the book opens when she is a small child. The language of the narration is stylized to reflect the distortion in time and the other-worldliness of unknown memory. The child would not remember her early years. So the author uses poetic license similar to that used in *Sweet Whispers, Brother Rush* where the protagonist seems to look into a mirror and enters into the time of her past.

Quoting from chapter one, page one of *Arilla Sun Down*:

Late in the big night and snow has no end. Taking me a long kind of time going to the hill. Would be afraid if not for the moon and knowing Sun-Stone Father is sledding. Way off, hear him go, "Whoop-eee!" Real thin sound, go "Whoop-eeee!"

If Mother could see me, she would say, "What you doing up? Get back under the covers. Catching your death." But Mama sleeping on. I can slip on out to the moondust snow. She not seeing everything I do, like she say.

Now hurry to follow all of the tracks going deep in the snow. Knowing there is some big hill where all tracks of children go. Downhill is deep in a moonshade and ends at a cliff. Only Stone Father can stop a sled in time. I can't stop it. Jack Sun Run wouldn't care to try. I am smallest, knowing nothing for sure. But I think my brother, Jack, is a horse. Jack Sun Run still sleeping. He is bigger. But I am who slipping away. (Arilla finds her father and persuades him to sled with her down the dangerous hill at the bottom of which there is no fence, only a deep gorge.)

"Arilla, now hear me," her father tells her. "If the creeps come over you, don't let me loose or I'll never catch you in the present time."

"Knowing that for sure," I saying. Downhill ends at a cliff. Over the cliff is another time. Having seen no one go over or coming back. They say three people have gone. Two boys and an uncle, so they say.

In Arilla and her father's lifetime cycles, death is not the end of time, but simply not the present time. It is described as "another time", all things in their circle of life being equal.

By the second chapter, we are back into what can be thought of as a present time. Arilla is no longer a child. But let her speak and you will see how she sounds in her present.

For sure, my Birthday would be a disaster. I mean, worse than the time they tell about when that Learjet piloted by some rock-and-roll star-boys crash-landed in Wilson Onderdock's Black-Angus pasture a mile outside of town. Knowing something about Black Angus and Onderdocks gives a clue to what kind of engagement went on in that cow pasture for half the night. Even if one of the star-boys was bleeding all over the place, Wilson Onderdock said nobody was getting any blood transfusion and an ambulance ride until his prize bull hanging in little chunks on the fence was paid for.

My Birthday was shaping up to be the same kind of for-real bust. I would be surprised if there wasn't a little blood and guts somewhere in it, too. Because any event that had me at the edge of it when I was supposed to be dead center, and had Jack Sun Run at the center when he shouldn't've been there at all, was doomed any sixteen ways you wanted to look at it. It was just that with my brother being the Sun if the day didn't naturally revolve around him, then it couldn't happen. It hadn't even been formed yet. Or it was a piece of clay; and no matter how I might want to mold it, my brother, Sun Run, would come along and have to flatten it. He'd smack at it, beat it and work it over into whatever kind of shape suited him. That was his power.

The power of the sun. We reckon time by the earth's rotation around it, and so too, do Arilla and the whole book, actually, revolve through the time of this fictional world around Jack Sun Run Adams. Between the time of the child and the first section that I read to you from *Arilla Sun Down* and the section about Arilla grown to teenhood, lies time and its passage, change over years, parts of which Arilla may actually recall. But she cannot recall all of it. Time in which a gentle Indian man by the name of James False Face whose secret name is Talking Story has profound influence over her development; so that, by the end of the book, when he, through a shadowy, ghost, or dead time — he, himself is dead — reveals to her, her secret name, she is already aware of it, she knows she is the Wordkeeper.

"Wordkeeper?"
"Hearing you, too."
"Think of a time, any time, and I will be with you."
"But you going now?"
"Yes."
"Can't I going with you?"
"Yes, if you want to."

"Is it far — going?"

"It is only going in a circle."

"Then you coming back again?"

"I am here and now, then and there, in all things."

"You just going around."

"Yes."

"Then I thinking to stay here."

"Stay, then. Live with honor. And Wordkeeper?"

"I hear you."

"Remember who you are." (Arilla Sun Down pp. 179-180.)

Time as a circle is an ancient concept. Think of Cronos devouring his own children, the offspring of time itself. It is also an Amerindian concept and that of countless other peoples. Ashes to ashes and dust to dust.

Because of the stylized language of this section, the psychic distance is not distracting. In fact, the psychic distance between the characters and the reader is almost nil. The reader feels that she or he is somewhere there between Wordkeeper and Talking Story, who is himself speaking softly either in Arilla Wordkeeper's head or in her ear. Stylization and a close-up psychic distance enables the author to avoid sentimentalizing Arilla's profound sense of loss over James False Face's death. We can use all manner of distancing to present events in time. "It was Saturday, Arilla Adams stood waiting." (That's one distance, rather remote and somewhat formal.) "Arilla hated being on a horse." (That's a closer distance) "Lord, the smell of the horse made her ill." (Still closer) "The rain seeped down her neck, it covered her hair, freezing, turning her lips blue." (Very close, indeed, we're right up front.) Psychic distancings are moves of a camera. Books usually begin with remote or medium shots; and as we focus in on the protagonist, we are closeup and intimate or personal. The mind created the camera and as we see our characters in action, in time, place and space, we see in terms of the camera eye.

I would guess that I am intimately involved in this Wordkeeper section I've quoted. The symbolism is great here. James False Face is a veiled reference to the James Weldon Johnson poem — We Wear The Mask:

We wear the mask that grins and lies

It hides our cheeks and shades our eyes
With torn and bleeding hearts we smile...
We wear the mask!

James is also my father's middle name. It is certainly true that the exchange between Wordkeeper and Talking Story is somehow a farewell to my deceased father. It is I, the author, saying, "Never fear, what you desired all of your life for yourself and was thwarted and for your children will be carried on. There is a keeper and the keeper protects the flame through her time, and passes it along."

I think there is usually a story behind a studied event marked by effort and effect in a story and the short Wordkeeper vignette is a deliberate study in stylized simplicity. It's not important that the reader know the hidden story or the events that were its cause. Not if the story up front is complete of itself and does what it intends in the plot. Often, the artist doesn't know for years about the hidden story. But it's good that it should be revealed to her because it continues the integration of the personality. I think all symbolic, stylized writing derives from a need to interpret the somewhat skewed parts of the individual writer who would be an artist.

It has been some time since I set my sights again on novel writing. The last novel that I wrote was *A White Romance* published by 1987. Seems like a long time ago from my present vantage in time. 1988 saw two books, one the collection of creation myths entitled *In the Beginning* and the other, the historical reconstruction of a fugitive slave's life and times as a biography entitled *Anthony Burns: the Defeat and Triumph of a Fugitive Slave*. In these three separate works, from *A White Romance* to *Anthony Burns*, I move the reader through contemporary time, into prehistory, the dawning of ancient times and civilization and the time of slavery in America. Thousands of years in all. I find it difficult to write only in contemporary time. I find it almost impossible to sustain one time period in a single book. My books are composed of generations. The generations speak in terms of the times that were vital to them.

Here is the voice of Talley Barbour's

generation speaking through her in *A White Romance*:

Too much always going on inside her. Where was inside! Talley didn't know. Sometimes, it didn't seem to be in her head. Some kind of longing she had seemed to be on the landscape or on the windows of buildings, on the street signs, anywhere she looked. She guessed it was pressed there wherever she looked so it could touch her heart and make her so sad whenever it felt like it.

What is longing? It is the space, the distance over time between desire and attainment.

And from *Anthony Burns*, May 1 1854:

The weight of the past and the darkness of its night enclosed Anthony until slowly, with the growing light of day, he returned to the present... He tried retreating again into the past, but all that would come to him was the time of sadness in Mamaw's cabin. With him these many years was the same question, born out of that night. Who am I?

And from the collection *In the Beginning*:

All was dark. There was water everywhere. There was no sun and no moon and no stars. Then a raft came from the north... There were just two in the raft. They were Turtle and Pehe-ipe. Down from the sky came a rope of feathers and down the rope came Earth Starter... "Where do you come from?" Turtle asked.
"I come from above," Earth Starter said.
"Make some dry land, Brother," said Turtle. "Can you do that? Sometimes I would like to come up out of the water."
When Earth Starter didn't answer, Turtle asked, "Will there be people in this world?"
Earth Starter thought about that. Finally, he said, "Yes."
"How long will it be before you make some people?" Turtle asked. "I don't know," said Earth Starter.

Apparently the name as first translated from the Maidu Indian language is Earth Initiate, but I felt that would be too difficult for young readers to say, let alone understand. So I changed it to Earth Starter and I think the meaning is close enough. But here you have some of the external times of my most recent works. I have the Christmas book coming out in the fall entitled *The Bells of Christmas* and though it is fiction which takes place in 1890, it is not a novel. It is a short story book with one story and of course, again generational. I designed the text length after Dylan Thomas's *A Child's Christmas in Wales*, although not the construction The construction is my own personal pattern and not quite sixty pages with

fifteen full- and fifteen half-page color illustrations. It is probably my way of experimenting with the short form since I am working on a book now that is approximately a hundred pages long — a loosely told story connected in the fictive manner of a novel, *Sherwood Anderson's Winesburg Ohio*. I think I am now at the point in the book where voices and sounds dominate. Not so much pictures. But voices, the way people say what they have to say. Movement is mental and talking. The elder protagonists are more or less confined. The young lead character in one of the stories may be the central protagonist, but I am not sure. I have a year and a half to figure out this book. In that period the sound of the book may change many times. It is contemporary and, in some ways, timeless. In this initial phase, I write by instinct and go with my instincts. I don't try to figure out too much. I simply write until my mind gets snagged on the raspberry bush thorns and I have to gingerly figure my way loose.

And I quote from *Cousins*:

"Mister Owen asked me to help him build him a hog house. Gram? You hear that. He just said so." Gram Rudman cackled like a hen.
Cammy sidled up to her bed and hopped up on the side rail. She smacked a big kiss on Gram's cheek.
"There!" she said. "I planted it, Gram. Now don't wash it. Let it grow."
Gram couldn't wash her own face, poor old thing, Cammy's ma said. Well you're not poor anything, thought Cammy, Are you, Gram? You just need me to snuggle your face. Cammy didn't dare snuggle her cheek up against Gram now. She always did that before she left, though. And it always made Gram cry, too.
"Gram?" Cammy leaned close. "You ain't dead yet, are you?"
Gram kept her eyes closed. She broke into a grin. Said, weakly, "Fooled ya!" and shot her eyes open.
"No, you didn't," said Cammy. "I knew you was here and always will be."
"Suspect I will, the rate I been here," said Gram.
"Ninety-seven years!" exclaimed Cammy.
"Oh, surely, not that long!" Gram murmured.
Cammy thought to let it go, found she couldn't. "Gram, how old are you?" she said. "Got ten fingers," Gram said quickly.
"But how old?" Cammy persisted.
"Don't scold me," said Gram.
"I'm not scoldin', Gram," Cammy said.
"Well, somebody is," Gram said. "Wish they'd leave me alone," she cried, plaintively.
"She hears voices, honey," Ma had told her. Cammy couldn't quite fathom that.

"You're ninety-seven years old, Gram," Cammy said.

"Oh, surely not," whispered Gram.

Cammy did let it go now. "Gram?"

What, honey? She imagined Gram would say that if she had the strength to speak just then.

"Did you hear what I first said? Otha Owen is building a hog house and needs some help. You want to help him?"

This time, Gram did rise to the occasion. Murmuring quickly, hoping to get the words out before all her strength left her. She had horded it since after breakfast, knowing that Cammy would come, talking a blue streak.

Gram's dry lips parted: "Tell that ole man he'll never make another pigsty nor wallow in the mud-manure, either," Gram said, softly.

"I hate hogs," Cammy told her.

"But you love them ribs smackin their taste in your mouth..." Gram murmured.

"...And sour dough bread with the butter drippin out of it," added Cammy.

Gram done made her last meal on this earth, her ma said, last Sunday. They all missed Gram's cooking, as though it had been something alive. When she no longer could cook before she went to the Care, Gram sat in the kitchen at home and Cammy's Ma cooked while Gram directed her. It had tasted good, too. But not as good as Gram doing it, Cammy thought. Never that good. Oh, - Gram!

"Maybe we can have it for Christmas," sighed Cammy. It looked as if Gram really had gone to sleep. Her mouth sort of lay slack on one side of her face.

But she fooled Cammy. "That's ain't Christmas dinner," she said, turning her head with effort. "You want turkey and duck for Christmas, like the old times."

"Truly, Gram? Will you come out and make it for us?" Cammy asked, all eagerness.

"Child, you wear me out in five minutes ... I done cleaned the whole house today ... what more ... Oh, Lord, where is thy light?"

"Gram," Cammy said. She knew very well that Gram got out of bed only for breakfast and dinner. She watched Gram closely. Saw that Gram was still with her. Her eyes rolled back and forward, then focused. She came back.

"Don't talk, Gram, cause it wears you down. Just listen. I was telling you that Otha Younger Owen is outside. Hear his chair squeak? Here he comes — Gram! Shall I let him in?" She knew how to turn a straight room chair over on its side in the doorway so not one wheel chair could come in, least of all, Otha's.

"Does he have his pajama bottoms on still?" asked Gram, her voice whistling from her chest.

"Gram...sure he does. They won't let him walk around silly."

"Say yestididdy he took his night clothes all off in the hall."

Cammy knew that had happened a month ago. Gram lost plenty of time. But she could speed it up, too, when she felt like it.

"Let him in," Gram said. "Mebby he knows me today."

Cammy went to the door, directed Otha in by saying importantly, but quietly, so as not to alert the nurses, "My Gram will see you now."

He rolled in, a sagging, pale little man, surrounded by

the chair, his small beady eyes hard and dry. He had no hair to speak of. He was tied in the chair with a sash across his waist and around the back of the chair; he shrank further into the chair each day. He stopped to the left of the sink and took in Gram's 'home'. He looked at the television on low at the foot of the bed, tuned to Oprah. He looked at the bed crank to judge Gram's condition. The top of the bed was up, keeping her lungs free of fluid. He took in the bed last, with Cammy standing on the rail, craned around to look at him. Without warning, Otha came up swiftly behind her and pinched the plump of her forearm.

"Ouch! You old..." She made a spit ball. He saw her mouth working and raised his hand. But she wouldn't use a spit ball on an old farmer in a wheel chair. I'm ten and I do know better than that, she thought. Ma would whip her tail for doing that, to say nothing of what her brother, Andrew would do to her if he found out. She was usually in his care, when he could find her. He never told on her when she slipped off because it was his fault for not watching her closely enough. And if he admitted to anybody that she ran off, he would have to admit that he never went to find her. Her brother Andrew was sixteen and hard as nails. She reserved the best spitballs for her cousins, who were the worst little pests in the universe, so her ma said.

Otha Younger gave her one of his blind kind of looks although he wasn't blind. But he would fall down when he tried to stand up. That was why he was tied in the chair.

"Got sixteen cents?" he asked Gram.

"What for, Otha?" she said, "Where's your manners — don't you know how to say good morning?"

"Gram, it's after four o'clock in the afternoon, goodness sakes," Cammy told her.

"To get a bus so I can go home," Otha said. "I'll give you a dollar if you arrest my son. Puttin' me here."

"There's no bus," Cammy said. "They don't run the bus to your house. Anyhow, your house is sold."

"You better get outta here. Nurse! Nurse! The kid is messin' around!"

"Shut up, Otha," Gram said, "Or you can't visit me no more!"

"Oh, hush up! Don't see why everybody's so cranky. My wife's mad at me, too, today. Stayed away all day," Otha said, glumly.

He don't remember his wife's passed, Ma had told Cammy. She also said it was funny the way he fits to his gravity and because it was, he would fall and do things sudden like. Cammy had seen Otha standing in the door of his home once, that being what they called their rooms at the Care. Each one had a separate home, and suddenly he was blown forward like out of a cannon. He just shot himself across the hall. And his head hit on the railing the old folks hold to when they walk, and pull themselves along when they're in wheelchairs. Didn't hurt him.

"So," Gram was saying, "Otha, what you up to?"

"He's building a hog hut, I told you," Cammy said.

"Oh, will you be quiet?" Otha said. "I'm talking to your mother."

"No you're not," she and Gram said almost at the same moment. Cammy squealed with laughter, just as Lilac Rose, the wing attendant this week, stopped to study the three of them.

"Party time," she said, coming in to check on Gram, feeling under her the way she would to see if Gram was still 'comfortable' as she put it. That meant dry.

"Hi Lilac," Cammy said. "Don't tell on me, please."

"I ain't seen nobody," Lilac said. "And I ain't hear nothing."

"Thanks, Lilac," Cammy whispered. Cammy placed her cheek on the dark coolness of Lilac's arm as she took care of Gram. Lilac never minded her and never told on her.

"I'm goin tell," Otha said. "Kid!"

"Otha, you ain't gone tell nothin' to nobody," said Lilac, "don't always be so mean. Miz Thompson likes having her gran-baby come visit."

"Well, I will," he said. He backed his chair carefully to the door, sensing when he was at the opening. Then he shot out and across the hall, holding his feet high off the floor. He hit the railing with force. Then he gave out a hog call that Cammy would've envied if it had been ear-splitting, the kind the young hog callers did at the county fair. After that there was a thud as the chair with Otha fell over on its side. All the unexpected noises started a series of cries, plaintive "help, help"s, all down the cool, quiet wing.

Lilac continued about her business with Gram. But at once, Miss Mimi came wheeling out of her 'home'. Cammy saw her when she peeked out to make certain ole Otha was all right. Miss Mimi had on lipstick all on her face and her hair was rolled in a fresh pompadour.

"I'm coming, girls, don't fret," she called down the wing in her high voice.

Gram sighed and said to the air, "We take care of our own."

This is a small section of the work entitled *Cousins*, which in my mind means connections, history, family and, again, generations. Time.

In *Cousins*, I hope to engage the reader as a participant in my imaginings. That is, I leave room in the text for the reader to enter and imagine part of the story. Maybe I will describe Lilac at some point, but maybe I will not, leaving it to the reader to decide what she looks like. I won't tell at once whether Otha hurts himself when his chair tips over. Let the reader imagine how he looks for a moment — a little bug made of iron, perhaps.

I don't believe reading is very much fun unless something exciting is going on in the reader's brain. We read and fill in the spaces; we begin to notice patterns, a sense of structure, a banding of feelings; and slowly we begin to make sense out of what we are reading, to recognize a kind of system full of recognizable signposts to which we can relate and which makes us feel comfortable as we find our way. This is a creative process and a dynamic which has to do with time, subject, changes, and conclusions. What the author attempts to do is surprise the reader while at the same time satisfying certain expectations drawn from the text. This is not a smooth or easy process. We read and constantly change our minds, in the very way an author makes revisions when she is writing. The reader revises her opinions depending on what is happening, has happened, and is going to happen in the text.

I have winter books and summer books; some are filled to bursting with dark and cold; others with sunlight and shade. *Cousins* is a summer book. The contrast between the cool halls of the Care Center where the old folks live and the free outdoors of summer are like two entities that actually have spirit and character as far as little Cammy is concerned. Cammy, through observation and learning how to move down the wings unseen, is able to visit her gram nearly everyday by herself, which is against the rules. Her mother works. She feels a special obligation to the fading elder senior as only a loving child can.

Actually the scene in the Center is only about four pages of the first story; the rest is Cammy and her friends and enemy cousins. But she will return time and time again the center; it is the somber counterpoint to an otherwise fairly sunny book. I know this even though I really don't know what the book is about in its entirety. Again, in a way I am speaking from hunches, unconscious sensations. Words that come into my head about the book and language for writing it have to be based on some truth. I believe that. I believe the book is inside, waiting.

Again, I learn how to write a novel by writing it. I learn the structure, the characters and the kind of time it takes. Sometimes I feel like a fortress and inside there are all these little soldiers lining up, doing muster, making ready to do battle — with what, they never know in the beginning. But they are lining up now and I feel indeed like a fortress under siege. My supports are the warm weather, sunlight, summer heat. My writing thrives in summer. First drafts of books are done from spring through September, October. By the time winter comes, I will have done the basic research on three books and will have a first draft of *Cousins*. Knowing my modus operandi doesn't make it any easier. The labor is always cut out for me. It is what happens day by day over long periods of time. I do not stop writing. I write something every day, something toward the fulfillment of some literary obligation.

Knowing that I have three projects that must be done over the next two and one half years or three years makes it impossible for me to really create anything further at the moment, although I am preparing for other future projects with publishers. One tries very hard to limit the activity and to stagger it; otherwise, one feels as if one's life and time is slipping through the fingers.

Ernest Hemingway thought it very bad for a writer to talk about how he writes. "He writes to be read by the eye," said he, "and no explanations nor dissertations should be necessary;" and also "that it wasn't the writer's province to explain or run guided tours through the more difficult country of his work." He also said, and I quote: "A writer can be compared to a well. There are as many kinds of wells as there are writers. The important thing is to have good water in the well and it is better to take a regular amount out than to pump the well dry and wait for it to refill.

But the best thing he said, I think, and although in no way am I comparing myself to Hemingway, it applies to me as well — is this, "Read anything I write for the pleasure of reading it. Whatever else you find will be the measure of what you brought to the reading."

And if I may add, if you have the time, take your time.

DIANA PAOLITTO

The child's perception of time in childen's books

AS THE LONE psychologist at this institute, I see my task somewhat differently from that of the other speakers here. As much as I might like to give you my personal reflections on my assigned topic, the child's perception of time, it is assumed that as a social scientist I shall provide evidence for whatever statements I make. At least this is what my American colleagues would expect of me.

In preparing for this institute during the late winter and early spring I asked myself, what could a psychologist's perspective offer this impressive group of writers, literary critics, librarians and educators? I concluded that the single most important contribution would be to represent the child. This I hope to do by attempting to enter the child's world and bring children's voices into this great hall.

As this audience most certainly knows, the wisest statements about human nature have been made through the ages by writers of literature. It is only in the last century that psychologists have set out to prove what writers have known intuitively all along.

Thus for example, Penelope Lively in her essay 'Bones in the Sand" delivered at a previous summer institute, states:

Children live in another country; and although it is one we have all passed through, to pass beyond it is to have lost, irretrievably, I believe, its language and its beliefs. We have lost the sense of a continuous present. (*Innocence and experience*, p.19)

How elegantly and simply expressed! This happens to be one of my most cherished beliefs as well, that children do indeed inhabit another country. She and I, however, probably arrived at this conclusion in very different ways: she, primarily through he own subjective experience gleaned from personal memories and keen observation; and I mainly through intensive study and observation of children via scientific investigation.

But scientists and writers may not be as far apart in our methods as one might first suppose. We both collect story fragments to reframe for our own purposes. Thus, in the process of preparing for this lecture, I found myself listening to stories about children and time that adults wanted to tell me when they learned I was struggling to formulate something definitive on the subject. My favorite one is this. Out of the blue one morning, a five-year-old inquired of his teacher, "When were you born?" "1944," she replied. "Was that before there were people?" he wanted to know. As adults we may chuckle, but the child was perfectly straight-faced in asking the question.

Part of my task this morning is to help us understand how it is that a child can come to ask such a question in just this way. Using the exact words of children themselves, I should like to provide evidence that children do indeed live in another country when it comes to how they perceive time.

There are virtually hundreds of psychological studies and theoretical articles which attempt to describe the child's perception of time. Jean Piaget's classic book *The Child's Conception of Time*, first published in French in 1927, continues to serve as an inspiration to numerous investigations of time as duration influenced by speed and distance. The majority of the studies center on Piaget's cognitive developmental framework. The other major stream of psychological thought, the psychoanalytical tradition, has been the basis for only a handful of theoretical and research papers on the child's perception of time.

But nearly all these studies seem peripheral to the central question that a psychological perspective could offer this institute: How does the child reader perceive time in literature? According to my search of the field, there is not one study which tries to understand how children make sense of time in children's books. I was inspired to conduct my own small study, therefore, as I became captivated by the books on our reading list, and began to discuss the time dimensions in some of them with my own children.

Let us look at what I decided to do. First of all, I begin any study of children with the basic premise shared by most developmental psychologists that the child's ability to construct meaning changes with age. The growth of a child's mental capabilities does not occur by amassing knowledge or by taking in more and more information about the world. Rather, children possess distinctive mental processes that transform knowledge itself in increasingly complex ways as they grow older. Their mental capacities change as a result of the interaction between the maturation of the nervous system and the stimulation offered by the child's environment. A child's mind is not simply a smaller version of an adult's.

It is true that every child, and each of us as well, does come to know and understand the world in a unique way. But undoubtedly Piaget's greatest contribution had been to document his hypothesis that people's patterns of reasoning change in a developmental progression, starting in infancy. Certain characteristics of thought cluster according to approximate age groupings that correspond to infancy, early childhood, middle childhood, and adolescence.

In relation to my own study of children's understanding of time, I found two very different developmental patterns, according to age. These are summarized with examples in a chart on pages 44 & 45. The first pattern occurred in children between ages four and six, and reflects the general characteristics of Piaget's so-called preoperational period of intellectual growth. The second pattern of responses, beginning around age seven, and continuing until about age eleven, corresponds to Piaget's so-called concrete operational period of thought. I shall also briefly mention the changes that unfold at the start of adolescence, which reflect yet a third pattern. Please bear in mind that the ages at which these patterns occur are approximate, and that all children do not suddenly change their ways of thinking when they turn seven, or eleven. Developmental change is gradual and uneven.

I interviewed forty children ages four to fourteen one at a time for a half hour to an hour each about time dimensions in the same few books. These children attend the Shady Hill School, an independent school in Cambridge, Massachusetts, where literature has traditionally been at the core of the learning process.

Naively, I started out to illuminate the straight dichotomy suggested by philosopher and psychoanalyst Hans Loewald between objective time and subjective time. Objective time was to be defined by children's understanding of Western notions of the measurement of duration, especially as demarcated by the ticking of the clock. Subjective time was to be explored in Loewald's (1980) terms as "the experience of time" "the subjective sense of lapsed time" (p.138); that is, in the internal interplay of past, present and future. For example, my talk this morning will take one hour's time according to objective clock time. Some of you, however, will experience this same duration subjectively as an eternity.

But the ability itself to construct a distinction between objective and subjective time is very much an *adult's* abstract perspective on the matter. This dichotomous organization presupposes that the child has already incorporated and understood the same stable notions of objective clock time that have been culturally agreed upon by the adult Western world. Based on all my previous research, my hypothesis was that children's ways of knowing and experiencing time would not be so neatly and clearly divided.

So I abandoned this adultified view of time and instead tried to listen closely to the children's own words. It became immediately apparent as I started interviewing that objective time is indeed so tightly bound up in the child's unique subjective experience that I needed to elicit the most basic concepts of time ordering to understand all the rest. I am defining these concepts as, first, simple *narrative* time (how does the child understand the sequence of a story?) and, second, *chronological* time (how does the child understand the passing of measured time in a story?). The interviews also informed my decision to discuss two parts of chronological time separately; *clock* time, or the child's understanding of seconds, minutes, hours, days; and *calendar* time, the understanding of weeks, months, years, centuries.

The children's responses that I will discuss this morning relate to only a few of the books on our list, mainly picture books. I chose to focus on these books, because they elicited the most clear and articulated responses from children about narrative time, clock time, and calendar time. They are *Come Away From the Water, Shirley* by John Burningham, and *When I was young in The Mountains* by Cynthia Rylant. With children ages four to eight the classroom teacher would read one of these books to the whole class, or to a small group, and I would interview a few children, one at a time, in a quiet corner, following the story reading. Starting with the nine-year-olds, I shall discuss *Tuck Everlasting* by Natalie Babbitt, which the children had read on their own prior to my study.

First we will consider the four-to-six year old's sense of narrative time. That is, how do children in this age group understand the sequence of a story, in this case, the chronology of events in the picture book *Come Away from the Water, Shirley* by British author John Burningham.? In this humorous story we have a wonderful opportunity to ask children about both narrative and clock time. As you may recall, in this book a day at the beach passes very differently for Shirley than for her parents. On the left side of every page Shirley's parents sit in beach chairs uttering commands to their daughter: "Mind you don;t get any of that filthy tar on your nice new shoes," or, "Don't stroke the dog, Shirley, you

don't know where he's been." Juxtaposed on the right side of each page is Shirley, engaged in imaginary play - rowing a boat out to a pirate ship where she and that very dog do battle on board with swords, dig for buried treasure, and row back to shore by the light of the moon, triumphant, she wearing a gold crown. On the last page Shirley and her parents are walking away from the water with folded beach chairs.

To elicit the child's sense of narrative time I asked, "Could you retell this story?" Although every child's rendering was different, of course, what we are looking for here are any similarities, or patterns, in the children's story summaries. I found two types of narrative summaries by four-to-six-year-olds. The first shows a lack of chronological sequence, and a fragmentation of the story line. Here are two five-year olds' versions of retelling *Come Away From the Water, Shirley*:

> There's pirates on the other side of the page. They are sitting on the beach. [I ask "Who?"] The people.

> I can't; I don't get it. [I open the book for her.] Her parents are sitting on beach chairs, and she's sailing back.

These statements comprise their entire retelling of the story. Unless we had read this book ourselves, it would be hard to get a sense of the story line from these statements. The story does not move forward in time, but rather proceeds from one particular idiosyncratic detail to another. The elements of the story lack coordination and progression.

The second type of story summary does show a rudimentary sense of time awareness within the narrative. But the major thrust of the child's version of the story is a highly personalized statement about the child's intuitive and private experience of the world, not the world depicted by John Burningham. The child's retelling of the story tends to fixate on one moment in time and describe only one feature of the story. The narrative does not progress in time. Here is five-year-old Lizzie's version of the Burningham book. You will recognize some of Shirley's adventures in her narrative description. But mainly her story summary is a captivating rendition of how she herself might "play pretend" at the beach:

> There's a little girl. She's thinking about pirates. She's thinking she's in a pirate ship and her dad's dressed up in a pirate suit. She's on the beach, and she thinks she finds some pirate gold...She's really pretending in a cardboard box, pretending she's in a real boat.

An even more dramatic example of how young children's sense of the story line centers on their own private experience rather than as adventures progressing in time is six-year-old Katrina's rendering of the story:

> The little girl's doing things she's not supposed to. She's annoying her parents. She was sort of going too far on things, pushing it too far. She wanted to do things she wasn't supposed to do. She was having too much fun. She got into trouble and the time ran out. So she just played alone.

The main thrust of Katrina's narrative is a highly personalized statement about Shirley's activities as a reflection of her own private experience, not a retelling of the story as it moves through time on the pages of the book. It is in this sense intuitive and egocentric.

Egocentric is not intended as a pejorative term here, from adult to child. It is a psychological concept which means that children center their attention on themselves and fail to take the viewpoint of others into account, in this case the author's and even the characters'.

If young children four to six years old reveal a lack of chronological sequence when they retell a story, what happens when a seven or eight year old child is asked to retell *Come Away from the Water, Shirley*? Most striking is the finding that the narrative has a time ordered sequence. This is how seven-year-old Matthew tells the story:

> It's about a little girl named Shirley and she goes to the beach with her mother and father, and she goes on this adventure with pirates. She goes to an island, finds a treasure, and goes back home. This is a real place. It's far away.

The story is linked together by a sense of time passing. The use of "and" indicates progression, meaning "and then" or "next" as opposed to the straight linkage for com-
munication purposes that a younger child employs. Time is cyclical: Shirley goes to the beach with her parents, embarks on an adventure with pirates, and returns home again. To the child, the story has a beginning, middle and an end.

Other children this age did not center their story summaries around the progression. Instead they provided a synopsis of the action of the story, thereby compressing the passage of time. Here for example, is seven-year-old Judd giving a synopsis of the story sequence:

> Its about a girl. Her mom keeps telling her do things. But she's doing it in a different way. She's not doing things her mom says, except when its getting late and they're ready to come home.

To summarize the development of the child's understanding of narrative time from these interviews from early childhood through the elementary school years of later childhood, we can see movement from a fragmented, egocentric and intuitive understanding of a story to a narrative ordered by time progression, or, at the least, time awareness. Before we move on to discuss clock time, I should like to give a glimpse of what the next transformation in thought might suggest at the end of childhood and the beginning of adolescence.

In late childhood the children of ten to twelve whom I interviewed seemed preoccupied with detail and compelled to follow the exact order of events in their story summaries. I named this preoccupation with detail "the tyranny of accuracy and precision" as I developed writer's cramp trying to record word for word the two-page narratives of these older children as they retold *Tuck Everlasting* by Natalie Babbitt in their own words. Forward movement in time was the central organizing force. First Winnie found a toad, next she met the man in the yellow suit, then she met the Tucks, and so forth. One could almost hear time itself marching by, steadily and relentlessly, as I listened to their narrative summaries.

With the advent of adolescence, when abstraction first becomes possible, the adolescent is freed from immersion in specific facts. For the first time, we witness the young adolescent's ability to construe narrative as a synopsis of ideas suggested by the story as well as the events themselves. For example, fourteen-year old Jim's understanding of *Tuck Everlasting* centers on future time as central to an abstract controversy:

A boy named Jesse and a girl met at a fountain. He said she could live forever by drinking from it. There is a big controversy about whether to live forever or not, or whether one could. The main plot is whether they should live forever, whether to drink from the fountain or not.

The heart of the narrative, as this fourteen-year-old reader understands it involves abstracting from the story the open-ended question of whether one could or should live for ever.

In terms of how the developing child understands the sequence of a story, we have moved from the intuitive to the abstract.

Now we will consider the child reader's understanding of clock time, and finally, calendar time. Starting once again with the four-to-six-year olds, we see parallels to their ways of construing narrative time. The outstanding feature of their revelations about the meaning of minutes, hours, and days is the arbitrary nature of what constitutes a certain length of time. What appears arbitrary to us is perfectly logical to them, because it is based on their personal experience with time passing rather than what the clock objectively says.

Here is a sampling of responses by five-to-six-year-olds to the question "How much time passes in this book, *Come Away from the water Shirley*?":

Maybe five minutes
[Is that long or short?]
A long time.
[How do you know?]
I'm smart.

About half an hour, 'cause that's a little beach. That's how long it takes me to go to the beach.
[Is that long or short?]
Half in half
[What would make it a long time?]
If I made a big huge sandcastle because that takes a long time.

A lot, pretty much, medium, sort of long, but sort of short. I'd say two minutes go by.
A hundred hours, because I just know.

I could continue to enumerate as many different lengths of time as there were children in my study. Furthermore, if I asked each child the same question the next day, or even a few hours later, they would come up with yet another amount of time. Their lack of certainty has the mark of a wild guessing game. The point is that units of measured time are still fluid at this age; minutes and hours are interchangeable. There is no objective standard around which units of time are understood. Clock time is a personalized progression, largely dependent on the amount or type of activity for its experienced duration. There is an implied understanding, however, that the time passing in this books occurs within one day. No child mentioned days, weeks, months, or years. Hours and minutes are understood as small units during which a day's activities are organized.

To understand further the relationship between clock time and activity, I asked the children two other questions: "How much time goes by for Shirley?" then "How much time passes for Shirley's parents?" Children from four to six replied that more time went by for Shirley because she was doing more. That is, the busier you are, the bigger something is to make, or the more parts there are to an activity, the longer it takes. Shirley's parents just sit there, so time is shorter.

In contrast, the seven-or-eight-year old has a more accurate and stable comprehension of clock time. As children of this older age group respond to questions about clock time in *Come Away from the Water Shirley*, they can approximate the number of hours a day at the beach takes. They also show an attunement to the diurnal rhythms captured in the book by the vivid illustrations. Here are some of their responses to my interview question, "How much time passes in *Come Away from the Water, Shirley*?":

It takes from day to night. When it's time to go home it looks like sunset.

It takes about five hours because it went from the afternoon to the night; because at the end it was dark; at the beginning it was light.

Unlike the child a few years younger, these seven-and eight-year-olds notice on their own the concrete markers of time movement - light, dark, day, night, sun, moon. Some of the children told me spontaneously that there were 24 hours in the whole day, or that day time takes about 10 to 12 hours. In other words, they have incorporated the basic logic of Western clock time. It is in fact at this age that the child learns to "tell time."

This gain in understanding objective time measurement also affects the child's ability to see that clock time remains stable even while people engage in different activities. So when I ask seven-year-old Amanda to compare how much time goes by for Shirley and her parents, she is not deceived by the appearance of different activities as a five-year old would be:

[How much time goes by for Shirley's parents?]
Shirley's parents think it's four hours because they're just sitting around.
[How much time goes by for Shirley?]
For Shirley it's two hours 'cause she's doing things so fast. If things go past quickly it *seems* like it's two hours, but it's really three or four. It's interesting how it can be.

Amanda maintains the notion in her mind that four hours objectively pass by for Shirley and her parents, while simultaneously realizing that time can feel long or short depending on what one is doing. For the first time a child shows curiosity about time passing in the story. That is, with the development of stable concepts of clock time, the child gains the flexibility to think about time from different perspectives. It is as if the older child is freed up to play with clock time, now that she understands it.

As children in this period of development continue to expand their understanding of duration as measured by units of the clock, some older children's awareness of time becomes dominated by an interest in accuracy and precision. The details of clock time are attended to in a manner similar to their detailed narrative sequences described earlier. Here is an example of a ten-year-old's response to the question 'How much time goes by in *Tuck Everlasting*?'

One day for Winnie to meet the man in the yellow suit. The next day they found Winnie near the spring and had to take her back with them. Then they only slept there one night, so that's two days. It was about three days for the man in the yellow suit who took her back to tell her about the gallows. Then they describe about a month when its really hot out. Then there's another day when the man dies and they say Mae has to go to the gallows. That's another day, so there's a month and a day. The next day Tuck comes by and plans the jailbreak and Winnie decides to help them. That's about a night.
So, so far that's a month and three days. Then a week passes and she sees the toad and she gives the toad water. So that's a month, a week, and two days. Then it's sort of the end of the story. Then a lot of time goes by, 72 years. They see her grave and it's 1950.
Therefore 74 years went by, plus a month, a week, and three days. Because she died when she was 72.

There is a definite interest, and even a fascination, for this child in figuring out the precise mathematics of time passing. This is because the child now understands how clock time is calculated, and seems to enjoy applying this ability to novel situations.

The final category of time which I shall consider this morning is calendar time. How do young children understand the passing of months, years, centuries? As I mentioned earlier, I decided to subdivide the concept of chronological time into two parts — clock time and calendar time — after I found a marked difference in how children understand these two. By calendar time I actually mean calendar time in the *past* exclusive of future months, years or centuries. This is because the books I used focused on movement between past and present time.

The younger children in my study perceived the past as an amorphous period of time, *then*, which contrasts with *now*. The past is not demarcated by years but is rather seen in relation to when their parents, or at most their grandparents, were little. Otherwise, past calendar time has a fairytale quality to it.

Stimulated by the picture of Shirley fighting the pirates, I asked the question, "When did pirates live?" These respondents are five or six years old:

I wasn't alive but my mom was.
A very long time ago. The olden days.
Another history, a long time ago; I don't know how long ago in numbers.

The last child has a vague sense that past time has numbers assigned to it, but she was the only child in this age group who alluded to the notion of years. The others saw the past as either a generation ago or else long ago indeed.

When we listen to the responses of the next age group, beginning at age seven, we find children using concrete markers such as inventions or style of dress as a way of anchoring stories in the past. The best examples of this tendency came from asking how long ago the story in the book *When I was Young in the Mountains* took place. As you may recall, every page of this account of the author's childhood memories of summer in the mountains of Appalachia, the threshold to the southern United States, begins with the melodic phrase, "When I was young in the mountains..." The author, Cynthia Rylant, then describes treasured moments like swimming in the local swimming hole, witnessing a Southern baptism of total immersion, and Granny's killing a giant snake.

Despite the clear and repeated generational markers in the text, these older children, like their younger classmates, told me that this story took place in "the olden days', or when things were "old-fashioned" and "not modern'. How did they know? Because of the absence of familiar objects in the illustrations: there were no swimming pools, no skyscrapers, no big buildings, no electricity, no washing machines, and no sewing machines. Their list goes on. They anchor past time from the standpoint of what familiar surroundings are missing from the story, rather than what is actually depicted. And like their five and six-year old counterparts, most older children, even ten-year-olds, did not conceive of the past in years. It was still the vague "olden days.'

Some children eight and older do estimate past calendar time in this books by calculating the years mathematically. These children step back from the page-by-page details and think about the amount of time in the book as a whole. For example, eight-year old Charlie told me:

This book took place 70 years ago, since if it's 1989 now, it would be abut 1919 when she was a little girl.

This boy seems to know that years progress incrementally. He can calculate a generation ago by using arithmetic. He also has a sense of how long it takes for a person to grow from childhood into adulthood, even though it is longer than most of us might say.

One might therefore expect the older child to apply this same type of logic to understanding past centuries as well. But such is not the case. Instead, we find that the same kind of wild guessing game takes place when even a ten-year old discusses centuries, reminiscent of the five-year-old's knowledge of minutes and hours. For example, one eight-year-old said that *When I Was Young in the Mountains* took place in "maybe 1600-something, maybe 100 years ago; no, 65." Decades are also interchangeable, as in nine-year-old Victoria's answer to the question "When did the story *Tuck Everlasting* take place?':

Maybe the 1970s. Well maybe later, [longer?] because they drove a horse and cart, so maybe it was 1960 or 1950.

Moving forward developmentally, we find that young teenagers have a more exact sense of time in the near past, if they proceed backward, generation by generation. But they, like their younger siblings, are still confused about past centuries. Making meaning of calendar time or historical time more than a few generations in the past still perplexes them. I did find, however, that beginning with the transition to abstract reasoning ability in early adolescence, children could estimate the century of a story by comparing it to what era in the past they had already studied in school. In other words, they need a known point of reference.

So what do all these interviews tell us about children's understanding of chronological time? In the first chapter of his book *Revolution in Time* David Landes sandwiches into the narrative a very important reminder of our Western bias:

"The first thing one has to remember is that it is not 'natural' to want to know the precise time — that is, time as expressed in hours, minutes, and subminutes. We take such a need for granted because hundreds of years of time discipline have inured us to it." [*Revolution in Time* p. 25] He is referring to the revolution in time that has occurred on the cultural level, of course, but there is an obvious parallel to our conception of time on the psychological level. A quieter but equally profound revolution takes place in the mind of each individual as we grow from childhood into adulthood struggling to understand time with greater and greater precision. Basing my conclusions on my interviews, I would take his point yet one step further: it is not only our wish to know the precise time that is unnatural but also our ability to do so. We have to grow into this knowledge, so to speak.

The child's understanding of chronological time begins with intuitive and self-centered perception stimulated by the immediacy of daily experience with rhythms of duration. Only gradually does intuition expand to incorporate time measurement that is based on an awareness of the objective increments determined by universal Western standards. But this process is not easy or natural, especially once we move beyond the ticking of the clock to the flipping of calendar pages. The most surprising part of these interviews for me, in fact, was the enormous gap between the child's ability to understand clock time and calendar time.

There seems to be a "lag" effect at work here, in that even the more sophisticated mental processes of late childhood are insufficient to the task of mastering calendar time. Our current psychological understanding of the child's mind does not prepare us for the fact that even teenagers still have an amorphous view of past calendar time, once we leave markers of generational time behind.

Across all ages, these interviews suggest that the further away time is depicted from the child's personal experience or vicarious experience, the longer it takes for time measurement to develop stable, universal meaning. For younger children this process holds true for both clock time and calendar time. For older children clock time can be comprehended, but calendar time still lies somewhere in the past enshrouded in mystery. I do not assume, by the way, that children's understanding of future time would necessarily follow this same process or rate of unfolding. Reference points in the future have far fewer concrete markers based on known experience to help children bridge the gap between here and there.

The primary outcome of this little study is simple but profound, as I see it: we cannot assume that children understand time as we adults know and experience it. We saw that as the child grows, there exists a relationship between the age of the child and the way the child perceives time in literature. The maturation of the child's mind involves a transformation in one's meaning-making capacity. This proceeds from a relatively intuitive mode, through the ability to grasp everyday reality, and finally towards the abstract realm of ideas. One might conclude, therefore, that educators need to simplify the ways that we adults explain time to children. And further, that writers of children's books need to modify their renderings of time in literature, where time is a central theme. The question of whether these modifications are desirable would certainly stimulate lively discussion over this week at the Institute. I hope it will.

As for me, I would like to inject a slightly different interpretation into the interview results. Instead of necessarily changing our current approaches, perhaps we should expend more effort listening closely to the responses of children as we read the same books together. Just what is their experience of time? What is ours? What do our differing responses tell us about the many facets of a piece of writing? I think we shall find that the best works of literature are still those in which time plays a central animating role, books that can be read and explored on as many different levels as there are young and old to read them.

The Child's perception of time in children's books

PRE-OPERATIONAL THINKING
(Approximate ages: four to six)

Narrative Time	Chronological Time	
STORY SEQUENCE	CLOCK TIME (seconds, minutes, hours, days)	PAST CALENDAR TIME (months, years, centuries)

Characteristics:	Characteristics	Characteristics
Fragmentation, lack of chronological seqence Basis in idiosyncratic personal experience or intuition Egocentricity	Arbitrariness Measurement in terms of the meaning of personal experience Influence of perception of type of activity on duration.	Dichotomy between now and then Comprehension of generational time only; otherwise fairy-tale time No notion of years or centuries Confusion between months and years
[Retelling *Come away from the water, Shirley*]	[How much time passes in *Come away from the water, Shirley?*]	[When did pirates live, in *Come away from the water, Shirley?*]
"Her parents are sitting on beach chairs, and she's sailing back"	"Five minutes" [Is that long, or short?] "A long time." [How do you know?] "I'm smart."	"A very long time ago. The olden days."
"There's pirates on the other side of the page. They were sitting on the beach." [Who?] "The people"		"I wasn't alive, but my mom was." "Another history, a long time ago; I don't know how long in numbers."
"There's a little girl. she's thinking about pirates. She's thinking she's in a pirate ship and her Dad's dressed up in a pirate suit. She's on the beach and she thinks she finds some pirate gold.. she's pretending in a cardboard box."	"A half hour; that's a long time, because when I go to the beach it takes us a long time to get back." "A lot, pretty much, medium, sort of long, but sort of short - two minutes." "A hundred hours, because I just know."	[When did this book take place?] "Summer." [What year was it?] "June."
"The little girl's doing things she's not supposed to. She's annoying her parents. She was sort of going too far on things, pushing it too far. She wanted to do things she wasn't supposed to.."		

The Child's perception of time in children's books

CONCRETE OPERATIONAL THINKING
(Approximate ages: seven to eleven)

Narrative Time	Chronological Time	
STORY SEQUENCE	CLOCK TIME (seconds, minutes, hours, days)	PAST CALENDAR TIME (months, years, centuries)

Characteristics:	**Characteristics**	**Characteristics**
Sequence, time-ordered seriation. Beginning, middle, end. Time linkages: ("and then," "next") Synopsis of events, compression of time.	Awareness of diurnal rhythms, concrete markers of light and dark, day and night. Ability to tell time and estimate duration.	Use of concrete markers (inventions, dress) to anchor past time Use of arithmatic to compute years (but not centuries) Interchangeability of centuries Instability of concepts of calendar time
[Retelling *Come away from the water, Shirley*] "Its about a little girl named Shirley, and she goes to the beach with her mother and father and she goes on this adventure with pirates. She goes on an island, finds a treasure and goes back home. This is a real place. Its far away."	[How much time passes in *Come away from the water, Shirley?*] "It takes from day to night. When it's time to go home, it looks like sunset." "It takes about five hours. Because it went from the afternoon to the night because at the end it was dark; at the beginning it was light."	[How long ago did this book take place (*When I was young in the mountains*)?] "This was the olden days, because... —no swimming pools— —no skyscrapers — —no big buildings— —no electricity, washing machines or sewing machines."
"It's about a girl. Her mom keeps telling her to do things. but she's doing it in a different way. She's not doing things her mom says,except when its getting late and they're ready to come home."		"It was seventy years ago, since if it's 1989 now, it would be about 1919 when she was a little girl."
Ages nine - eleven, add: Insistance on exact sequence of events.	Ages nine to eleven, add: Precise calculation of clock time. [How much time went by in *Tuck everlasting?*] "...so far that's a month and three days. Then a week passes and she sees the toad and gives it water. So that's a month, a week, and two days. Then it's just sort of the end of the story. Then a lot of time goes by —seventy-two years — they see her grave and it's 1950; therefore seventy four years, plus a month, a week and three days. Because she died at seventy-two."	Ages nine to eleven, add: Interchangeability of decades, centuries. [When did *Tuck everlasting* take place?] "Maybe the 1970s. Well, maybe later (longer?) because they drove a horse and cart, so maybe it was 1960. Or 1950." [When did *When I was young in the mountains* take place?] "Maybe 1600-something, maybe 100 years ago, no, 65."

REFERENCES

Babbitt, Natalie. *Tuck Everlasting* Toronto: Collins 1975

Burningham, John. *Come Away from the Water, Shirley*. New York: Thomas Y. Crowell. Co., 1977.

Duckworth, Eleanor. *"The having of Wonderful Ideas" and other Essays on Teaching and Learning*. New York: Teachers College Press 1987

Ginsberg, Herbert & Opper, Sylvia. *Piaget's Theory of Intellectual Development: An Introduction*. Englewood Cliffs, N.J.: Prentice-Hall, 1969.

Landes, David. *Revolution in Time: Clocks and the Making of the Modern World* Cambridge, Mass.: Harvard University Press, 1983.

Levin, Iris (Ed.). *Stage and Structure: Reopening the Debate*. Norwood, N.J.: Ablex,1986.

Lively, Penelope. Bones in the sand. In B. Harrison and G. Maguire (Eds.), *Innocence and Experience: Essay and Conversations on Children's Literature*. New York: Lothrop, Lee & Shepard, 1987.

Loewald, Hans W. *Papers on Psychoanalysis*. New Haven: Yale University, 1980.

Piaget, Jean. *The Child's Conception of Time*. New York: Dutton, 1982

Rylant, Cynthia. *When I was Young in the Mountains*. New York: Dutton, 1982

Spence, Donald P. *Narrative Truth and Historical Truth: Meaning and Interpretation in Psychoanalysis*. New York: W.W. Norton, 1982.

GREGORY MAGUIRE: SEMINAR

Memory

Thou still unravished bride of quietness,
Thou foster-child of silence and slow time.
— Keats.

THE WOMAN WHO answered the door to me had somewhat more spunk than it had sounded on the telephone. She was nearly ninety, a crosshatched shadow behind the screen, checking first to make sure that was indeed the graduate student who had called earlier to see about taking a room in her house in the other Cambridge, in Massachusetts. She checked the slip of paper in her hand. Was I Mister Maguire? I was. She pushed open the door of the late Federal-style house a few blocks north of Harvard Square, and I tiptoed in.

It was, I told my family back in Albany, like a visit to the set of a Masterpiece Theater production. A seventeenth-century Dutch cuckoo clock, its cuckoo bird long voiceless, ticked on the wall by the umbrella stand. In the front hall, on an elegantly carved mahogany table with rams' heads and laurel branches improbably entwined in bas-relief, stood the brass chest armor and helmet of some strange medieval costume. But Mrs. Reginald Seabury Parker took me beyond, into the parlor, where we settled on an Empire sofa to have a chat.

I had guessed we would talk about rent, house rules, and perhaps she'd interview me to discover any alarming habits I might have, but her eye was caught by the headline of the *Times* folded up on the coffee table, and she asked me my opinion of Jimmy Carter's Camp David efforts in the Middle East. I didn't have many opinions at the time. Luckily, my hasty inquiry about the cuckoo clock changed the

BOOKS FOR DISCUSSION:
James Berry *A Thief in the Village*
Eleanor Cameron *The Court of the Stone Children*
Janni Howker *Isaac Campion*
Penelope Lively *The House in Norham Gardens*
Margaret Mahy *Memory*

subject before any damage was done. We realized we'd both spent our childhoods in Albany, New York — a mere sixty-five years apart. Albany was settled by the Dutch, we both knew about that, and so we nattered on about the influence of the Dutch on the domestic architecture of the upper Hudson River valley, and then about the attitudes of the Anglican church in the push for the ordination of women, and other crucial matters. Sarah Parker brought out two glasses of lemonade and two Chinese paper fans. The armor, she explained, was brought back by her uncle who had been in the Philippines in the 1890s. She never knew whether it was ceremonial or utilitarian, and it had proven a trial to keep free of dust, but out of love for her uncle she had always displayed it prominently. And then she said,

"Well, my dear, I believe you'll do very well, and I do hope you will choose to come live here."

"But we haven't talked about rent," I said.

"My dear boy," she answered, "if I were to charge you rent I would have a serious responsibility to make sure all was superbly managed, wouldn't I? If we avoid rent, then I haven't a care in the world, which is as I like it."

She showed me the room, a back bedroom with a sloping roof, nice prints on the walls, old furniture. "This is a Parker dresser, this is a Horton chair sadly in need to sprucing up," she said, indicating the families from which the old pieces had come and to which, she implied, they would return after she died, for she and her late husband had had no children. There was a private bath with a little shower under a skylight, and a maid came in once a week to clean. "But I must insist you supply your own linens," she said, and gave a worried look as if I might back out at this indignity.

My friend and folks in Albany couldn't believe I'd landed on my feet in quite such a way. My father insisted I should have held out for an allowance.

In the first few weeks to follow, I made myself helpful by carrying sherry glasses in from the parlor when guests came in the afternoon, and I was always welcome to sit with guests and enjoy their company, too. One afternoon, however, after listening to a pompous retired minister pontificating about Our Lord, in those distinctive spoken capitals which assure you that Our Lord is more mine than yours, I ventured to say to Sarah, as we washed up the glasses, that while I had enjoyed his wife, I hadn't quite understood the minister's sense of humor. Sarah turned from the sink and said quickly, "Well, that's perfectly understandable, dearie, he hasn't got any."

Sarah Parker was a lot like Penelope Lively's Aunt Susan and Aunt Ann, in *The House in Norham Gardens*, which is one of the reasons I was so drawn to that book, and to this topic of memory in children's fiction. She was perhaps a bit more robust physically than those great-aunts were, at least when I first met her, and she got out a bit more. Her husband had been dead for sixteen years in that summer of 1977, and her beloved brother Tom some ten years earlier than that; the house on Avon Street was a kind of stole, a mantle she wrapped around herself, redolent with the aroma of the past, her past and her

husband's, but not masking the present, not disguising it nor distilling it.

It is that house on Avon Street, in Cambridge, Massachusetts, from which this talk begins; specifically, a photograph, now perhaps ten years old, of Sarah Reginald Seabury Parker. In this photograph you see Mrs. Parker at ninety or ninety-one, or ninety-two, depending on her mood when you asked her about it.

I'd like to propose this morning — and throughout this talk it will never be more than a theory — that our memories are dramatically affected not only by the conventions of art but also by the technologies of the times in which our art is created; I suppose that memory performs the same function in most cultures, by and large, and throughout most times in human history, but that the ways memory manifests itself in individual human consciousnesses in different cultures and times may be vastly different, so very different that if we indeed were able to dip into someone else's memory, it might seem to be nonsense — random, unintelligible, illegible.

Let me give you an example. Last summer, I took a trip to Nueva Segovia, in the northern part of Contra-ridden, impoverished, undeveloped Nicaragua. I spent ten days in Quilali, in a community under siege, divided in its loyalties to the Sandinistas and the Contras, and possessed of some of the most vigorous and hopeful children I have ever met. One of them, Sayra Rossy Lopez Molina, was a girl of perhaps thirteen, with the kind of needling clarity in her attention to her siblings, the weather, her studies, and me, which I have come to associate with pre-television culture. Sayra was that godlike creature in whom a pleasant nature and a beautiful face seem impossibly harmonious; it makes you feel you're being sentimental and gushy when you're really just observing the true facts about her.

When I was about to leave, Sayra Rossy Lopez Molina gave me a photograph of herself on her first communion day. It's a bit cracked from having been folded, and the letters she wrote on the back bulge through like Braille on the front. The Sayra in the picture is perhaps only half the age of the Sayra who stood there smiling, offering me what is likely to be the only existing photographic image of herself. (The photo was taken by an American who passed through Quilali years ago). All the blues and yellows have faded; Sayra stands holding up her white-pink skirt, with words on it I cannot read, in a brick-pink world. It's like the old sepia photographs, or the black-and-white ones; the past Sayra at the age of six, has no blush and no dimension, she is a fading coppery doll, pinned to a moment almost like a butterfly in plastic; she even looks like a butterfly with her pudgy hands holding out the skirt to show its fullness. She seems to be Exhibit A, unsmiling, yet all the physical beauty and cleverness and obedience she would demonstrate at thirteen is already present in this photograph.

So she gave me the photo, and I accepted it not to hurt her, but I felt I might be stealing the sole glimpse of her childhood. Sayra didn't have photo albums and videotapes to choose from; this single photo was it. I wondered if, as Sayra remembers being younger, she remembers it in a pink haze, in frozen moments of demonstration rather than in fluidity, light, color. I thought I might be stealing her memory. But I packed this card inside my passport and carried it safely home. In this photo is the "foster child of silence and slow time," in Keats's words, the girl who will not grow up, though the real Sayra will and largely already has.

Back from the rural village life of the highlands of Central America, home in the sweltering heat of last August in Boston, I turned around almost immediately and hopped aboard a British Airways flight to England, to meet with John and Jill and confer about arrangements for this 1989 conference.

So scarcely ten days later I arrived in Cambridge, and John and Jill met me and introduced me to their village home. For a lark, out we went on the river, skies high and clouds bright and occasional, willows bending picturesquely. John punted, and then I did, and then Jill took a turn while I trailed my fingers in the water. I said, "I expect that film credits are going to come rolling up over my face any minute now."

My point is this: as children of the middle part of the twentieth century, we cannot seem to help seeing, interpreting, recalling the moments of our lives in the language of cinema. We hear soundtracks in the music that plays on the radio, soundtracks of our own lives. We edit mercilessly, having learned our trade from observing a thousand and one films. For instance, when I recall Sarah Parker from ten years ago, I see her in soft-focus close-ups, filmed through cheesecloth, perhaps. I see the house lit more dramatically than it ever was; I hold the bits and pieces of conversation between us as a sort of montage, segueing from comic exchange to difference of opinion to poignant and emblematic epigram, stitched together with my own internal film editor's rigorous logic. I lived with Sarah Parker for two years, but most of that has ended up on the cutting room floor. Like it or not (and incidentally I don't like it,) the memory of this couple of years in my young adulthood is squeezed into conventional terms; for me, the terms of film.

Thinking about time and memory a whole year ago while wandering through the British Museum, I paid a visit to the Elgin Marbles. As you move from one end of the gallery to another, imagining the friezes in place in the Parthenon, you yourself supply, by walking, the movement in time to correspond with the intense kinetic energy of the procession. As a museum goer in London, you pause before, say, north frieze number 38. With your twentieth century familiarity with the work of Marcel Duchamp's "Nude Descending a Staircase," for instance, or the more contemporary photo-collages of David Hockney, you are used to cubist portrayals of time and motion, essence and ephemera. You may begin to see the horsemen as a single character in motion, almost as if you held up a strip of celluloid and looked at all the static images at once, like the photos of Edward Muybridge.

You do this if you like, having been born after the invention of the camera. It is however impossible for us to be sure how a citizen of Athens would react to a single frieze, isolated from the rest, or even how he or she might react to the whole organic ensemble. Did the sculptures tell the Athenians what to remember of their lives, and how to remember it? As the ritual of the procession gave form to their religious and spiritual hopes and longings, did the art of the time affect the way they would select, interpret, and store their recollections?

Would a young woman in seventeenth-century Holland, be she Calvinist, humanist, or Catholic, conceive of her life in moments of exquisite stillness and consoling light such as Jan Vermeer painted? Would her memory be trained to fasten on the sumptuousness of the pattern of carpets, the chill clarity of pewter, the forgiving resilience of water? This is not to simplify what is, of course, not so much a line of argument as a meditation: a Dutch girl of the seventeenth century who saw Vermeer might also find fascinating his contemporary, Jan Steen, whose depictions of ribaldry and revelry are anything but still and inward.

Charles Simic, in his "Notes on Poetry and History," focuses the thought a little better than I can. He says:

> If not for the invention of photography and motion pictures, one could perhaps still think of history in the manner of nineteenth century painting and Soviet Revolutionary posters. There you meet the idealized masses and their heroic leaders leading them with chests bared and sleeves rolled up. They are marching with radiant faces and flags unfurled through the carnage of the battlefield. The dying young man in the arms of his steadfast comrades has the half-veiled gaze of the visionary. We know that he has glimpsed the future of humanity, and that it looks good. Unfortunately for all concerned, people started taking pictures. I remember, for example, a black-and-white photograph of a small child running toward the camera on a street of collapsing buildings in a city being fire-bombed. The smoke and the flames are about to overtake her. She's wearing a party dress, perhaps a birthday party dress. One is also told that it is not known where and when the picture had been taken.[1]

Or, said by poet Robert Lowell,

> We are poor passing facts,
> warned by that to give
> each figure in the photograph
> his living name.

I hope you will forgive this rather lengthy introduction to the five books of our seminar.

For me the books are, individually and collectively, about the power of the created object of art to focus memory, to hold it, to train it to work in a certain way.

Of the history of memory we can say this: according the Greeks, Mnemosyne was the Titaness of remembrance, born of the marriage of earth and sky. The continuity of the world was insured by Mnemosyne; she bore witness and gave testimony. And I remember here the story of Prometheus, whose name means not Memory but Forethought, perhaps Memory's predecessor; I remember how Prometheus gave to his creation, humankind, the gift of fire which he had stolen from Zeus. He carried the fire of the sun in a hollow tube and made a gift of it to the race of humans. And this was how they were distinguished from the animals. Forethought.

But let us get on to the books at hand, for the authors of these books share some similar concerns, though the results are strikingly different. And let us look at each of the books with these foci, particularly: what is the perception and meaning of time to the children in these books? What do the objects of art they encounter suggest to them about it? How do they choose to speak, to tell others about their understandings? And finally, what do they steal? Somewhere, among those four questions, lies at least one set of assumptions about children and memory, about the ordinary and the immortal.

James Berry's collection of short stories is called *A Thief in the Village*; its nine stories take place in a Caribbean setting; the stories are told by children, often unnamed; even when the stories are written in the past they are presented in childhood's relentless present moment. More often than not the stories are told in the first person, too. The needs and desires of the children in these stories are so fierce that they eclipse most else, including the histories and memories of these children, with the force of feeling they engender. Becky wants a bike so she can join the Wheel-and-Brake Boys. Delroy wants a mouth-organ. Gustus braves the hurricane for his natal tree and cries "I did wahn buy my shoes, Pappy. I...

I cahn go anywhere 'cause I have no shoes..." Fanso wants to know what his father is like and is chilled when he realizes that on the evening of having finally met him he is already forgetting him.

These stories, so richly representative of the culture of the Caribbean, tell us little about the community memory or its history. Perhaps the little sidelight about the "blackheart men," the white slave traders who kidnapped Africans and transported them to the new world is the primary example of the past acting on the present in a way which is comprehensible to the child narrator of that story about a rare and representative Sunday, a Sunday like every other Sunday, a Sunday which will in memory become one Sunday: On Sundays we did this...

Interestingly, there is a bit of thieving going on, although I mention this only in passing. Becky steals her dad's sun helmet to trade it for a bike; Big-walk is accused of stealing coconuts. Delroy is accused of stealing a mouth-organ. Despite the title of the book, the stories are not about stealing, not really, except insofar as each story is about a child claiming for himself or herself some little bit of the world in a slightly stronger voice: This is mine, this is what it is to be me. I want my memory of my father, I want my shoes, I want my mongoose. I want my name Stephen, not Tukku-Tukku. I want to keep this story, and tell it in the Jamaican voices of my father's homeland.

For the other thing that ties these stories together is the persistent appreciation of the incidents as stories. In the title story Maxine retells the childhood incident of Nenna and Man-Man because having visited Jamaica she is "fascinated by my father's birthplace and home village." And having written the story, she is asked by her teacher to read it in her Jamaican voices. She has made the memory of her father her own, and when her father is gone, some bit of Jamaica from before Maxine's own time will stay with her and live on in her. In "The Pet, The Sea and Little Buddy," another glorious Sunday is marred by the catastrophe of a runaway horse and a helpless child. Once the danger is passed, the narrator tells us, on the way home "the men had already begun insisting on their own version of what had happened." They begin to anthologize the story according to their own needs, which are no less vigorous than the needs of children, but perhaps less transparent.

On occasion — only rarely — James Berry allows us a little breathing room out of the panting nowness of these children's lives to give us an adult's point of view. We hear from Granny Flo, momentarily; she is stunned and thrown off balance by the colossal need of her grandson. We alight inside of the weeping Mr. Bass who has come to rescue his child, and it is here that James Berry leaves us: inside the adult who carries around a greater knowledge about, though no greater involvement with, the causes and effects of the tragedies of the world. It is as if we are told that the perfect Sundays of our childhood will break open and hold inside them more anguish than children can bear; and that is the burden of being adult, and of knowing time.

Janni Howker's Isaac Campion also has fierce desires, although they are more abstract than mouth organs and bicycles. Isaac Campion, the child, wants to escape from the future projected onto him by the death of his brother Dan. Isaac Campion, the adult, wants to communicate to the future how he did escape. The young Isaac wants action; the old Isaac, communication. Both, in fact, get what they want.

Isaac Campion's memories are given dramatic shape; he recreates the feel of life by withholding information until its release corresponds with the narrative moment he's describing. He knows what he's doing, providing a caveat right off: "When you look back over all those years, you think that what happened was bound to happen. You can't imagine that it could happen any different." But of course Isaac as an old man knows full well what was going to happen to him, now at the moment of telling; he knows that he was to escape his father's tyranny, and the cycle of accusation and recrimination between his family and the Laceys would be broken. Isaac then revels in his role as a chronicler of his life, slipping in at times general comments about how life has changed from then to now, but rarely giving an advance glimpse of how the tragedy was to be righted, if ever it was.

The memories he brings up are rich in sensory appeal. He says of the day of his brother's death, "That day's fixed in my mind like a picture." Not like a snapshot, notice, not like a movie, but like a picture. Isaac tells us, however, that the references are stronger than merely pictorial; he says, "Do you know something? I can even smell that day. . . "

And he does smell it, and so do we, and we hear it and see it and perceive some of the lost foreignness of it.

"They used to make a lovely soft thundery sound, those wooden casks, when they were rolled across cobbles," Isaac tells us. It was "An April day — sun scudding out between grey clouds. A primrose sun, my mother would have called it, and clouds hung up like washing. But the lanes and alleys were all a churn of muddy cinders and cart ruts, and on the streets the cobbles shone like grease..."

And a bit later on: "I could smell beer and horses. Smell the sweat of fast bidding and money on the men's clothes. All jostling and arguing."

Of course this wasn't just any day; it was the day Dan was to die, impaled on a wrought-iron spike, and by the time Dan had died Isaac had cottoned on to the fact that this would be one of the important days of his life. As an old man he muses, "This is the only way we have, you see, to go back into the past. This business of remembering. But it is false. You can't go back because you know what is going to happen. But you didn't know what was going to happen then, you see? You did not know. You are just living your life, wondering what it is all about. You don't know what might be important. You don't know anything."

But by the evening of April 17th, 1901, Isaac Campion *did* know this was important, and at that early age he stored up the details of the time and arranged them so that eighty-four years later, he could remember them. Now of course it's anyone's guess whether the wooden casks ever made those lovely soft thundery noises on April 17th, 1901; perhaps

they did and perhaps they didn't. Maybe they made those noises every time Isaac went to town, and he has lifted the noises from his general pool of memories and applied them to this day. They aren't, after all, pertinent to the dramatic action of the day. Perhaps only later on, when beer stopped being delivered in wooden casks, did Isaac recall the sound and apply the metaphor of thunder to it. This is to say, only, that he is making a story of what he knows to be true.

He freely admits as much when he talks about standing in a quiet stable. "Have you ever stood in a quiet stable? They're calm underwater sounds you hear. Shod hoofs scraping on the flag-stones. Soft sputtery thumps of dung. Deep-chested gentlemanly snorts... I can hear all those sounds now." But of course it's not in the Hardacre Infirmary he hears them, and lord knows how long it's been since Isaac Campion stood in a stable. He wasn't crazy about horses, as you know.

So Isaac makes a story of his escape. It is such a short tale, and it is heartbreaking in the size of the changes it portrays. For the child Isaac, slowly perceiving the "pattern of all our lives," continues to think on the same subject as an ancient man. "What would become of us all? " The cruelty and sham which was part of dealing with horses had its counterpoint in how people dealt with each other, too, and Isaac knew it. "Ever since I was born, I'd seen all the indifferent cruelty that was inflicted on horses to make them work, or to trick a buyer into thinking a poor slow animal was frisky and spirited. And how patiently they bowed their heads to their lot, those working horses. I just knew that even if I tried all the days of my life I'd not stop feeling this awful pity for the lives and deaths of animals and men."

And Isaac never does stop, not at the time of day in which he was born nor in which he dies. He comes near to feeling pity for his father, but he cannot sacrifice himself for pity, and we learn that he does escape his father's domination.

Isaac hasn't stolen anything, for his own life belongs to him, and the gift of it to the author and to us is a gift outright. Yet it is interesting, parenthetically, to notice that the only other storytelling that goes on in the novel outside of Isaac's narration to us is the story that Isaac's mother has teased him with in childhood, and this story is the narration, please take note, of robbers.

"One dark and stormy night, three robbers sat in a cave, and the youngest robber says to his chieftain, 'Tell us a story.' And this is the story he told. . .

'One dark and stormy night,' says the chieftain, 'three robbers sat in a cave, and the youngest robber says to his chieftain, 'Tell us a story.' And this is the story he told...

I don't want to make more of the motif of theft than it deserves, for of all things Isaac seems to be, it is honest and forthright. He lobs the golden sovereign into the river, he gives Dick Lacey the lost whistle back. But the tale his mother tells is a story about telling stories, and so too is Isaac telling stories, and one may then wonder if it is only robbers who can tell stories, for it is only they who have the nerve to steal from their own lives or the lives of others, and pass the goods along. In the pattern of all our lives, we may only guess at what will become of us all if we allow ourselves to be the receivers of stolen goods, the fence through which the stories of the Isaac Campions and Sarah Parkers and Dominique du Lombres may pass.

Which brings us to *The Court of the Stone Children*, with its abundance of art, its collection of interpretations of a life and of lives in the handwriting of one artist particularly, the fictional Jean Louis Baptiste Chrystostome. In Eleanor Cameron's richly textured tale of the receptive child Nina Harmsworth and her strong "museum feeling" — that attachment she has to the lives of the people whose things are left behind in museums — there is much passing back and forth of information and sensation, through strange and peculiar ways of knowing: premonitions, reminiscences, and dreams.

In a sense, Nina stands in the confluence of these mighty forces, receptive to the past and the gentle haunting of Dominique; confident of her future as a person in a museum; and all the time guilty and capable,

too, of the grand larceny of dreaming about others. And what a grand, grand larceny a dream is; it is dreams which make the strongest connections in this story. The Chagall painting is described "like a fairy tale or a dream," and Dominique, in discussing her feelings about her home being moved to San Francisco, says it is like a "strange, twisted dream of (her) home", with all the wrong views out the windows. And of course Nina understands Domi. After all, not long ago she had run into the wrong house, into the identical building next door, and seen a group of strangers apparently occupying her own home. Would that not be what it felt like to come from the past and observe the future, watch strangers make themselves at home in your space, with your things?

This is a sad book, or perhaps it might be cleaner to say it is very much a book about sadness, for all the competent life of Nina and her committed associates and friends. She knows as much, she puts it into words herself when she glimpses a reproduction of the Chagall painting inside Gil's scrapbook. "Time is a river without banks" — yes, immeasurable and indefinable. And she understood, with no need for words, that it was the paradox and, somehow, the sadness of Time that drew her to the possessions of those long gone: "objects unthinking, unfeeling objects that have their own voices and that outlast the loving flesh that created them.".

Nina is captivated by the past perhaps because she is young enough not to have too terribly much of her own past yet to remember. Yet young as she is, she's malleable; the Moment with a capital M keeps occurring to her, and the image is of a painting becoming fully fleshed and real.

"As she stood there, she felt someone behind her-- and there it was: her Feeling, the sense of timelessness, an acute awareness of being freed of the moment. She held her breath, looked down at her own hand resting on the window sill, and it seemed scarcely to belong to her. She looked at the shadows on the wall and they seemed not shadows any longer but living shapes of an indescribable beauty against color so deep as to invite her to enter it, as if it were no longer solid but some depthless medium in which she might become lost." The ordinary and the immortal.

With her sensitivity to the sorrows of lost times, Nina Harmsworth is likely to endure much indeterminate grief, starting from the conclusion of the novel, when once again all the children were stone and the Moment had passed. For if the capital-M moment is gone, the instant of communion and connection, in the next moment is a poignant echo, a lapse, which will diminish. In the words from Odile's journal, "We think the memory of them will never escape us, but they are like our dreams, which are often vivid on the moment of awakening, but blurred an hour or two later when only a haunting impression remains."

Jonny Dart, of Margaret Mahy's *Memory*, is perhaps the most roguish of our protagonists, the most capable of stealing, and he meets up with Sophie, the angel of wisdom, for whom time has regained an unusual elasticity. Jonny Dart is a child of popular culture, too; he is deeply affected by melody, only for him music provides the soundtrack by which he can remain somewhat isolated from the world. "DREAM CITY, DREAM STREET, ALWAYS AT MY DOOR," sings the band in his walkman, providing the counterpoint to his wanderings. "SHUT YOUR EARS BUT THE VOICE GOES WANDERING ON," it jeers.

Jonny runs into Sophie, and something about their mutual mistrust of the present moment binds them together. When Jonny first steps out of Sophie's house without his walkman, quite late in the novel, he thinks more clearly about his past in conjunction with hers. "Jonny wondered what would happen if he went into Cognito Systems and tried to order a new memory for Sophie. She would have to be personally fitted.... For that matter he might as well put his own name down on the new-memory list himself, for certainly part of his own past had been recorded falsely. Though memories were often regarded as careful files in a catalogue, Jonny now believed they could just as easily be wild stories, always in the process of being revised, updated, or having different endings written

on to them. After all, even Sophie's file on Alva was still open, for he, Jonny, was being added to it, even if the entries faded into nothing almost at once."

Mahy's central concern, it seems to me, is about the value of witness and testimony. Early on, Jonny Dart explains why he's looking for Bonny Benedicta — whose name might wittily be translated as good blessing — he explains it to himself, but that's enough for now.

"Because," he was saying eloquently inside his head, "because she once told a lie for me, and I want to be sure why, because sometimes I've got two memories and I can't be sure which is the right one, and she was the witness."

Interestingly, the first memory of the death of Janine, Jonny's sister, comes when Jonny awakes from his drunken sleep, "lying flat, spread out like the spokes of a wheel, crucified face downwards... Then he began to go in and out of the old memory which he knew by heart, but which to him was always extraordinary." Jonny eventually leaps off the balcony rail onto Nev, attacking the past, witnessing again the memory of Janine's fall, and only when his defense of the rather defenseless Sophie is complete does he receive the testimony of Bonny Benedicta: "I thought you had enough to cope with. I wanted to protect you, that's all. But she tripped. She tripped and fell."

"Once you start thinking something like that," Jonny stammered, "how do you stop? It makes itself real."

It is Mahy's singular success, to my eye, that Sophie maintains her incredible Sophie-ness clear through to the end of the novel, and beyond, getting ready to venture out on the last page of the novel in a crocheted bedjacket. "Are you the one?" she asks Jonny, for the second time, and this time he answers "I think I am the one. I truly think I am."

And he is; he is for Sophie what Bonny has been to him: the good blessing, the witness who will verify that that long rich life with Errol and Uncle Brian did in fact occur, that extra ear to receive the testimony, that adjacent memory to receive the testimony.

"No one quite like one of your own," Sophie has said, and in the final book of our discussion, Penelope Lively's *The House in Norham Gardens,* we have in bracing polarity the two extremes meeting in this, the fourteenth year of the life of Clare Mayfield. On the one hand we have Clare's attachment to her ancient aunts, who are very much her own — dear and exotic and eminently knowable; and on the other hand we have Clare's dreamy speculations about the New Guinea tribe from which the totemic tamburan has been taken, a people who become harder and harder to know as their own past seems to fall away from them.

As it is for Nina Harmsworth, Clare Mayfield's young life is stirred up, in her case, by the physical object of the mask; like Nina's, Clare's is a story of the birth of a sense of loss; also like Nina's, dreams become the avenue through which the past and future approach each other and meet. Too, and perhaps more obviously than in any of the other novels we've considered, *The House in Norham Gardens* is about the theft of memory. In the italicized introduction to chapter six, we learn

"The valley is a place without a past. The tribe do not know how long they have been there: a hundred years, a thousand, five thousand. Their future is entrusted to the spirits of the ancestors, who care for them and watch over them. One day, strangers come to the valley and the tribe welcome them as these spirits, returned with rich and wonderful gifts. They are honored, and given all they ask for."

So it seems Clare's great-grandfather, on the Cooke Daniels expedition of 1905, may have asked for the tamburan, and under the circumstances we might consider it a kind of theft.

It becomes for Clare a symbol, as for the tribespeople it had been a symbol for Clare it is weighty with the implication of what is lost when memory is not shared; for Clare it is the fading colors of the riotous lives of Aunt Susan and Aunt Anne. And when Clare, alone of her tribe, tries to honor the past and return the tamburan, in that rich dream from church to jungle, she learns that it is already too late; the people have lost the significance of the tamburan, and do not want it.

But it is not too late for her, and she goes back to her own life, knowing she "can't make it stop at now... and you shouldn't want to, not really."

And Clare does what Isaac Campion has done, in noting the cabbage-leaf veins of his father's hands; what Nina Harmsworth has done, in studying "Mrs. Staynes minutely, as if memorizing her"; Clare does what Fanso needs to do: see his forebears. "All his life — thirteen years — he'd never seen his dad. And no true picture of him was in his head or anywhere to be seen." Clare is coming to the realization Jonny names, that sober truth which lies at the heart of all of these books: "On the face of it, it wasn't likely that he would be able to live happily with Sophie for long, yet she linked up with knowledge he already had: that in their essence people were born and lived and died alone," yet, nonetheless, as Jonny explains, "I'm one of your own."

Clare looks at the aunts "intently, at their faces and their hands and the shape of them. I'm learning them by heart, she thought, that's what I'm doing, that's all I can do, only that."

On the night of her heart attack, Sarah Reginald Seabury Parker did not cry out, but I woke up at three a.m., uneasy, and for the first and only time while I lived there I wandered through several adjoining rooms until I got to the front of the house and saw a light from her bedroom. I called out lightly, not to frighten her — "Sarah, are you awake?" and she answered immediately, "Oh dear boy, thank heavens you've come. I didn't care to call and wake you up. I believe I'm very ill."

I got the doctor and the ambulance, and while I waited for them to arrive I sat with her and tried to remember all the things I hadn't paid attention to when people talked about dying. I tried to console her — "This is a passing thing, you've got a good ten years yet, I know you," I said, and she started and said in horror, "Good Lord, I hope not. There is such a thing as enough, you know, and I've kept Reggie and Tom waiting too long as it is." It had been sixteen years, I remembered, since her husband had died. I made other ineffectual consoling noises, and she said to me, "Dearie, it has meant more to me than I can say to have you here in the house with me these two years. You mustn't get yourself stirred up for I have been very happy to know you. The gloves on the sofa downstairs belong to Mabel Colgate, and should be returned to her, she left them at tea on Saturday."

She wouldn't hear of my coming in the ambulance with her to Mount Auburn Hospital, but I wouldn't hear of not, so she directed me to her Bible where there was a twenty-dollar bill hidden; I was to use it for taxi fare home and get back and get my sleep, for I had classes the next day which I wasn't to miss.

I wandered in to the hospital each day for several weeks. She looked better and better. When she started complaining about the food I knew she'd pull through. "The macaroni and cheese," she said to me one day, "I thought, what can they do to macaroni and cheese? Well, my dear the macaroni was all dried out and the cheese had gone home."

She was well enough to spend the summer at the shore. The last day I saw her, I took the commuter train for a day visit, bringing with me a thermos of Manhattans, because Rockport is a dry town. We sat in the gardens and looked at the sea, and I swam and went home. She died about ten days later, the day before she was to leave the ocean to return to the city.

Her distant niece came, and such family as there was did everything very properly. I wasn't invited to sit with family nor comment on any arrangement. I took a pew at the back of Christ Church, but sang out, in the heat of late August, the song Sarah had requested for the opening hymn of her funeral. The pastor quoted her: "...with full gusto, please, and irrespective of the liturgical season."

It occurs to me that Sarah, finally dead, was at last really breaking the hold of the calendar over her, of time over her — "irrespective of the liturgical season"! The song, in the heat of August, was the Christmas carol "Joy to the World."

And the family did ask me to stay in the house for a week or so until they found some available relative to come and remove the valuables. Like the painting over my bed, which I learned only then was an original Winslow Homer. The Dutch clock, ticking three centuries away. The Filipino armor from the Spanish-American war.

I spent my five days there writing obsessively, cataloguing room by room and memory by memory the place and the time, trying to capture the face and the character of Sarah Reginald Seabury Parker, who now is dead a full decade. I do not know if I started early enough; like Clare I really might have memorized her. Perhaps, unlike Isaac Campion, I lived in too fast and igorous and cinematic a world, my senses were too dulled and sated to pick up the nuances of Sarah Parker's life. All the Sundays have begun to be one Sunday in Sarah Parker's house, for me.

But the photo I showed you at the beginning was in an envelope on her desk. And although I was set there to guard against the theft of the coat of armor and the Dutch clock, I slipped the photo of Sarah Parker out of the envelope. Unlike the photo of my Nicaraguan friend, Sayra, this was one of hundreds of photos. I looked at that fleeting, lying image of one instant only, created by light and captured in a hollow tube, that foster child of silence and slow time. And I stole it. Like Prometheus, I took the light of the sun trapped in a hollow box, to make myself human.

Isaac Campion and Sarah Parker speak with one voice.

"It's the same for the young ones, they think they are going to live forever. And good luck to them, I say! Good luck to the young ones, let them live to ninety-six! Let them live to a hundred!"

Let them steal what they can and make themselves human, to assuage the sorrow of what is lost, and to ponder with nerve and heart on what they may yet allow to be stolen from them, for the good of the turning tide and the inexhaustible flood of our young, which repeats freshly the ordinary and immortal pattern of all our lives.

Let the pattern, as often as it can, for the memory of Sarah Parker and the future of Sayra Rossy Molina Lopez, for the past and future in all our lives, let the pattern

Repeat the sounding joy,
Repeat the sounding joy,
Repeat, repeat the sounding joy.

1 *The Uncertain Certainty* pp 124-25

PETER DICKINSON

Time and times and half a time

WE HAD A MOULDY old summer last year. The greenhouse effect seems to be causing excessive condensation in these parts. But there was one fine afternoon late in August when I was standing in the middle of one of my borders attempting to poison some bindweed without poisoning the rose it had wrapped itself round — a tricky business involving rubber gloves and an old sock and a jar of diluted poison and another jar of clean water with a sponge to wipe off any poison that fell on the roses, while at the same time maintaining a slightly poncy posture dictated by the other plants in the border which mustn't be stepped on. In the middle of all this the telephone rang. My children had given me one of those cordless things so that they could get at me when it suited them, and not only when they guessed I might be within earshot of a fixed telephone. This gadget was attached to my belt, above the right buttock. I won't detail the procedure required to dispose of my two jars safely, and get the poison-sodden sock off my hand, and get the telephone out of my belt and answer, without overbalancing, but I managed it.

The caller of course was Jill, from the other side of the Atlantic, asking me to be here today to talk to you about time in children's books, and telling me not to dither about it because of the cost of the call. I tell you this not simply to excuse myself for being here today, when I may have nothing of interest to say to you at all, but because it's a good enough example of the instantaneousness of most things nowadays. It seemed to me then, as I stood balancing in the middle of my own private, dreamy Eden — a place dominated by seasons but not by times — quite unreal to be talking to a friend a third of the way round the world, a five-day journey to most people for many years after I was born, and discussing what I might be doing in twelve months' time. But this is the world our children — or in my case grandchildren — will regard as normal.

In addition to my house in Hampshire I have a small flat in London. Driving the familiar journey between my two homes I sometimes think "Less than half an hour to go, now," and then, routinely, having thought this, I become aware that if my car broke down and there were no other form of transport available it would take me a full day to reach my destination. I don't believe my children think like this. In fact, I doubt if they are aware that since we began making this journey, when they were small, the two houses have moved many miles closer together. Not literally, of course, but good as. Thanks to the improvements in roads and cars, the journey takes us half an hour less than it used to. Say twenty miles. Those lawns, those chimneys, that cellar, those trees, the slope of parkland seen from the front windows, all lifted up and flown towards London. The actual money value of the house hugely enhanced by the shrunken distance to the metropolis. Real money in a real bank. Extraordinary.

Children may not think about time much, but they are more aware than we are of its strangeness. The child is a hero who has to adventure into and ultimately make his home in the magical world of adults. The entrance to that world is guarded by two great giants whose names are Cause and Time. To live in the adult world you have to come to terms with them and accept their rules, though looking back over your shoulder once you have passed them you see them only as two natural stone pillars on either side of the ever-narrowing gap through which you journeyed out of childhood. Unless you happen to become a theoretical physicist, in which case you actually have to engage your adult mind with the nature of their power and strangeness, you henceforward take them for granted. Only in dreams, and in the logic of dreams, do you know them for what they are.

Sometimes when I talk to children in schools we get onto the subject of time — usually by way of the obvious question of why it seems to matter that certain things — poems, pictures, cathedrals — should endure and retain a meaning for new generations long after their creators have become dust. I have a riddle to help them think about this. Imagine you are the owner of the oldest man-made object in the world. Woman-made actually. It's a piece of leftover rib which Eve picked up and whittled some notches in so that she could be combing her hair with it when Adam woke up and found her beside him on the young green grass of Eden. It is absolutely guaranteed authentic. Now, a friend of yours has invented a new gadget, a sort of three-dimensional photocopier which can replicate small objects molecule by molecule, and as a test piece you let him try it out on your comb. So now you have two. You label them carefully, so you know which is which. Then another friend, one of those pop-science TV producers, hears what you have done, and realizes it might fill a bit of air-time, so he asks you to come along and show your two combs to the viewers. He sends a taxi round, and off you go. It's a wet night, and the streets are slippery, and half way round Shepherd's Bush an idiot cyclist cuts under the nose of your taxi. There's a squeal of brakes, and a slither of tires, and a crash as the taxi skids into a traffic island. Nothing apart from the taxi and the traffic island has been damaged, but when you pick yourself up you find that both boxes have come open and the combs have come out. It is a ghastly moment, but you keep your wits, put one comb back in each box, and close them, and carry on as if nothing has happened. The program goes out,

your friend's first copy gets wide exposure, and as a result he is able to set up a little company to manufacture them, and gives you a block of shares in gratitude. The company does very well, and you become extremely rich. You collect art, and found your own museum, whose prize exhibit, of course, is Eve's comb. Actually, the one which everyone thinks is the real one is kept in a vault for safety, and the other is on display. But you, and you alone, know that there is a fifty-fifty chance that you've got them the wrong way round. You go with the secret to your grave. The question is, of course, what if anything has been lost? I don't know the answer.

Now let's get back to the instantaneous world. As one gets older one tends to believe more and more that it is somehow important that people should have a sense of time, of themselves and their moment by moment existence having this enormous context of other existences behind and ahead of them. There are obvious practical reasons why it should matter. Most of us want to live in a comparatively stable society, which is also a democracy. A proper sense of times and causes will, we think, help a democracy — help the voters not to rush headlong for every apparent quick fix. The knowledge that there was market collapse in the late twenties and a hideous depression afterwards — or perhaps not even knowledge, just a vague half-grasped public awareness — is of some use in trying to avoid the same thing happening again. And there are similar kinds of argument about the greater richness of life, and so on. In fact, I believe our wish for others, particularly children, to have some feeling for time is largely rationalized into such arguments. As we get older we simply become more conscious of time passing. I am now over sixty. A year for me is a sixtieth of my whole life, less than two percent; blink and you miss it. But for a child it is a huge ten percent, a whole desert of misery to be trudged across, or a whole continent of riches to be explored. You know those lines they paint across the road on the approaches to roundabouts, setting them closer and closer as you get nearer to the danger point, so that even if

Peter, in view of Eva, has, like Ursula, a fascination
with Otherness —
Quite Otherness not
just mild Otherness.

you're slowing down you still get an impression that you're going faster than you really are? Time is like that. More and more precious. It's only natural to want to pass that feeling on.

When Jill telephoned me that sunny afternoon and I'd said yes, I'd come, she then told me to pick a couple of my books to be put on the reading list. This hasn't happened to me before. There's a sort of Humpty-Dumpty-ish feeling of false grandeur about being on a reading list, but I didn't have any time to think, so I chose a couple of books which seemed pretty obviously about time.

Given more time — here we go again — perhaps I might have chosen differently. One of the curious by-products of having written quite a number of books is that one can in an idle moment leaf back through them and become aware of preoccupations and obsessions of which one which one hadn't before been consciously aware. I suppose it's a bit like relating one's dreams to a psychiatrist, if there are still psychiatrists who go in for that sort of thing. Fiction is in any case a form of controlled public dreaming. For instance, I must have written more than a dozen books before I realized that in something like two-thirds of them a language is spoken which the principal character, through whom the story is experienced, doesn't understand. Sometimes this is a plot device, for instance, a way of concealing facts from one character while revealing them to another. Sometimes it is merely a thickening of atmosphere, adding to the strangeness of circumstances. But the fact that it happens so often, and that the passages in which it occurs tend, to my ear at least, to be written with extra energy and attention, makes it clear to me now that I do have some kind of hang-up about languages. Does it go back to my early childhood, and hearing the servants in my parents' house in what is now Zambia speaking their own mysterious language among themselves, and with that the subconscious awareness that not only the language but the lives were mysteriously different, wholly other? Or is it more straightforwardly something to do with my never having been much good at

language at school? English was always my element, transparent and buoyant as the air is to the raven, while French, Latin and Greek — the last two after years and years of study — remained largely stifling and opaque.

Anyway, it's there, an oddity in my literary make-up, something that bothers me even though I'm not often aware of thinking about it.

Of course we all have hang-ups of this kind, some of which we know about and come to terms with, some of which we find it hard to perceive, but those near us are more aware of, and some of which will remain unrecognized, coelecanths of our inner deeps, for all our lives. Almost chief among these for most people must be the strangeness of time. It is one of the great preoccupations of fiction. Every novelist is a kind of Proust. I think if Jill had given me more time to think about the famous reading list I might have chosen rather more subtly. In a way it is when one is not primarily attempting to deal with a subject that one may without knowing it have had the most interesting things to say about it. The real Proust may do what he chooses, but among us minor writers the unconscious Prousts may well know and feel more than the conscious ones. One of my adult novels falls into two halves, the first recounting a love-affair in the fifties and the second set in the eighties, the same woman looking back and realizing that what had really happened then was different from what she'd imagined. There is almost no account at all of the intervening years. You learn that she has married and divorced, you meet her children and so on, but for the most part you are left to guess. I didn't do this on purpose. It was a plot device. I wanted to use my own experiences on the staff of a magazine in the fifties as a setting, and since I was writing a kind of detective story and have no grasp at all of how real detectives work, I needed some kind of viewpoint from which it could be seen that what had appeared to happen had been different from what did happen. But when I'd finished it turned out that the most interesting section of the book is the one that isn't there, the gap in the middle. How did that eager, buoyant, impulsive girl become this controlled and controlling woman?

That's an adult book, partly because the question is an adult question. In fact, by no means all adults are prepared to face it. More than one reader told me they'd enjoyed the book, but added, "I do wish you'd written more about what happened in between." I'm not going to say I wouldn't attempt to do the same thing in a children's book, because there's nothing at all one wouldn't attempt if that inner voice which a book has when it's going well told me to give it a try. But it's easy for adults to forget how difficult time is for children. Not long ago I was sent a batch of letters from a class who'd been reading a book of mine called *Healer* in which the first few chapters alternate between what's happening now and earlier events that explain what's going on. Almost every child said they found this confusing, though I'd have thought the flashback was by now so much part of the ordinary grammar of narration — seen, surely, almost weekly on the average soap — that they'd have cottoned on at once. This doesn't mean I won't do it again. Among other things I might tell myself that a child in a class asked to read a book as form-work is going to be prepared to find confusion and difficulty when the same child, picking up that book by chance and choosing to read it for his or her own interest would have no trouble at all. Next time, perhaps, though, I'll try to signpost the time-shifts more clearly.

Healer, like most of my other books for children, concerns itself with the strangeness of time only as a side issue. The flash-backs were no more than a plot device. As I've said, perhaps if I'd had time to consider when Jill phoned me last year, and if half my mind hadn't been concerned with the business of poisoning bindweed — only about seventy percent successful, the passage of a year reveals — I would have suggested that you look at books in which the obsession with time is largely unconscious. As it was, I did the obvious thing and chose two books which are not in any way typical of my work, and which also attempt, particularly in the case of *City of Gold,* to deal almost explicitly with the

passage not of years, but of centuries, of whole millennia. I don't know whether you've found them rewarding, but at least you've had some lovely pictures to look at.

Before I try to talk about *City of Gold* I had better make my own position clear. No doubt many of you are believers, Jewish or Christian. Probably some of you believe in some form or another in the literal truth of the words in the Bible. Now, I am not a believer. I spent the first forty or so years of my life trying to persuade myself that I was, but then I came to the conclusion that I would be happier if I tried to be a bit more honest with myself; so I am now an agnostic, and as such I have to apologize to any of you who may have been angered or saddened by reading this book. Though I am an agnostic, I do have some beliefs, and one of them — the most important of them, to me, I suppose, — is that what makes us human, what really distinguishes us, as far as we know, from the animals, isn't tool-using, or language, or anything like that, because all these human-seeming things are emanations from one central human development, which is the power of the imagination, the ability to use the word "if . . ."

"If I were to tension a cord between two ends of a springy stave, and use it to propel a sharpened stick..." "If my neighbor were to filch meat from my larder, as I propose to do from his, and I were to find out, how would I feel?" And in this particular case, "If I were to believe unquestioningly that there was a single supreme being who had chosen my group of tribes for his especial purposes..."

City of Gold is in that sense, I assure you, a completely sincere book. It isn't a case of an author using a sacred text as the raw material for a display of his skills — though I have to admit it was great fun to write — it is an attempt to convey to the modern questioning mind what it might have been like to hold a set of unquestioning but changing beliefs through a huge expanse of time.

What happened was this. I'd told my editor, Joanna Goldsworthy of Gollancz, that I wasn't certain what to write next, and she telephoned me one morning and explained that they had

She never been concise & using plot device

embarked on a series of traditional stories, illustrated by Michael Foreman. So far they'd done Grimm and Hans Andersen, and now she wondered if I would be interested in doing stories from the Old Testament.

"You can't be serious," I said. "Stories from the Old Testament? Noddy in the Holy Land? Big Ears meets Moses? Its an absolutely rotten idea. A, there's no way in which it could be done these days, and B, you're dealing with something of a quite different order from Hans Andersen and Grimm. I wouldn't touch it with a barge-pole. What's more, I forbid you to ask anybody else to do it. You'll have to think of something else."

That's the way to talk to editors. Well, I turned back to my typewriter, and went on with what I had been doing, but twenty minutes later I picked up the telephone again, and rang Joanna.

"That Old Testament idea," I said. "Have you asked anyone else to do it?"

"No," she said. "I was too frightened."

"Well, I've thought of a way."

When I explained Joanna didn't sound too keen, but I did a couple of stories to show her — I don't remember which ones I did first — and then she caught on. After that . . . well, of course, it didn't come out quite as I had expected. Nothing ever does. Bits which you expect to come easy and be impressive often go dead on you, and other bits which you thought were going to be more or less transitional passages actually acquire a life of their own. And then there's the sheer weight of previous tellings, which force you to find some kind of fresh note or voice, without betraying the original. It wasn't always possible to envisage what the oral tradition might have been, and where I could envisage it, it seemed to me important that the story should exist in its own time, as part of that time. That, with rare exceptions, it should be told for some purpose other than simply that of passing it on to the next generation. When stories are told like that, they have already begun to solidify into Writ.

Writ, you see, is timeless. It has to be. It has to claim to apply not only to its own time, but to all times, unambiguously. It follows that

the events it relates, though obviously they have taken place in some historical time, and have their own inner time-sequence, must still in another sense be somehow timeless, taking place in a kind of universal and unending now so that they can apply to all the localized nows. The Renaissance painters who dressed their Madonnas and saints in contemporary robes were painting the events of Writ. The painters of the Victorian period who located their biblical scenes in the Middle East and in what research might show to be the dress of the first century, were, however pious their intention, at least partially denying the universality of Writ. There was nothing else they could do. The spirit of their times dictated that. But at the same time the denial was only partial. The clothes on the carpenter's son might be the authentic dress, copied from notebooks scribbled in a veritable woodworker's shop in Nazareth, but the face would still be the face of the Squire's eldest son at Steeple Bumpstead, with its round blue eyes and golden lashes and pink, unweathered skin. However historical our enterprise, we are still prisoners of our time.

I don't claim anything else for myself. *City of Gold* is quite clearly a product of the late twentieth century, both in style and subject matter, though some future scholar trying to date it might put it rather earlier on stylistic grounds, noting the strong influence of Kipling, and tracing that back to Robert Browning's monologues. If I'd been doing the New Testament stories in the same way (which was, I think, suggested, but which I decided not to try) I might have thought of approaching the raising of Lazarus in something like the manner of Browning's *Epistle of Karshish*. But I'm sure my imaginary scholar would note many things, not only the relativism of my approach to belief, which tie the book firmly into the nineteen-eighties — things which only those looking in from outside the culture, from at least two generations on, will perceive as peculiar to our time. To us they are so taken for granted as to be transparent.

I don't think I've got much more to say about *City of Gold* beyond a point which isn't really relevant to our main theme but always strikes me as odd. I'm lucky enough to have my books liked by a number of schoolteachers, and sometimes when I go to schools they claim to have read the lot. But time and again it turns out that they haven't even heard of *City of Gold* because it gets put into the shelves and categories concerning religious education. If it's about religion it can't be literature. I haven't talked to religious education teachers, but I suspect they take a mirror-image view. They glance at it, and perceive that it might count as literature, and therefore be somehow untrustworthy. Perhaps, after all, I was right in my first reaction. Bible stories are Big Ears meets Moses.

Merlin Dreams arose in much the same way as *City of Gold*. Chris Kloet, who'd taken over from Joanna at Gollancz, telephoned to ask me if I'd like to tackle the King Arthur stories. My reaction, though, was different — less cool to start with, and less warm later. Again you have the problem of the endless retellings and the need to find a voice which is both true to the original and new and right for you and your own time. I immediately rejected the notion of doing a fake medieval, high-style prose version. I think I toyed briefly with a very brutal, down-to-earth version — fake realist, like the film "Excalibur." I reread Malory and the *Mabinogion*. But from the first, though I didn't know much about it, I was most interested in the mystery of where the stories came from, and how they grew to the shape they are. How does a religious belief embody itself into a myth, and how does the myth then change and become something different — in the case of most myths something barely recognized as such, a familiar shape on our joint mental landscape, like a long barrow plowed and replowed across the generations till it is no more than a vague swelling in the reaped stubble, with everything else about it — names, lives, fame, tragedy, — forgotten. Even the bones gone.

But in the case of the King Arthur stories something else, an astonishing and still-flowering tree, its roots only guessable at in the dark Celtic soil, but its flowers remaking themselves time and again, as though each generation were a fresh season.

So my first really serious thought was that I would attempt to do something roughly similar to what I'd done with *City of Gold*. I would take and retell the stories at different stages in the growth of the tree, one perhaps from right down among the roots where the sacred lance that hangs over the couch of the wounded but undying king is recognizably the same weapon as that used for the sacrifice of the corn-god; then others, from up the growing trunk, more changed, and so on through branch and twig to the flowers.

I couldn't do it, of course, luckily for me. Attempting to do anything like what you've done before is a recipe for failure. Without exception I think my least satisfactory books have been those which I began with the thought that this was my sort of story, and I should be able to deal with it out of my previous writing experience. But, as I say, luckily for me the idea didn't work. There was no tree. There were the guessed-at roots, a shaving or two of bark from the trunk — I defy anyone to get much of a story from *The Gododdin*, if that's how you pronounce it. And then there were the flowers. There wasn't much I could do with them, except rearrange them in the vase.

"The hell with it!" I thought, "I'll grow my own."

And having done that, I might as well grow my own roots too. I made them up, of course. There is very little good Celtic scholarship in the linking passages of *Merlin Dreams*. I didn't feel anything like the same sense of responsibility towards my material as I had in *City of Gold*. I suppose, too, I felt I was playing truant from my proper job. I think I said that *City of Gold* was very enjoyable to write — so was *Merlin Dreams*. I don't mean it was effortless fun, though one or two stories did seem to slip onto the page almost unaided. I can't tell whether this sense of holiday, of freedom, of fresh air, communicates itself to the reader, but I hope so.

All this is highly personal. The books exist, and now have their own life in the public mind, and for a few years at least, independent of me and Joanna and Chris and

Michael Foreman and Alan Lee. How they came to exist should be of only casual interest to the reader, and I've talked about it at some length only because I was pretty well ordered by Jill and John to do so. But there's a point of much more general interest which arises out of the contrast between them. The stories in *City of Gold* still matter. Some of them are central to one of the world's major faiths, and important in at least two others, and they have relevance in the physical as well as the spiritual world. I retold only one story from *The Book of Joshua*, barely mentioning the obvious one about the walls of Jericho, in passing, because I found and still find the book repugnant. But unless you are aware of it you won't understand one crucial strand in the hideous tangle of the modern Middle East. It is genuinely important for us, and not only for our children, to have this awareness, and with it the awareness of the centuries between those historical events and what is happening on the West Bank today. For a promise to last three thousand years!...

No wonder I told Joanna that the Old Testament was something different from Grimm and Hans Andersen.

By comparison the King Arthur stories are a complete frivolity. What I can discern of the religion of the Celts, the roots from which the pretty flowers suck their food, is at least as repugnant as anything you'll find in the Book of Joshua, and there is none of that extraordinary sense, deeply moving even to an unbeliever, of a whole nation struggling to explore and express its relationship with the divine, erratically and with many lapses, across century after century, to culminate in the exalted vision of the major prophets.

Perhaps the Celts believed in their own Gods with the same conviction as the Jews of early Palestine did in Jehovah, but if they did it no longer matters. That faith is gone. Efforts to revive it, however sincere, seem to outsiders merely whimsical.

So is my own use of the lost faith in *Merlin Dreams* equally whimsical? Largely, I think, yes. As I say, I made most of it up. Who knows what happened to a man who touched the sacred horses in the grove of Epo, supposing there were such horses, and such a grove? But all societies are fuelled by their own myths. Myths are a means of explaining to ourselves what we are. Without the idea of Camelot my own feeling of what it means to be English would be different. The difference may be trivial compared to that of what the idea of Jerusalem means to the Jew, but it is there, real, despite the fact that no place may ever have existed of which one could now say "This was once Camelot."

Though the cohesion of societies is important, the shared myths by which that cohesion is authenticated are neutral. An idea is not necessarily good because it is embodied in a myth. We can take the murderous energies of a head-hunting group of clans and turn them into an ideal of chivalrous manhood. We can take the life-giving forces of birth and lactation and turn them into a vampire queen. We do this unconsciously, generation by generation over the centuries. Surely it must be useful for our future citizens to have some feeling of how this happens.

Three thousand years, say. How can a child think in such numbers? How can you and I, if we are honest with ourselves? Wave after wave of invaders, burning great shrines, or adapting them to their own new religions. The Gods dying from the minds that had once known them immortal. The very languages being no more spoken. But all the while, something persisting, changing from tongue to tongue and renewing itself through change, still part of the minds that remake it...

Think of it, if you can. But if you can't, no wonder. Time and Cause are twin giants, and they still guard the pass in all their strangeness.

PENELOPE LIVELY AND BETTY LEVIN

A continuous present

Lively — I really want to address the subject rather than individual books — the subject of how we look at time and above all how we write about it. In my own work this is a subject that's woven its way in and out of children's and adult books, albeit in a slightly different way. To give you a brief rest from our argument or discussion we will read passages that we hope will be a kind of prompt or sparking point for what is to follow. Reading from *Moon Tiger*, the protagonist addressing the pilgrims at Plymouth:

You are public property — the received past. But you are also private; my view of you is my own, your relevance to me is personal ... There was a spaniel on board the *Mayflower* ... What I find remarkable about this animal is that I should know of its existence at all, that its unimportant passage through time should be recorded. It becomes one of those vital inessentials that convince one that history is true.

Levin — The speaker is a historian, and she says in another part of the book, "Unless I am a part of everything, I am nothing." Two viewpoints seem to emerge from all of your books: that the past is unknowable, that we, like the people in the past, are imprisoned in our own time, that we cannot shed what has happened since but also that we are shaped by the past, that the past is true, and that we need it. Is this a paradox that you keep plumbing? Do you see these two views as irreconcilable?

Lively — Not at all. To me they mesh. I would put it like this: I think the past is unknowable in a literal sense; we cannot recover the exact experiences of other times because we are unable to shed our own assumptions and expectations. We can make what I would call informed guesses about what it was like to live in another time. But it is nothing more than

an informed guess because we cannot strip the imagination of all the knowledge and assumptions.

There's an analogy here with the way we look at childhood, which is something we might want to talk about later on. And I'm always seeing analogies between the way we look at the collective past and the way we look at individual pasts. Just as our own pasts are extraordinarily unrecoverable, so the collective past is unrecoverable in the same sense. We're so imbued with the moral assumptions and beliefs and the scientific knowledge of our own time that we simply cannot recover the state of mind of another time. But, along with that and, I think, parallel, there goes the simple fact of the existence of the past, that we know this. When I have Claudia saying, "Unless I am a part of everything I am nothing," what she means is that knowledge of the past, knowledge that there is a past, is what dignifies humanity, which is something of huge and central importance; so that even if the past is unreachable, the very fact of knowing about it and of being concerned about it is what, in fact, makes us human. It's the huge distinction, aside from language, between being a human being and being an animal. I'm never quite sure what this does for you. In the deepest sense, certainly for me, it wonderfully concentrates the mind.

Levin — There's also a feeling of dualism in the statements that some of your characters make, for example in *Moon Tiger* "the benign historical eye," and in *According to Mark* "the cold eye of the future," or "He felt like some cold, omniscient Olympian eye." In what way does the novelist's eye differ from the biographer's and historian's?

Lively — I'm hastily assembling these quotations in my own mind. There is a paradox there, but whether it's an intended one or not, I think it's possibly an interesting one. Benign historical eye or the cold eye of history. It seems to me it depends on the viewpoint. We think of ourselves when we're looking back as imposing order of some kind. The historian's purpose is to try to impose some order on what would seem to be a process of random events. In one sense historians are looking for order; they're also looking for meaning. And I think there is an analogy with the novelist.

In writing a novel I'm trying to impose an order out of random processes of human existence, which seem to me intolerable unless you can look for some kind of order in them. "Humankind cannot stand very much reality." That's what in a sense it's about. In fiction what you're able to do in this omnipotent and manipulative way is to impose an order where in fact there is none. Reality, it seems to me, has no order at all, whereas good fiction has of course an absolute order. We judge a novel on how well it works, on whether it has an internal cohesion. Now life, of course, doesn't have that, which is what is tiresome about it and makes it so difficult to live. But one of the things the novelist is trying to do is to create that kind of order and to give that kind of meaning, and so there I would see some sort of analogy between what a novelist is trying to do and what the historian is trying to do.

Biographers, on the other hand, can't do very much of that at all. No doubt the biographers in the room will rise in a body and contradict me. Obviously they have to use a historian's skills. They're searching for evidence — marshalling evidence and seeing what's to be done with it. Their role is much like the historian's, but I cannot see it as being very much like a novelist's, unless they're going to be the kind of biographer that none of us would respect. They're not going to manipulate to the point of distorting, which is what the novelist does.

For the novelist everything is open.

But I've answered the second half of the question first. I wanted to speak to the distinction between the benign eye and the cold eye of history. There, it seems to me, the distinction is between viewpoints. When we are looking at the past, whether as historians or anybody else, in a sense the eye could be called benign. It is trying to make some kind of sense of what it is able to see. Whereas when we think of the cold of the future, we are thinking of something of which we have no part. There is a paradox here. To know that you are a part of the processes of time is a solace and essential; it is also slightly chilling — that there is a future in which we will have no part. Not many people really say, "Après moi le deluge" because in that sense we are also a part of the future, even though we shan't be here.

Some people care more about this than others. I don't personally care at all, but patently most public figures do. Many of them write autobiographies in which they are very clearly trying to manipulate the future, manipulate the record. That's the sense in which most people feel themselves to be a part of the future, which of course they won't inhabit. They are actually, it would seem to me, afraid of the future. I suppose in a sense we all are.

Levin — This leads to another question: If the past is true, is the future true as well? Have you considered writing about the future? And if not, why not?

Lively — I think we have to assume that the future is true. I've certainly never been interested in writing the novel of the future, perhaps simply through feeling unequipped to do so. Most fiction of the future has become the admonitory fiction of our time; it's the exemplar, a sort of cautionary tale. Science fiction and literary fiction that does the same kind of thing (Orwell or whatever) — while I read them with guarded pleasure, it's not my favorite kind of reading. I never was tempted toward it, I think because I'm not interested in admonitory writing. I don't feel that I would do it at all well.

Levin — Parenthetically, do you think that *Riddley Walker* is an admonitory novel?

Lively — Ah, I'm glad you brought that up. I suppose of all the futuristic novels of recent years I would admire *Riddley Walker* more than any other. No, in a curious way, I don't think it is. I can't quite pinpoint why. I think in a sense it's a rather despairing and sad novel and has the characteristic Hoban down-in-the-mouth flavor to it. I have to say that I admire Russell Hoban barely this side of idolatry. But to me it has a completely different quality from the flavor of Orwell and Huxley and Doris Lessing in her recent novels, which are so political. What is admirable about *Riddley Walker* is that it doesn't have a political quality. To me above all what it's about is the preservation of memory, which is what I find so moving about it.

Levin — About the impenetrability of the past — do you see it as akin to the wall of common sense that prevents James Harrison from trying to explain to his father that there's a ghost bullying and blackmailing him?

Lively — Not really. I would see the father there as being in a sense the literal reader who refuses to suspend disbelief. What in fact James is arguing for — I'm now getting rather fond of this interpretation — is the suspension of disbelief, which after all we all do as readers. It's why we read fiction, why we want it. I would see the father there as the carping voice of the literal-minded reader, who sort of crept into the book. When I used to visit schools, children used to ask, Do you believe in ghosts? The answer I would sadly give, being an honest woman, is that I'm afraid not. What you cannot say to a child audience is that the ghost is a marvelous and convenient literary device, as many writers greater than I am have found, and it can be used on every kind of level. Whether you're using it in a Henry James way or in a more prosaic way, it's a wonderful, manipulative fictional device. In a book like *The Ghost of Thomas Kempe* it's simply a device for the discussion of the past, or rather for the discussion of the operation of memory. It can be dressed up in a children's book to seem like what on a crucial level it is, just a story about a ghost, although all the rest of it is seven-eighths of the iceberg. These are all the things you can never say to children.

I should add that this lighthearted and frivolous children's book arose from a deeply serious and seminal work of history, Keith Thomas's *Religion and the Decline of Magic,* a book that came out two or three years before I wrote *Thomas Kempe* and was in a sense cataclysmic in English historical writing. It shoved aside the tradition of political historical writing and brought in the kind of historical writing that is more fashionable now — the history of ideas and historical sociology. And I fell on this book and devoured it — it was the kind of history I'd been waiting for all my life. It certainly did something traumatic to me in an intellectual sense, but what it did was produce a mouse, as it were. A mouse that's run a long way, I must say, and run into a lot of different languages. I've never been able to tell Keith Thomas this; I hope he wouldn't mind too much.

Levin — It was the mouse that roared, Penelope. Now let's come to children. Are children impenetrable too? Will you read the passage from *Moon Tiger* that begins, "Children are not like us."

Lively — Reading from *Moon Tiger:*

Children are not like us. They are beings apart; impenetrable, unapproachable. They inhabit not our world but a world we have lost and can never recover. We do not remember childhood — we imagine it. We search for it in vain through layers of obscuring dust, and recover some bedraggled shreds of what we think it was. And all the while the inhabitants of this world are among us, like aborigines, like Minoans, people from elsewhere safe in their own time-capsule.

Levin — I can't possibly ask you what do you mean, children are not like us, which is what you told me to ask, because you're so patently clear in that passage. You've said it.

Lively — But you see that's one of the problems for the novelist, that you can say what you mean in the novel, but you can't say what you mean in other ways. I mean that in exactly the same sense as the historical past is unreachable. We can only view childhood through the accumulation of knowledge and experience, and it's quite impossible to strip our minds of these. We cannot view childhood in the sense that it was when we were within it. It seems to me that you think you remember childhood, but what you're actually remembering is an experience that is already clouded by the perceptions and assumptions and the prejudices and the knowledge of life. It's a bit like looking at old photographs in an album; you see them obscured by all the subsequent events. Certainly you cannot recover the vision and understanding of childhood. It's a state not by any means of innocence (I do intensely dislike that word, innocence, when applied to childhood). Childhood seems to me anarchic, because it's without expectation and without prejudgment. Children have no idea what to expect; therefore they can expect anything. That's what makes them so vulnerable and so exciting. It's also what makes them so manipulable. We try to instill them with our assumptions and expectations. Children, of course, resist this. They do quite remarkable things, it seems to me.

If we're thinking about this in terms of writing for children, one of the problems is the absolute impossibility of recovering the child's vision. We write for children, but practically no one has tried to write both of and for children with the anarchic vision of the child, except perhaps Lewis Carroll. Carroll tries to show the child's eye view of the world. Alice stands for the rationality of the child confronted with the inconsistencies and the incomprehensibility of the adult world, which is Wonderland. The reason it's so perennially fascinating is that all the layers of meaning are in it. It often seems to me that none of us can write for children in the wake of Alice, but of course few of us have ever attempted to do that kind of thing again. Betty, you may have something to say about this, about Alice.

Levin — Since all of Alice is dream, it can also be read as the adult subconscious memory of childhood, which may be the only way in which childhood can be recovered — not through volition, but through accident. That's just one other way of looking at it.

Lively — I have doubts about that, but part of the interesting thing is that we don't know about Carroll; we don't know which it was he was trying to do, or even if he himself knew. It seems to me that he was one of those rare people who may have had glimpses of what

the anarchic eye of childhood is.

Levin — Reading from *Going Back*, from paragraphs separated by other parts of the book:

Remembering is like that. There's what you remember and then there are the things that have never stopped happening, because they are there always, in your head...

People's lives tell a story, I thought once: and then, and next, and then... But ... if it's a story at all, then there are two of them, running side by side. What actually happened, and what we remember. Which is more important, I wonder?

Which is more important?

Lively — Ah, well, and how are we to sort them out? I think that's the problem. It's getting back to the central problem of what we can know. Take that book. I knew I was wanting to write a book which in its structure would reflect the processes of memory, and in terms of its narrative would be discussing the processes of memory. It seemed to me that you could do that more effectively if you used your own memory, not as in autobiography, but in the book's setting — a house and garden that was deeply familiar to me, my grandmother's house in West Somerset. It seemed to me that I could incorporate this in the book and therefore I would be using this sort of skill of memory to write a book that was also reflective of memory.

The interesting thing is that as I did this, I wasn't actually in the house or indeed visiting it very much, but I found myself wondering if I had things accurately. I just wrote the book without checking, but then went there perhaps a month or two after, as it were, to check up on details. Deeply familiar as this place was, I had things wrong. And I left them wrong deliberately, because it seemed to me that in a sense this was more accurate. Because after all I was using memory.

Levin — In so many of your books a place seems to contain memory. In *The House in Norham Gardens*, the house a huge head packed with events, experiences, conversations, and Clare feeling that she's a part of all that. Place as receptacle for feelings and thoughts.

What do you really think about this? Because again and again, you use this image in your children's books and in your adult fiction.

Lively — I think that places are completely meaningless. I think that place has no significance whatsoever, that in a sense it doesn't matter. That being said, of course, it matters profoundly, because what gives it meaning is what we think and what we know.

One of the things that most infuriates me is the mystical view that certain places are imbued with atmosphere or with feelings or with significance of some kind. This seems to me the wildest use of the pathetic fallacy. It's we, of course, who are projecting what we know and feel onto such places.

I've always written of place as having great significance and being charged with feeling, but of course in fact it's the people who are giving that meaning or who carry it. And this actually is the theme that's totally occupying me in a book that I'm writing now — an adult novel which is about the way in which cities (or a city in particular — London; any city, actually, would be equally appropriate) are projections of human experience. The past, in fact, is always there.

I realize I'm beginning to change the ways in which I look at the past. I'm now convinced that the past is a continuous present projected from the eye of the viewer, and it seems to me that the life of a city lies in the knowledge and the response of the viewer, of the participant. All these buildings, this place, this interesting ancient city, if none of us were here, if nobody else were here, would have no meaning. A world stripped of humanity would be a world that had ceased to have any significance whatsoever.

PHILIPPA PEARCE

Time present

Fellow Travellers in Time – in Time Present, thus companionably I address you, and ask for a particular favour: that you will remember my form of address. I shall return to it later.

But now I begin very personally by admitting to a limitation – a physical limitation: I am very short-sighted. Of course, I can see into the distance as well as most people, but only with the artificial aid of spectacles which I harness to my nose first thing in the morning, keeping them there until I go to bed at night. (It's interesting – significant, I think – that we myopics never need our glasses in our dreams. Then, indeed, vision can become supernaturally powerful.)

In writing fiction, as in everyday life, I am similarly short-sighted. I have had the best of artificial aids – an excellent academic education. I seem to know a lot of rather obvious things about the distant Past – that is, in history; but I cannot see it with the imaginative vision that would make the writing of historical fiction possible. There must be other writers with my limitations. We quail at the thought of the equipment of the historical novelist – that immense accumulation of detailed knowledge together with all the usual skills of the fiction writer – the ability to create character, dialogue, scene, and all within an aesthetically significant structure.

All this is not for me.

I am short-sighted, and my range is limited to my own personal present time. Note, however, that one's present time is not really oneself just at this isolatable second. For instance, my body is still digesting a meal eaten some hours ago; my mind is still digesting conversations at the Conference reception some days ago. I am also the books

I have written – or read – some of them many years ago. I am also my childhood; and, because my parents brought me up, I am also my parents; even, more dimly, or more subtly, I am my grandparents.

Easily, I date back to the reign of Queen Victoria.

What I have just said applies to many people – years ago I might have said, to most people. But what I have said about childhood and parents and grandparents implies a set of very stable family relationships, a very stable social setting. All this is changing – or has changed – at least, in the West. And this, of course, is reflected in contemporary fiction, both for adults and for children.

My very first book, *Minnow on the Say*, was written over a quarter of a century ago, and looked back in time for another quarter century. I was celebrating some of the joys of my childhood – especially the joy of living by a river – the same river (then unpolluted: we picked wild watercress for our tea) – the same river that flows through this city of Cambridge (then officially still only a town). I wrote of recollected joys, and with love.

I also wrote from a kind of angry principle. In those days, a good many stories for and about children started with a child (boy) or a couple of children (just possibly boy and girl) going on holiday to some picturesque and remote spot in the British Isles. There they would find waiting for them a mystery, a treasure, or a crime. During the period of that holiday they would unravel the mystery, find the treasure, or truss up the criminals for the police to cart away to jail. Then they would return home (usually to London).

I don't think such stories are so common

nowadays. But, then, I used to feel indignant for the local children. What did they feel when they saw total outsiders come down in a whirlwind to deal with their exciting problems, and then vanish? Was there something wrong with the local children: were they lacking in intelligence or initiative or guts, or what?

Shame!

So the story of my very first book is about two boys, both born and bred in the village of Great Barley, who get together with a canoe on a river to find a family treasure — a treasure strictly within the family history of one of the two boys. This family history, and the village that goes with it, the river through the village, the countryside itself, including its bus service — they all interlock. The two boys and the whole local setting unite to foil the predatory outsider — a wicked art-connoisseur and dealer from London. (I'm afraid that the plot, in the end, became almost as unlikely as the plots I have been criticising.)

The sense of my story of family and anchored community came from my own experience of family and village life in childhood. Deliberately, in this book, I used the names of my brothers and sister, of my nieces and nephews, of my parents, and of people in the village who were notabilities at that time. The funeral of the aged and reclusive Mr Codling becomes the focus for all this:

'Everyone was there,' said Mr Moss. 'Mark Tey came, to represent the Parish Council; and someone came from the cricket club, and the bowls — although some of the younger ones can't have known him at all, even by sight. Old Alice Hellin was there, and Roger Ramsden and Gertrude from the Codling Arms, and Arnold Alexander — Ernest Alexander's son. Frankie Ellum was there, from the paper shop. Edward Nunn was there. Even Squeak Wilson was there: he crept in late and sat in the back pew and looked like a mouse the cat has caught. I saw Miss Codling spare a word for him afterwards, and shake hands with him, too.'

'She must be in a sad way,' said Mrs Moss.

'A sad way,' agreed Mr Moss, 'but she has spirit. Like her father — although the Barleys won't see his like again.'

He shook his head and sighed; and David wished intensely that he had known old Mr Codling in the old days, when he had made his century at cricket, and played bowls, and ruled the Parish Council, with Mark Tey. Now Mr Codling had withdrawn into a remote and golden past that he would share forever with Robin Hood and Bonnie Prince Charlie and Nelson at Trafalgar.' (*Minnow on the Say* Chapter 17)

This story of mine, which has (I think) the most unrealistic of plots, also has the closest local realism and sense of local time. (I should stress, perhaps: for *me*. My family — on my father's side — had lived in that village, or in neighbouring villages for many generations.) The families I wrote about were embedded in local society, with a small s. Our own social group could be described as upper lower middle class. Or perhaps middle middle class. Class distinctions in English society were — and to some extent still are — very delicate and very important. Also, often, very cruel. But I viewed all this through spectacles I had tinted with rose, or with that glowing gold that seemed suitable for the late Mr Codling, Robin Hood and the others. I realize now, as I certainly did not want to then, that I was partly idealizing a past.

I must add, however, that my two heroes led more humdrum lives than other heroes in contemporaneous fiction. Not only did they have their adventure on home ground, but they were under home discipline: one with a mother and father; the other with aunt and grandfather. The heroes of other books were usually free of such cramping control. Even in the decline of the British Empire, writers could send fictional parents off to staff Imperial outposts, leaving their children free for the adventurous holidays in picturesque places that I described earlier. I have noticed that the lessening availability of work in Imperial outposts coincided with — if not actually caused — a rise in the fictional parental death-rate in road, rail and air accidents. There is a brutal logic in this: if children are to be free for adventure, caring parents have to be got rid of, temporarily or permanently. Nowadays, fortunately, if both parents are in full-time employment, fatalities are less necessary.

After what I have said about such heroes, and about the first book I wrote, it may seem unprincipled of me in the very next one, *Tom's Midnight Garden,* to have brought a child from far away to solve the mystery of the midnight garden. But there was a good reason.

On the one hand I had a late nineteenth century child who lives in the bosom of an unloving family not her own: she is friendless, lonely, longing for companionship. And I wanted to match her with a twentieth century child also unhappy, lonely and longing for companionship. So Tom has to be an exile from the warmth of his family and the comradeship of his brother, although he is certainly no seeker of adventure in picturesque places. A community of longing brings the two children together over a span of Time that would otherwise separate them forever.

I pause over the story of this book because it exemplifies in several ways what visions and insights even a short-sighted writer such as myself can hope to have.

I begin with the way in which my little nephew laughed. I had told him some anecdote of the doings of his father — my brother — when he was a little boy. The child laughed, and I suddenly perceived in the quality of the laugh a kind of genial incredulity. He didn't really believe that his patriarch of a father had ever been a little child like himself.

What a natural mistake to make!

Over the years I have looked at adult audiences and thought — and even said, in desperation: Is it really believable that you — that *we* — have ever actually been children? Yet that (and death) are the only human certainties.

I wanted to make a childhood of the past a living reality to a child of the present. (Oh, and vice versa, of course!) I was already interested in writing highly localised fiction: the bringing together of different childhoods over intervening time seemed exactly to fit with this. I had just the right setting to hand. I (and my two brothers and sister) had spent our childhood in the same house, played in the same large Victorian garden, as my father. He had been born in that house in 1876. I knew about our childhood at first hand; and, from my father's tales and allusions, I knew about his childhood in the same garden. One garden; two time-separated childhoods: that is the basis of the story of *Tom's Midnight Garden*.

Notice an elaborate Time complication. I wrote the story in the nineteen fifties: that was my personal Present. However, I set the story slightly in the future — say, the nineteen sixties. This was because, in the fifties, I thought the house and garden — hardly changed from my father's childhood — was under threat, and I wanted to imagine that threat executed — the house split into flats, the garden built over. This fictional Future of mine is, of course, Tom's Present, just as the Past of my father's childhood is Hatty's Present. The story is caught and supported in a network of Time.

And now, today? Well, of course, the whole thing has slipped into the Past, anyway, leaving a confusing impression, perhaps, on anyone who reads the book too carefully. George Orwell's *Nineteen Eighty-Four* published in 1947, was set in the Future, became for one year an unconvincing Present, and since then has entered the Past — and still lives.

I like the tos-and-fros of Time; but I don't want to seem to over-rate the attractions of what one might call generational fiction. Some of the most banal novels in the world must be family-sagas. Family soap-operas are as bad. And, in the actuality of my own life, when I was old enough to go to London to earn my living, I felt a wild exhilaration to be out of sight of parents, aunts, uncles and great-aunts and the whole of our village society, who thought they knew all about me simply because they had always known all about my family.

But, against this view, there are wonderful imaginative opportunities, which have sometimes been wonderfully taken. In adult fiction there is *Wuthering Heights,* with its interplay of the generations: in children's fiction, *The Borrowers.* The exquisite intricacies of genetic inheritance are plain in the Bennet family in *Pride and Prejudice.*

There is something very comfortable in writing about not only one's own childhood but also about the immediately preceding period. This is the period of one's parents: their early experiences and attitudes are still in the air, still available to us.

I once wrote a short story, with surprising

ease, about the ghost of a young soldier killed in the First World War. I say 'with surprising ease' because, although I was born after that war, I seemed to know the feel of it. In my mother's family, one of my uncles was blinded, another killed. The word 'telegram' was a fearful one: it still has emotional weight for me.

It seems quite possible to share, to some extent at least, in the sensibility of the period nearest to one's own. Writers gifted with long sight feel at home in further distances of Time. Leon Garfield has spoken of the human emotions that are recognizably the same over centuries; but even he admits he doesn't want to peer back further than about 1700. I suggest that cumulative changes in sensibility, rather than any changes in basic human emotions, may be what daunt him.

A novel I much admire that goes back the furthest I know is William Golding's *The Inheritors*. The protagonists are prehistoric people — Neanderthal Man and Homo Sapiens. We seem to recognize Homo Sapiens quite easily, even in a very primitive stage of history: we recognize the elements of tenderness, lust, curiosity, and so on. We see basic human emotions in the Neanderthal family; but we also see a people whose relationships with each other and with the outer world are almost unimaginably different. 'Almost unimaginably' — but William Golding succeeds in imagining it. He shows us, for instance, a people who communicate only partly by language, in sounds. Otherwise their communication is by mind-pictures, in a kind of visual telepathy.

This has brought me a long way indeed from my own close-at-hand fiction. I go scuttling back — or forward, if you prefer — to the superimposed childhoods of *Tom's Midnight Garden*.

At this point, inevitably, we reach the Time theories of J W Dunne. In my growing-up time, his books, especially *An Experiment with Time*, were still popular and influential. I'd heard about them; I'd even — it seems — read them. I say 'seems' because when I look at the theorizing now, I don't really understand it. Frankly, I wonder whether I ever did.

But, in *Tom's Midnight Garden*, I wanted to bring those two childhoods — each to be as absolutely real as the other — together; and there had to be some rational justification. So I adopted Dunne's theory — or seemed to. I think I must have felt a certain self-doubt in this, for I added the bolstering suggestion that dreams can work a time-shift. I also threw in an elaborate reference to Time from the Book of Revelation.

This ambivalent attitude to the use of the Dunne theory is obvious from my putting part of its exposition — in an almost direct quotation from Dunne's book, *Nothing Dies* — into the mouth of Uncle Alan, who is a bit of a fathead:

'After supper he got out pencil and paper and began to draw diagrams for Tom. 'Imagine, Tom, that this is a point in Time ...' Later he asked Tom to imagine a painter standing in a landscape and painting it, and a second painter coming behind him and painting the same landscape with the first painter's picture of the landscape in it, and yet a third painter coming up and painting the same landscape with the first painter's picture of the landscape and with the second painter's picture of the first painter's picture of the landscape, and then a fourth painter ... I hope that parallel has made things clearer to you, Tom,' said his uncle. 'Or look at it another way. Suppose ...' Tom's face was beginning to go stiff all over with the expression of understanding he was putting on it; and really, by now, he wanted to cry, like a baby, because he understood nothing, and yet it was all so important to him.' (Chapter 21)

It's clear, isn't it, that the writer of this particular fiction is in rather a muddle — a resentful muddle, satirically displayed? Or rather, is covering up an ignorance — an ignorance of how and why, but not an ignorance of the fact itself. I may not understand Dunne when he draws diagrams, but I understand him absolutely when he says that a rose that blooms once blooms forever. (*Nothing Dies*, Chapter 5). This is the fact of Time — its overwhelming mystery.

I asked you, when I began talking, some forty minutes ago, to remember my opening words: Fellow Travellers in Time — in Time Present. Where have those words gone? Certainly, I've written them down for future reference; the tape-recorder may have snatched them into what one might call temporary immortality; you may even — and if so, thank you — have remembered them.

But the words — the actual sounds of the words — belong to forty minutes ago, to the Past. You may think, as Candia McWilliam says: 'It didn't seem like the past, at the time.'

But the Past of forty minutes ago is as irre-trievable as the Past of Hatty Bartholomew in the eighteen eighties or of Nelson at Trafalgar or of Bonnie Prince Charlie or Robin Hood or Neanderthal Man.

Time is a mystery; and I suggest that we should be very respectful of it.

DAVID LOWENTHAL

The past is a childlike country

AMERICANS who come to England often step back in time. It can be personal time, a reverse Dorian Gray effect that makes one an oldie at forty, a wrinklie at fifty, a crumblie at sixty. But not for good.

As a Senior Citizen I travel cut-rate; you buy a British Rail card by showing proof of age, and turn it in each year to be renewed. The second year I was again asked for proof of age. "But you have my old card", I said. "Ah", says the canny clerk, "but how do I know you're *still* over sixty-two?" I'm lucky to avoid the deeper identity crisis of Dorothy Eady, who thought she reincarnated as an early Egyptian temple maiden and went back to live there with such success that, as she put it, "sometimes I wake up in the morning and can't remember whether it's B.C. or A.D."

More common is stepping back in social time. Not just a trip to the nineteenth century or the fourteenth or whenever, but joining a people hellbent to prevent change, to deny it has come about, and to put the clock back should it slip forward. An instance is turn-of-the-century folklore. In many English villages folklorists found vestiges of "ancient and unchanging links with a lost rural past". Villagers unknowingly preserved fragments of primordial truths wrapped in later perversions; it was the folklorists' self-imposed duty to make the fragments whole and restore them to life.

Folk life was by definition static, the folk living depositories of ancient history. When folklorists realized that, contrary to this theory, folklore *had* changed and was changing still, they termed these alterations and accretions degenerative. As late as 1968, experts asserted that "folk society does not accept, reflect, or value change."

Since they considered only the most ancient elements authentic, folklorists exhorted villagers to strip off later corruptions and go back to original truths. And though few villagers had heard of Celtic fertility rituals, they deferred to the professionals and changed things accordingly. Thus the annual souling play at Antrobus adopted the view that characters reincarnated the Halloween ghosts of their ancestors; the Marshfield Mummers' perambulation was "revived" as an inviolate magic circle; the local belief that Castleton's Garland Ceremony goes back to Celtic sacrificial rites stems from a persuasive Celticist who visited Castleton in 1977.

To understand British folklore today, you have to retrace the recent steps of the folklorists whose purifications it today embodies. The 1938 president of the Folklore Society reproached the leader of the Padstow Hobby Horse Festival for 'spoiling' an ancient and unchanging fertility rite; she might now be mollified to hear a villager, half a century later, intone that the ritual 'still means the same to us as it did a thousand years ago.'

In every walk of life change is thought bad, avoided when possible, and renamed tradition when not. British reverence for precedent is immortalized in F. M. Cornford's classic *Microcosmographia Academica* of 1908, a mock guide for academic politicians. With all Cambridge committee matters referred back to how things had or had not been done in 1882, the past served as a rock on which every prospective alteration or improvement foundered. Any impulse toward change could be throttled by an appeal to three rules of inaction. The *Principle of the Wedge:* "you should not act justly now for fear of raising expectations that you may act still more justly in the future". The *Principle of Unripe Time:* "people should not do at the present moment what they think right, because the moment at which they think it right has not yet arrived" — and as we know, time has a trick of going rotten before it is ripe. The *Principle of the Dangerous Precedent:* "you should not now do an admittedly right action for fear you, or your equally timid successors, should not have the courage to do right in some future case". This led Cornford to the conclusion his countrymen still cleave to: "Every public action which is not customary, either is wrong, or if it is right, is a dangerous precedent. It follows that nothing should ever be done for the first time."

A few years ago I wanted to look at the will of Christopher Codrington, a seventeenth-century West Indian governor; the will is in the Codrington Library of All Souls College, Oxford, Codrington's major legatee; the librarian invited me there to see it. We chatted; he brought papers to my antique desk; half an hour later he came back, perturbed. "By the by", he asked, "you've used our library before, haven't you?" "No", I said, "I haven't." "Oh", he said, "then I'm afraid you can't use it now." (It was all right in the end; an All Souls Fellow was hauled away from tea to identify me.)

To be sure, self-mockery often cloaks obsession with British heritage — these days derided as "the heritage industry". A satirist lampoons the hawking of genealogical bona fides:

'Get your ancestors here! Get your ancestors here!' The cry came from a raggedy old man, pushing his barrow up the Bayswater Road... 'Get your ancestors here! Lovely, fresh ancestors!... Cross my palm with traveller's checks and I'll find you an ancestry you'll be proud of for the rest of your life... By the greatest good fortune I have a piece of the old family tapestry here'... He blew his nose on it and offered it to me, together with the title deeds to a disused railway line in Clackmannanshire. 'You are now Honorary Lord of the Station of Newtonmuir, and Porter Extraordinary of Gaskhorn. God bless you, Sire! That will be 75 guineas.' 'You're a grand old fraud', I said, flashing my Ancestry Fraud Squad badge. 'I must ask you to accompany me to the station. I believe you are the Mr Big we have been looking for.'

The moral: "Don't be like Mr Big of that Ilk - leave the selling of our heritage to the appropriate government department."

But beneath the jokey facade the British take pride in uniquely durable attachments. In 1931 the historian Herbert Butterfield had demolished Whig history, the classic nineteenth-century view that saw modern England as the culmination of centuries of institutional progress. In the dark hours of the Second World War he repented to extol English strength of tradition:

English institutions have century upon century of the past, lying fold upon fold within them... Because we English have maintained the threads between past and present we do not, like some younger states, have to go hunting for our own personalities. We do not have to set about the deliberate manufacture of a national consciousness, or to strain ourselves, like the Irish, in order to create a 'nationalism' out of the broken fragments of tradition, out of the ruins of a tragic past... Our history is here and active, giving meaning to the present.

I wonder what Butterfield would have thought of the British Army's present contempt for history. A recent recruitment ad reads:

You're pinned down by enemy fire. WHAT USE IS A DEGREE IN MEDIEVAL HISTORY? A lot of use. You have a trained mind. The capacity to absorb information rapidly and to act on it. Join, and... soon, *instead of reading history YOU might be helping to steer its course.'*

In June I went to a symposium on Nostalgia in Helsinki; Finn after Finn lovingly recalled their pasts. Two aspects of life stood out: country life and childhood. These seem obvious choices: for most Westerners the countryside is now far enough back to belong firmly in the past. Here in England, where ninety percent live in cities and few have immediate rural roots, nostalgia for the land is especially potent — and illusory. The Finnish countryside lies within the memory of most adults; when they go to it on holiday, they consciously seek out semblances of childhood. What about childhood? For most of us it is self-evidently past. But what are we nostalgic for? Many aspects of childhood seemed at the time sad or unsavory; even the fortunate had to put up with grown-up imposition, incomprehension, and tyranny over time, place, and event. Yet nostalgia for childhood may even embrace these conditions. We nostalgize what was different about childhood, however good or bad it may have been or now seems.

That's the essence of nostalgia: we yearn to

recall (though not usually to relive) a time when life was different. What we are nostalgic for is not the past as it was or even as we wish it were; but the condition of having been, with a concomitant integration and completeness lacking in any present. No one ever experienced as "the present" what we now view as "the past"; the reconstructed past is more coherent than when it happened. We interpret the ongoing present as we live through it; we stand outside the past to view its more finished forms, including its now known consequences for what was then the unknown future. For all its strangeness, the past thus feels definitive and magisterial. History reveals — and nostalgia celebrates — an ordered clarity contrasting with the chaos or imprecision of our own times.

One quality childhood shares with other nostalgic pasts is that is it over: unlike the present, it has been finished, completed, summed up. No doubt we never come to terms with all aspects of childhood. But in memory it feels unlike our present messy and incoherent existence; it is a narrative with a fabulous structure, a beginning, and an end. Our childhood saga itself has the shape of fable: it starts with "once upon a time" and prototypically ends with "living happily ever after". One narrative convention sees change as progress; for most this holds true only in childhood, when we acquired length and strength, facts and skills, self-conscious experience.

Books and experience also awaken children to wider worlds, close up and far off, past and future. As neophyte explorers, children become global citizens. Hence my dismay at the film version of L.P. Hartley's *The Go-Between*. I had used Hartley's opening line, "The past is a foreign country", as the title of my own book; my main theme is his next phrase, "they do things differently there". Both lines are packed with meaning for life, life histories, and history proper. But the film script omits these lines and scuttles their implications. The past is not foreign or different. The movie's whole weight is made to rest on the crippling shock of sexual revelation, the calamitous gulf between the world as seen by young Leo, and by the lovers and other adults. But Hartley had meant much more. He meant the gulf between childhood and

maturity to echo that between then and now, the *historical* changes in English manners and mores.

Ability or failure to heed such changes and to build them into their own behavior crucially counterpoints his characters' personal stories.

In neglecting the novel's social and historical dimension, *The Go-Between*'s film script resembles many popular tales set in other times or traversing both past and present. Characters are distinguished only by age and gender or maybe minority and majority status; the same motives, mentalities, machinery of the mind appear to animate mythical or medieval or modern folk. In stories devoid of meaningful place or context, only timeless elementary habits and elemental passions are enacted on an essentially present-day stage.

Historians as well as storytellers (and the best are both) themselves further a fallacious faith in an easy, anachronistic recovery of the past. The immediacy of *Montaillou* and *Martin Guerre* has thrilled millions. But what readers and viewers gain from these exotic forays into the lives of remote peasants is not cultural actuality; it is a voyeur's view of distant private lives. Vivid intimacies promote empathy but limit understanding; they underscore the constants of human universals; but they obscure or ignore the historical trends that both link and differentiate past and present.

This is why the historian Natalie Zemon Davis rewrote her film script of *The Return of Martin Guerre* as a scholarly book. It troubled her that the film departed "from the historical record... These changes may have given the film the powerful simplicity that made the Martin Guerre story a legend in the first place". But they weakened its contradictions and glossed over the sixteenth-century religious and social realities.

Our growing love affair with the past jettisons its cultural distance. Historic sites, museums, and costume romance revert to Thucydides' dictum that human nature remains constant, that "in essential features people have not changed from one age to another". Though historians scoff, heightened popular interest in history augments that myth. The past is seen in the same terms as the present.

The audiovisual prelude to the Minute Man National Historical Park, in Massachusetts, shows the events of April 19, 1775, as a staccato modern newscast. The intimacy engages the visitor. But it hides a crucial difference: news two centuries ago spread more slowly and was received in ways unlike our own. Conned into thinking they are reliving the event exactly as it happened, viewers gain rapport at the cost of hindsight. The first exhibit Minute Man visitors see features a wooden darning egg, a needle holder, a detachable pocket, and an old comb, with the legend: "Life was a daily thing. Battles only temporary. But both went on while colonists waited out the war." This domesticates the Revolution. But it offers no historical events – only universal processes. At Valley Forge, too, history is just timeless human nature. The display label tells us that the soldiers who encamped there over the winter "demonstrated the universal desire of the human spirit in its pursuit for freedom and self-determination." As Daniel Czitrom puts it for comparable Civil War displays, "Instead of social history we get *Dynasty* set in the 1860s."

Outdoor history museums expressly liken past to present. The Nebraska's Stuhr Museum of the Prairie Pioneer feels it "important that the visitors know that the problems of the people in 1880 are still very much the same problems of the people in 1980" – that is, farm prices and energy. The evident absurdity highlights the reason for saying it: erasing the time gap puts the visitor in the pioneers' frame of mind. A 1975 history text "clarifies" past issues by dragging them out of context into the present: "People in all our communities today have serious problems, just as slaves had problems before the Civil War."

Felt needs for relevance and empathy require historical fiction and drama to show "that people in the past were much like those in the present". Behind the exotic facade of swords and galleon rigging are familiar relationships expressed in modern terms. Yet we desperately need to recognize that people in the past were strange. It is as much a part of growing up as recognizing our own past selves. We are enlarged by the differences and distances of other times, other folk, other creatures, not just by empathy with them. Only enduring and welcoming what is strange, even beyond comprehension, frees us from blind submission to the idols of the tribe.

But personal time comes first – first in childhood, first in the child's concern, the first model for other senses of time, as Rousseau and Wordsworth showed. It is through our own childhoods that we learn to tell the repetitive or the cyclical from the unique, to spot sequences, to balance cause and effect, and to find our own persisting selves in the stream of memory.

Children come to engage innumerable aspects of time. I will address three. One is locating themselves within longer time-spans. When do we realize that our life is bounded within a wider realm, a brief crack of light between two eternities of darkness; and that others came into this world before us and will live after we are gone?

Some cannot endure this awareness: Nabokov's *Speak Memory* describes a chronophobiac who could not bear that his parents and older siblings had lived when he was nothing. Looking at home movies taken a few weeks before his birth he was stunned "that he did not exist there at all and that nobody mourned his absence... 'A brand-new baby carriage... on the porch had the smug, encroaching air of a coffin... as if, in the reverse course of events, his very bones had disintegrated". My own daughter's retrospective angst comes as torrents of grief for not having done something she long ago wished to do.

Children usually aim to live forever, or at least as long ahead as they can imagine; no future must escape them. The brevity of our own being, compared with the earth's or even our own family's, and the unique contingency that gave us life just here and now, are never fully assimilated; but they must be confronted.

I turn to a second time awareness: discovering memory's manifold uses. All parents recall children's repeated pleas to retell early events in their lives or ours. Through this public ritual they mythologize themselves. Some develop a near-Proustian regard for memory, not as a substitute for the present, but as a precious enrichment of themselves.

Memory can feel irreplaceable. Against the growth of the blank and darkening past piling up behind her, Annie Dillard felt she had to remember everything. "If one day I forgot to notice my life, and be damned grateful for it, the blank cave would suck me up entire". To hold that looming loss at bay she plans on total recall — to "trap and keep every teacher's funny remark, every configuration of leaves, every dream, and every scrap of overhead cloud. Who would remember if not me? (Unaccountably, I thought that only I had noticed time... Children may believe that they alone have interior lives.)" This urge to preserve memory foreshadows the elderly custodians of family lore — the gerontologists' "Last Leaf" syndrome. "Unable to pass on her inherited store of memories, the lone survivor of an ancient lineage bears the heavy burden of being the Last Leaf. [She] is all that the past has to rely upon — and she knows it." (Only a few opt for oblivion. With so much feeling bound up in her past, Anna Freud in old age could not bring herself to share her recollections "with the reading public... so I allow myself the privilege of taking it all with me.") But while the old look to the immortality of collective memory, the child's is sharply self-centered.

Third: children need most of all to link with their past selves. Defying the manifold changes of time and growth, they build up an identity grounded in continuity. By extending themselves over time, children come to anticipate the familiar, to stabilize change, and to assess how thought leads to action, action to consequence. They begin to learn that some of what happens to them stems from innate nature, some from volition; they weigh the impacts of habit and chance, outside force and inner will.

Only later if at all do children connect their own pasts and futures with collective history. Even for many adults history has no significance; for many more it remains abstract and ephemeral, used only as a frame for personal events — 'you remember, the war had just started when we moved to the new house', or 'it was the winter of the great snowfall that Kate caught measles'. To others academic history — or the science-fiction future — may be fascinating in themselves but bear not at all on their personal time.

A child's private life unwinds inside her skin and skull; only as she sheds childhood... can she locate the actual, historical stream, see the setting of her dreaming private life — the nation, the city, the neighborhood, the house where the family lives... We children lived our... Pittsburgh history without knowing or believing any of it',

writes Dillard in *An American Childhood.*

I breathed the air of history all unaware, and walked oblivious through its littered layers.

More accessible than this actual background history are the imaginative, even imaginary, pasts and futures of literature. Fictional time-lines are not littered layers that need tedious excavation; they are narrative gems whose shaping resonates with the child's unfolding. Unlike the public history that fashions and constrains the child's environment, fictional time also has the virtue of being somewhat within his control. To be sure, these tales are already told, fixed, and shared; but they can be privately absorbed, in the child's own time and at the child's own pace. And the personal time of the stories' inhabitants meshes with the worlds they are set in. Thus they help children to link with their own encompassing histories and suggest how they may reshape them. So children learn to become not just consumers or subjects but active makers of history.

History remains the amateur activity *par excellence.* Each of us is his own historian, in Carl Becker's phrase, forging unique invaluable findings. Emerging hindsight reopens the past to ever new views. And each new day's past reminds historians that all their insights are evanescent, doomed to give way. A "Mysteries in History" show at the Indianapolis Children's Museum conveys the thrill of open-ended sleuthing. "We're not saying, 'This is the past. Believe it!' We're saying, 'Given what we know, this is our best interpretation of the past.'" Doubt is extolled:

Traditionally, youngsters have been taught history as they were taught math — as a finite subject with definite right or wrong answers. But by exposing them to the methods used to find out about the past, youngsters will see that history and the way we interpret it is not carved in granite. They'll find out we're constantly finding out things that change our perception of the past. They'll learn that what we know about the past today is not what we'll know about the past in the future.

They also learn there are some things we can never find out. Best of all, they, too, "make discoveries and reshape how we look at things." Like these children, each of us can shed unique light on the past — both private memories and broader historical insights.

The future has fewer imaginative prospects than the past. And it lacks the past's dense specificity and its invaluable tension between the actual, the possible, and the invented. Even the archetypal time traveller H. G. Wells was put off by the future's thinness and absence of individuality. Its handsome but characterless buildings, its healthy and happy people devoid of personal distinction left "an incurable effect of unreality'; however rational, it seemed 'strange and inhuman". By contrast, any past institution, however irrational or preposterous, had for Wells "an effect of realness and rightness no untried thing may share. It has ripened, it has been christened with blood, it has been stained and mellowed by handling, it has been rounded and dented to the softened contours that we associate with life."

The Elizabethan bobbin boy in Alison Uttley's *A Traveller in Time* beautifully conveys the quality of things smoothed or roughened by time. But our program epigraph worries me. Time's continuity makes her Penelope feel "a part of events past, present, and to come, and I could choose my way among them". But being able to make that choice does not *confirm* the continuity; it *denies* it. Freely to visit any past or future is to hold aloof from the stream of time, to dissociate oneself from inheritance and stewardship.

Penelope herself comes to realize this; her deep involvement at length precludes stepping back at will, and confirms her present identity. Like Ralph Pendrel in Henry James's *The Sense of the Past*, she learns that a past too vividly felt imperils sanity and even life. It is the nightmare evoked by Borges while conjecturing an earlier childhood. Suddenly "the facile thought *I am in eighteen hundred and...* ceased being a set of approximate words and deepened into a reality. I felt dead, I felt myself an abstract perceiver of the world", unable to separate "one moment belonging to its apparent past from another belonging to its apparent present."

Delusive familiarity tempts some to see the past not as precedent but as alternative: not what has happened but what could happen, an option still open. Characters in films like *Blazing Saddles* and *Blade Runner, Star Wars* and *Zelig* reenter the cinematic past as authentic natives; the popularity of *Back to the Future* reflects the cult for reliving the personal past. Until recently the believing time traveler was a rare eccentric; today the credulous are the mainstream. One student recently confided to her California philosophy professor that "you were a Cheyenne warrior in a previous existence, and I nursed you back to health after you'd been wounded by an arrow through your heart" (all he could manage to respond was "thank you"). A "medieval kissogram" messenger hauled into court in Harrow as a drunken rowdy refused to remove his costume on the ground that he was a medieval knight; the usher explained in vain that "This is not a medieval court."

(The time-travel disease is catching. At Plimoth Plantation, where actors impersonating seventeenth-century inhabitants are supposed to profess ignorance of the post-1627 future, a recent visitor who asked permission to take a picture met with blank incomprehension. Forgetting that his auditor was in fact a twentieth-century impersonator, the visitor embarked on a lengthy explanation of the mechanism of the modern camera.)

A dilemma of our time is that we know more about the past than ever before, but seem less and less able to use it creatively in the present. Instead we recapture one or another historical moment to play with it, inspecting it like a museum specimen. Each recovered moment is unique, but they have a family resemblance: they are all remote, and dead. We do not live with the past; we collect it.

Once-lost pasts are scrupulously revived; but we do not engage with them as natives or re-create their original auras. As Robert Morgan says of early music retrievals, we can never replicate how a contemporary performer related to a language he absorbed unconsciously, encoded as a determinant of his very way of thinking, hearing, and speaking. "Writing my books about the Edwardian period", says a character in Peter Dickinson's *Death of a*

Unicorn, "I mark each page with some pungent signal — a brand name, song, form of speech, public person or event in the news — to bring the odor of the period to life. Cheating, of course. Few people living in a period notice such things. Their real sense of their time is as unrecapturable as the momentary pose of a child."

Nor can we ever see the spinning wheel in the museum as those who used it did. For us it is not a new tool, but a *former* tool, left stranded in the present by the tides of industrial change. As Arthur Danto notes, its proper place today is the antique shop, the *authentic* reproduction, the deliberately atavized decor. For people to see spinning wheels as they were once seen, the whole history of spinning jennies, Crompton mules, and so forth would have to be unknown by them. Moderns may enjoy the past's differences, but as Brecht reminds us, our delight in comparisons, in distance, in dissimilarity should echo a delight in what is close and proper to ourselves.

My concern here is the opposite of what I said about the film of *The Go-Between.* To see the past as truly foreign, we must remember it is unknowable. That is hard to bear in mind, because the past is often enclosed in "a terrible carapace of false familiarity", to cite Michael Baxandall. We think we know Italian Renaissance paintings as contemporaries did because their familiar themes are well studied. But we come to Piero della Francesca with eyes that have seen Picasso. And Piero had no need to spell out the sixteenth-century conventions we have had to make explicit — making them also coarse, rigid, and clumsy. To love Piero properly, Baxandall suggests, we must respect his remoteness from us, continuing to use such archaic terms as *colore, diseqno, commensurazione,* which have no precise modern equivalents, to remind us of what we do *not* understand.

Does this seem too ambivalent? Ambivalence toward the past is inescapable. Children grow up immersed in ideas and artifacts that antedate their own birth; they necessarily copy, emulate, and venerate their elders. Yet to become adult they must throw off these models and make their own way, denying or transcending parental

legacies. Those who fail to do so remain fixated on the past and never achieve autonomy. Like nations, children must draw sustenance from their past, yet also put it behind them.

They do so not just by confronting the present, but by constructing their own past and future. That mental process begins long before children can physically act on it. Here books are critical: they teach modes of travelling in time that encourage children to overcome subordination to adults and to the confines of familiar worlds. To read chronicles of others' times is not simply to escape for a while from our own time, but to embellish and magnify how we apprehend it. But passing time then renders childhood itself ever more foreign. We have to recover or reinvent the child within ourselves to keep the clockwork constraints of adult existence from taking over.

Luckily the past is biddable. We do well to embellish it. E.L. Doctorow tells of an elderly Texan woman who took issue with his novel *Welcome to Hard Times,* set in the Dakota Territory in the later nineteenth century:

"'Young man', she wrote, 'when you said that Jenks enjoyed for his dinner the roasted haunch of a prairie dog, I knew you'd never been west of the Hudson. Because the haunch of a prairie dog wouldn't fill a teaspoon.' She had me. I'd never seen a prairie dog. So I did the only thing I could. I wrote back and I said, 'That's true of prairie dogs today, Madam, but in the 1870s...'"

Historical latitude marks English tradition too. Butterfield echoes Cornford: since the seventeenth century, "our greatest innovators had tried to show that they were not innovators at all but restorers of ancient ways... Even when we have a revolution we... try to carry it out in accord-ance with ancient precedents". How fortunate that these would-be seventeenth - century restorers knew so little history, and used it so cavalierly, that for all its antiquarian fervor the seventeenth century

did not resurrect and fasten upon us the authentic Middle Ages... In England we made our peace with the Middle Ages by misconstruing them; 'wrong' history was one of our assets;... precisely because they did not know the Middle Ages, the historians of the time gave the seventeenth century just the type of anachronism that it required.

Thus creative error enabled Whig history in tandem with the common law "to tighten the bonds that hold the Englishman to his past — foster our love of precedent, our desire for gradualness in change, our adherence to ancient liberties."

Liberties denied to children, though, at least until *1066 and All That* punctured the pomposity of the custodial past. For children, the British Museum remained a byword for the past's repressive and suffocating presence. It is immortalized in the cartoonist H.M. Bateman's *The boy who breathed on the glass in the British Museum* (1916). Confronting an Egyptian mummy a misguided youth succumbs to temptation; he takes a deep breath, and puffs vigorously on the glass case. A warder hauls him off by the scruff of the neck; the poor boy is arrested, tried, and sentenced to prison for life for this heinous desecration of the preserved past. The past may be a childlike country, but children visit it at their peril.

Slippery time

Time present and time past
Are both perhaps present in time future
— T.S. Eliot

"I KNOW what time is," said St. Augustine, "but if a man ask me what it is, I cannot tell him." Few of us today, even if we have read Stephen Hawking's *Brief History of Time,* are confident that we know, and even fewer would venture to tell. Yet the mystery of time has held endless fascination for a great many minds through the ages. I want to say a little about changing ideas on the subject because of the effects they have had upon writers, including writers for children. Whether these ideas were or are correct belongs to a different discussion, in which I am not qualified to engage. Since I am dealing with matters on which countless thousands of words have been written, you will understand, and I hope forgive, the crudeness and brevity of my summaries.

The view of time traditionally taken by Judaism, Christianity, and, I believe, Islam is a linear one. God created the world, and in doing so set time in motion. Time runs in a straight line from the Creation to the resurrection of the dead, when it will come to a stop and be subsumed in eternity. Time, in short, is temporary. There are difficulties, of course, even with such a simple concept as this. People have asked, Was there not time before the Creation? or, What did God do before he created the world?

St. Augustine, who was the greatest of the early Christian thinkers, when asked the latter question, replied in effect that it was a meaningless one. Time was a property of the universe that God created, and before the beginning of the universe it did not exist.

BOOKS FOR DISCUSSION:
Penelope Lively *The Ghost of Thomas Kempe*
Alan Garner *Red Shift*
Jane Langton *The Diamond in the Window*
Philippa Pearce *Tom's Midnight Garden*
John Rowe Townsend *The Visitors* (U.K. title: *The Xanadu Manuscript*)

Interestingly, Stephen Hawking observes in almost the same words that "the concept of time has no meaning before the beginning of the universe."

Buddhists and ancient Greeks viewed time as a cycle rather than a straight line. For Buddhists there is an endless succession of rebirths, aspiring towards the timelessness of Nirvana. Reincarnation and endless recurrence had their place in ancient Greek philosophy, too: among the Pythagoreans and Stoics, for instance. Eudemus of Rhodes, not a Pythagorean, told his pupils that if the Pythagoreans were to be believed, "the same things come again and I will talk, staff in hand, to you sitting like this, and everything else will be alike" for ever and ever. He may have been ridiculing the idea. However, since everything from the heavenly bodies down could be seen to move in cycles, it did not seem an unreasonable view that time would also be cyclical and would come round again. Professor Cornford, in *Plato's Cosmology,* sums it up: among the ancient Greeks, he says, "time was conceived not as a straight line, but as a circle." He quotes Aristotle as saying that this view is held because "time is the measure of a circular motion and is itself measured by a circular motion" [that of the heavens.] Several Greek philosophers, including Plato, developed the idea of the Great Year: a period in which all the heavenly bodies would return to their former alignments. Cornford quotes Protus as saying, "The whole of time is contained in a single revolution of the whole universe." Greeks also, I think, supposed a historical cycle of destruction and starting again.

Both of these views — the straight line and the circle — left room for prophecy, which to me is the most fascinating feature of ancient thinking about time. Those of you who know your Bible will know that the Old Testament is full of prophets and prophecies, and the New Testament is insistent that prophecies have been fulfilled. The first two chapters of St. Matthew's Gospel, dealing with the birth of Christ, contain five times, with slight variations, the words "that the prophecy might be fulfilled;" it was very important to the early Christians to establish that Jesus really was the prophesied Messiah. And the moving conclusion of St. Luke's Gospel, telling of the risen Christ, has him saying to the disciples, "These are the words which I spake unto you while I was yet with you, that all things must be fulfilled, which were written in the law of Moses and in the prophets and in the psalms concerning me . . . thus it is written, and thus it behoved Christ to suffer, and to rise from the dead the third day." Prophecy is crucial; the point I shall return to is not connected with the truth of the Resurrection or of the Christian religion generally, but is that a valid prophecy must place a lien upon time: if something *has* to happen, then the future is not a blank page; it has been written on already. To put it another way, the future is there, waiting to happen.

In this context, I want to go back briefly to the ancient Greeks. As everyone knows, they believed — though there were skeptics among them — in the foretelling of the future; we are all familiar with the phrase "consulting the oracle." I want to refer particularly to Greek drama, so hugely important in western literary culture. I need hardly remind you to what extent Greek tragedy is rooted in the concept of destiny. The opening motif of many plays — the *Agamemnon* of Aeschylus, the *Oedipus at Colonnus* of Sophocles, and others — is "The time has come." Time brings doom: unavoidable doom. "All things the long and countless time first draws from darkness, then buries from light"; that is from Sophocles' *Ajax*, and it has to mean that events lie hidden in the future, they become for an instant present, then they are fixed for ever in the past. In Aeschylus, according to Jacqueline de Romilly's book *Time in Greek Tragedy*, time is an instrument of divine justice. In Sophocles, time, or rather destiny, tends to be the enemy; man fights against his destiny, but fights it in vain. In that lies his nobility, but in that also lies his tragedy, for destiny is stronger than he is. I suppose the world's most famous story of implacable destiny is the *Oedipus Rex*; whatever the twists and turns, the dreaded prophecy that Oedipus will kill his father and marry his mother will be fulfilled; and, as the Chorus tells Oedipus when the truth is revealed, "Time the all-seeing has found you out in your despite." In Euripides' *Orestes*, the Chorus sings, "Alas, miserable tribes of men, creatures of one day living among tears, behold how unpredictable are the ways of destiny!" In short, we do not control our fate; everything is written in our stars. Read the Bible, read classical Greek drama, those primal sources of our literature, and you are confronted again and again with prophecy, with destiny, and therefore with time that is already mapped out.

I used the phrase "written in our stars" just then in a figurative sense, but of course astrology would have it that this is literally so. Astrology began, according to the *Encyclopedia Britannica*, with the cataloguing of omens in ancient Mesopotamia, a matter of which I confess I know nothing, but it developed with great complexity in ancient Greece as astronomical observation became more accurate. It seems not at all unreasonable that the heavens should provide a key to events on earth — should indeed control them — and that if you knew how to read the heavens you would be able to read the future. However, since the movements of the stars are predictable, astrology appears to rule out free will; in fact it appears to rule out divine intervention, though some early Christians claimed that the stars could be seen as displaying to us the will of God. The heavens were God's picture book, as we would see if we could but decode it. But Christianity in general, I think, hated astrology.

The point I want to make about all these destinarian systems of thought is that, first, events in the future must be already there, even if time has not yet, in Sophocles' phrase, brought them to light, and, second, that they are incompatible with free will. The problem of free will was well understood by early Christian thinkers, and it is a difficult one: if God is omnipotent and omniscient, he must know what is going to happen, he must have ordained it, and we have no say in the matter. St. Augustine put what we may call the God's-eye view very clearly:

What is future to God who transcends all times? . . . He does not in our manner look forward to what is future, or contemplate what is present, or look back at what is past, but works in another way removed far above the habits of our thinking . . . He comprehends in a stable and eternal present all the things that happen in time, whether they are yet to be in the future, or already present, or already over in the past . . . For his knowledge of the three times, present, past and future, does not change in diversity, like ours, since with him there is no change or shadow of movement.

Augustine was driven in the end by his own honesty to accept what he saw as the logic of this: namely, that moral praise and blame are irrelevant, since we respond to God's grace as God knows we will respond. He came to believe in predestination. I think most people find this a chilling doctrine. A great deal has been written about the problem of foreknowledge and freewill, and solutions have been found which do not require predestination and do allow freewill, but the question can give a lot of trouble, as John Milton realized when he struggled with it in *Paradise Lost*. In Book III of *Paradise Lost* God explains that he knew that Satan and his followers would rebel,

but they cannot complain that he as their all-powerful, all-knowing Maker decreed it and is therefore himself responsible, because, God says, he gave them free will and

> . . . they themselves decreed
> Their own revolt, not I: if I foreknew,
> Which had no less proved certain unforeknown.

God is saying that he knew they were going to do it, but he'd given them free will so it was still their fault. It is a neat bit of dialectical footwork, but it doesn't really convince; if God knew they were going to do it, then surely they were not free *not* to do it; and anyway he has just observed that he was their Maker, so he must have made them with the evil in them. Milton's aim in *Paradise Lost* was "to justify the ways of God to man," and I have never been able to feel that Milton achieved this aim, though it is of course possible to conceive a quite different God from Milton's God.

Milton and *Paradise Lost* were, however, at the end of a line. The new thought of Copernicus and Galileo, soon to be followed by Newton, was changing everything. Science was replacing dogma; the world was no longer at the center of the universe; it and the planets went round the sun and, in Hawking's words, it became natural to suppose that the fixed stars were objects like our sun but very much farther away. Newton put forward the theory — essentially the theory of gravity — and also the mathematics to account for the movement of bodies through space. He seemed to many to have sewn it all up:

Nature and Nature's laws lay hid in night.

God said, *Let Newton be!* and all was light.

Thus Alexander Pope. He spoke too soon, but we'll come to that later.

With the dawn of the scientific age, soothsayers and all that stuff were discredited. According to the *Encyclopedia Britannica*, "Newtonian physics eradicated a belief in astrology among the educated." I'm not so sure of that; I have met educated people who believe in it, and there are parts of the world where it is still taken very seriously today. We still have "What the stars foretell" columns in our newspapers, and most people can tell you what sign of the zodiac they were born under. (Mine is Taurus.) And there's a certain amount of fatalism always around. *Che sarà, sarà* — what will be, will be. In World War I, and perhaps in World War II, there were soldiers who would say, "If there's a bullet with your number on it, it will get you." I am a cautious man, but I will declare without hesitation that astrology and all forms of fortune-telling, with tea leaves or Tarot cards or what you will, are bunk; and I am glad that I have no belief in them, because if you do believe in them you are on a logical slope which ends with the acceptance that you are a cipher without free will and therefore without responsibility.

I come now to time-slip and time travel. They belong essentially to modern fiction, to the age of the novel, which is more or less coterminous with the era of the children's book. But as students of children's literature, you will not be surprised that they have their antecedents in legend and folk tale. The simplest form of time-slip could perhaps best be called the time capsule: a person falls asleep and wakes up many years later, like the Seven Sleepers of Ephesus, who were walled up in a cave by their persecutors, fell asleep, and woke two hundred years later thinking they had only slept for a few hours. They couldn't recognize the place where they were, and when they tried to buy food, their strange dress and obsolete money drew attention to them and a miracle was proclaimed. In some versions they then expired; in others they went back to sleep and are still asleep, awaiting the Day of Resurrection. Such tales as "The Sleeping Beauty" and "Rip Van Winkle" are on the same theme.

There are many stories of sleeping warriors — King Arthur, Charlemagne, Barbarossa and others — who are effectively enclosed in time capsules. And there are many stories of visits to Fairyland in which fairy time is different from our time. In 1890, Edwin S. Hartland wrote a book called *The Science of Fairy Tales*, in which there are three chapters crammed with such instances. One of the tales is of a young Pembrokeshire shepherd who joins in a fairy dance and finds himself in a glittering palace surrounded by beautiful gardens, where he lives happily for years among the fairy folk. But he's been told he mustn't drink from the fountain. He feels an increasing urge to do so, and one day he plunges his hands into the pool, whereupon the whole scene vanishes and he finds himself back on the hillside, the episode having taken only minutes. More often, however, it works the other way, and while one is in fairyland for an apparently short time, many years go by in our world. For instance, two fiddlers in Strathspey were inveigled into going into a hillside and supplying the music for a brilliant fairy assembly, which seemed to them to last for a few hours, but when they came out it was a hundred years later. Seeing this as a miracle, they went to church, but when the clergyman began to read the gospel, at the first word he uttered they fell into dust. There are also fairy lands where time stands still, like Tir Nan Og, where the grass is always green, flowers and fruit come together, feasting and music, love and hunting go on all day and there's no such thing as death.

Stories of fairyland avoid the problem of time travel within our own world, which is that you can't go into past or future without thereby changing them. Fairyland is outside our time. Similarly, stories on the Rip Van Winkle theme avoid this difficulty, because while the protagonist is simply asleep he can't interfere with anything; he passes out of time and comes back into it at a later point. No problem. If, however, as a writer of fiction, you send John or Jane Brown from the contemporary world into, say, the time of Queen Elizabeth the First, you have to face the fact that everything they do there will have a cumulative effect through the intervening years and will change the world of today, which is impossible.

I must return to what has happened to time, and fiction involving it, since Newton. Newton himself did not in fact propound any new theory of time. "Absolute, true and mathematical time," he wrote, "of itself and from its own nature, flows equably without relation to anything external." He looked on time as a continuous sequence of moments; all other motions, he said, "may be accelerated and retarded, but the flowing of absolute time is not liable to any change." That is essentially the common sense view. Newtonian science did however encourage development of a philosophy of determinism, which said in effect that every event had a cause or causes, and if we could know all the causes that were operating we would know what was going to happen. Everything that happens, in fact, *has* to happen as the sum of all its causes, and, as a corollary, what doesn't happen could not have happened. This is a kind of predestination, mechanical rather than arbitrary, and can be reconciled with religion by the familiar image of the great clock; God, as it were, set the system going but doesn't have to intervene in its operation.

The great changes in thinking about time came in the nineteenth and still more the twentieth century, though there were beginnings in the eighteenth; and the background to the new thinking was the expansion in the perceived *extent* of time. It had been supposed that the world was about six thousand years old; but by the nineteenth century geologists and evolutionists were indicating a time that stretched back millions of years — a time as vast as space. And the question was waiting to be asked: was time the same kind of thing as space? And if you could travel around in space, could you — fictionally, at least — travel in time?

The first time travel novel that I know of was written by a Frenchman, L.S.Mercier, and published in 1771. It was translated into English by a Dr W. Hooper and made quite a stir, though it's now forgotten. It has prefixed to it a quotation from Leibnitz: "Le temps présent est gros de l'avenir" — the present is big with the future. Its second chapter, the effective beginning, is headed "I am 750 years old."

The narrator dreams that ages have passed since he lay down to rest; he went to bed with black hair and a florid complexion, but when he gets up his brow is wrinkled and his hair is white: no wonder, at that age. He finds that a newly erected monument and several notices that are displayed bear the date MMD —

2,500. A passer-by, surprised by his dress, asks in what year he was born. "In 1740," he replies. "Indeed. Why, then you are 750 years of age," says this phlegmatic questioner. "We should be astonished at nothing."

The society described is in effect a utopia, a hugely improved society, and obviously the main aim is to condemn by contrast the writer's own society, which is pre-revolutionary France. So the people in Paris 2500 wear simple, sensible dress in place of fashionable foppery; mostly they go on foot, so rashly driven coaches don't cause traffic jams and injury to pedestrians; coaches in fact are reserved for those full of years and honor. There are no mechanical wonders; the idea of technological change seems never to have occurred to the author. In essence the book is an exceedingly liberal blueprint for the future. Down with tyranny, it says; honor to the hardworking peasant.

The ending is fully in the spirit of time-slip fantasy. The narrator goes to Versailles, which is in ruins, and finds an old man there lamenting the abuse of power that it represents. The old man turns out to be none other than Louis XIV himself, brought back by a Divine Justice to contemplate "the outcome of his deplorable enterprise." It's a chilling moment, which is followed immediately by the abrupt ending of the book: the narrator is about to ask the revived Louis Quatorze a question when "one of the adders, with which this place swarmed, darted from a broken column, stung me on the neck, and I waked." So we never learn what Le Roi Soleil had to say for himself.

The idea of time as a fourth dimension seems to have been put forward in the eighteenth century by two Frenchmen, D'Alembert and Lagrange, whose work is not known to me. For most of you it will be a familiar idea, and not difficult to grasp, but for a brief explanation let me jump forward to the first well-known and still-read piece of time fiction, H.G.Wells's *The Time Machine*, published in 1891. In its opening chapter, the Time Traveller explains to a group of his friends that "any real body must have extension in four dimensions: it must have length, breadth, thickness, and — duration." And he goes on to say — it is italicized in the book — that "there is no difference between time and any of the three dimensions of space except that our consciousness moves along it." So instead of Newton's equable flow of time, we have our own movement along the time dimension.

In case anyone does find it hard to conceive of time as a dimension, let me give a simple illustration. Consider the difference between a work of visual art and a piece of music. A painting, as we see it hanging on the wall, is two-dimensional; it has height and width. If it isn't too big, we can perceive the whole of it at once. But a piece of music — let's simplify this and say a tune — is not all perceived at once. It is a pattern, and our recognition of its nature as a tune is totally dependent upon our ability to distinguish that pattern. It is, however, a pattern in time, whereas a painting is a pattern in space. Musical notation will allow us to show the pattern spatially, but that is only a notation; the reality is still perceived serially in time.

We have a way of storing patterns in time; we call it memory. And out of memory, or other records such as photographs, we can construct patterns which we could not perceive in the passing moment. This process too is cited in *The Time Machine,* when the Time Traveller says to his friends: "Here is a portrait of a man at eight years old, another at fifteen, another at seventeen, another at twenty-three, and so on. All these are evidently sections, as it were, three-dimensional representations of his four-dimensional being, which is a fixed and unalterable thing." And we do to some extent have a four-dimensional sense of what a person is — supposing a much-photographed famous person, or a relative who figures repeatedly in the family photograph album dies, we can put together in our minds a kind of composite portrait.

Wells's Time Traveller declares emphatically that there is no difference between time and a space dimension, but one of his companions instantly draws his attention to a crucial difference: "You can move about in all directions of space," he says, "but you cannot move about in time." We are, or so it appears to us, stuck on a narrow moving belt that is carrying us inexorably at a steady pace to our ultimate destination. At this point I think Mr Wells puts one over on us. The Time Traveller retorts that civilized man can now go up against gravity in a balloon — this was before the age of the airplane — "and why should he not hope that ultimately he may be able to stop or accelerate his drift along the time dimension, or even turn about and travel the other way?" Well, it isn't as simple as that, and I'm afraid that for very good reasons the rapid technological progress that took us within a century from ballooning to space flight is not going to take us with similar speed from living out our mortal days to shooting back and forth in time.

Wells, however, as a novelist had the primary concern of setting his story going, and having given this somewhat slippery answer to his questioner the Time Traveller goes on to say that he's made a machine that is to travel indifferently in any direction of space and time, as the driver decides. And here's his machine — a good stout Victorian contraption made of brass rails and nickel bars and ivory and quartz rods; and when he's ready to go he tries all the screws again and puts one more drop of oil on the quartz rod, presses the starting lever, and bingo, he's away into the future. And there I think we will leave him.

There were other time travel novels in the late nineteenth century, of which the only one I'm going to mention is Edward Bellamy's *Looking Backward,* which made a great stir when it was published in Boston in 1888. The narrator, Julian West, a rich young Bostonian, suffers from insomnia and has himself put to sleep by a mesmerist in a sleeping chamber that he's had built in the foundations of his house. Overnight, the house is burned down, and Julian is supposed to have died. But he hasn't; he's still in his bunker in a mesmeric trance. When he wakes up he's in Boston in the year 2,000. It's a city with miles of broad streets, tree-lined squares with statues and fountains, and "public buildings of a colossal size and architectural grandeur unparalleled in my day."

This future Boston isn't a great place for technological marvels. Its streets have all been covered in, so that people don't have to walk in the rain and poke each other in the eye with their umbrellas, but that isn't really high-tech. Goods are delivered through vacuumatic tubes, which is somewhat more so. There isn't, so far as I can recall, anything to suggest development in means of transportation. The most interesting innovation is that there are several music-rooms in the city in which day-long programs are performed, and you can listen at any time, in the privacy of your home, to any one of four concerts on the telephone. A useful amenity, but, let's face it, unsophisticated in comparison with the compact disc or even with the radio.

However, Mr Bellamy isn't really interested in mere mechanical details; his book is mainly an account of a superior future society in which capitalism and competition have been abolished and there's a total welfare state. It sounds good until you learn that in this utopia everyone is obliged to serve in what is called the Industrial Army, with its many ranks culminating in generals at the top. It's a kind of national socialism, and not very appealing. There's no trading and there are no shops: just huge identical megastores in each of which the choice is exactly the same. Shopping doesn't sound like much fun.

There is, however, one romantic detail. Julian falls in love with a sweet, and I must say very Victorian young lady called Edith, and finds that she is the great-granddaughter of his own lost love, also Edith. He folds the lovely girl in his arms and never goes back to 1887; he stays in the year 2,000 and presumably lives happily ever after with Edith Mark 2. In eleven years' time, some of you Bostonians who are taking part in this program may get to meet them.

There were several other time-travel novels by American and British writers in the latter years of the nineteenth century; the notion was becoming fashionable. On the children's lists, the first, and I think still one of the best, is E.Nesbit's *Story of the Amulet*, which features the children from *Five Children and It* and the crotchety, sand-loving, wish-granting little beast called the Psammead. The children, prompted by the Psammead, have picked up in a junk shop half of an immensely powerful amulet; they can step through it into the past and they seek to reunite it with its missing other half. In the course of doing so, they have various cliffhanging adventures in times and places in the past and are eventually successful; it's good gripping stuff and it's also informative, for E. Nesbit had the help of the justly celebrated Dr. Wallis Budge of the British Museum.

The time aspect is very interesting. E.Nesbit was clearly well aware of the difficulties of the genre, and she allowed herself to take some liberties, no doubt with tongue in cheek. Thus she has the children encounter Julius Caesar in 55 B.C., gazing across the Channel toward England. He's just decided it's not worth the bother of invading, but when the children have told him about such marvels as electric light, hot-air balloons and Madame Tussaud's waxworks, he decides he will invade after all, if only to find out what it's really like. So this family of children in Edwardian London are responsible for our island story of the last two thousand years. It's a closed loop; and there's at least one more when the children find a way to put the two half-amulets together by going forward to a future time when they will have done it. There are several hints at ways of thinking about time; for instance, at one point the Psammead tells the children that if they were only made the right way they "could see everything happening in the same place at the same time."

Einstein, to whom I shall be coming in a minute, found it natural to think of time in dimensional terms, but this has not been universally accepted even in fairly recent times. In particular Henri Bergson totally rejected it and maintained that the flux was the only reality. The past has gone, the future doesn't exist; only the present moment is real. The stream-of-consciousness novel attempts to capture this flux. Bergsonian philosophy was a powerful influence on T S Eliot's early work, as Nancy Gish points out in her book on *Time in the Poetry of T.S.Eliot*. Eliot found this idea that nothing is real but the flux, going on pointlessly for ever, profoundly depressing.

> The worlds revolve like ancient women
> Gathering fuel in vacant lots

says one of his poems. As Gish observes, in any ultimate sense the old women's movements are purposeless; the daily task of gathering fuel leads only to another day of gathering fuel. Eliot, as we all know, progressed from this pessimism to a religious standpoint; his ultimate thinking and consolation are to be found in the *Four Quartets*, which are deeply concerned with time and in fact form a developing and complex discussion of time and eternity.

However, it was science, not philosophy, that reshaped twentieth-century thinking. If the nineteenth century had hugely extended the scale of the universe both in space and time, the twentieth can be said to have blown it apart: we gaze bewildered at the vastnesses of cosmology and the infinitesimal smallnesses of quantum physics. A few minutes ago I quoted Pope on Newton: "God said, 'Let Newton be!' and all was light." There is an almost equally well-known couplet by Hilaire Belloc:

> It could not last; the Devil, howling "Ho!
> Let Einstein be!" restored the status quo.

I shall not purport to explain relativity to you. I do not pretend to understand more than a bit of it, and that precariously. I shall restrict myself to ideas that have got into the consciousness and caught the imagination of fiction-writers. Here are a few of them. Closest to what we have already been discussing is the observation by Einstein himself in his account of the Special Theory of Relativity:

There is no more commonplace statement than that the world in which we live is a four-dimensional space-time continuum . . .
The world of physical phenomena is naturally four-dimensional in the space-time sense. For it is composed of individual events, each of which is described by four numbers, namely, three space coordinates, x, y, z, and a time coordinate, the time value t. That we have not been accustomed to regard the world in this sense as a four-dimensional continuum is due to the fact that in physics, before the advent of the theory of relativity, [time] played

a different and more independent rôle . . . According to classical mechanics, time is absolute.

That last, of course, is the Newtonian view, and Einstein rejected it. In doing so, he put the space-time continuum into the general consciousness. Several other inferences from relativity have lodged in the public, and particularly in the writerly, mind. One of these is that the mass of a body, increasing with its speed, would become infinite at the speed of light; consequently you cannot travel faster than light. This has put science-fiction writers in a difficulty; how can you ever hop around among galaxies innumerable light-years away? They have come up with various devices, the commonest one being a time-warp, now a cliché. I have in the past regarded this as a naïve cheat, no more than an assertion that the impossible has been done. However, as I understand it, the further postulate of Einstein in the General Theory of Relativity, that the space-time continuum is not flat as in Euclidean geometry but curved, gives rise to the interesting notion that if time-space is a kind of four-dimensional sphere, finite but unbounded, you might be able to take a short cut across it, as if between points on a globe of the world, rather than going right round by the surface.

Another intriguing inference from relativity theory is that if you could travel close to the speed of light, your clocks, including your internal clocks, would be slowed down relative to those at your point of departure, and you could make a long trip through space and come back very little older, though the people you left behind would have aged. Fiction writers like this idea. One use of it is in Ursula LeGuin's *The Left Hand of Darkness*, in which an envoy to another world, who is making no progress with his proposal that a backward ruler should join an intergalactic network, remarks that if he is sent packing, he can just go back home in his spaceship, turn round, and come straight back. The few hours he'll have spent on the ship will amount to thirty-four years on the world he's now in, and he can start all over again with a fresh lot of powers-that-be.

Soon after Einsteinian relativity came the

Heisenberg uncertainty principle: you cannot know both the position and the velocity of a particle. The result of this was quantum mechanics, in which particles have a so-called quantum state — a combination of speed and position — and which, instead of telling you the result of an observation, tells you what the probabilities are. This is introducing a random element into science, and Einstein didn't like it: "God does not play dice," he said. And then there's the quantum leap: quanta pop in and out of states and places without actually travelling between them. So here we have three potent phrases which have strongly affected the outlook of many people, including writers: the space-time continuum, the uncertainty principle and the quantum leap. You can give yourself a licence to dispense with the linear sequence of events and with the mechanical progression of cause and effect. Everything is all spread out there in a vast array to all parts of which you have instant access. As an example, here is the beginning, after various preliminaries, of Kurt Vonnegut's *Slaughterhouse Five:*

Listen.
Billy Pilgrim has come unstuck in time.
Billy has gone to sleep a senile widower and awakened on his wedding-day. He has walked though a door in 1955 and come out another one in 1941. He has gone back through that door to find himself in 1963. He has seen his birth and death many times, he says, and pays random visits to all the events in between.

And, as you will know if you've read the book, that is the narrative pattern, totally broken up in terms of the traditional order. Billy does indeed make unpredictable leaps and pop up all over the place in time. There is no explanation of this in terms of cause and effect. None is needed.

I come now to the books on your reading list which are assigned to this session. I apologize to any of you who may think I should have been talking about them long before this point. *Tom's Midnight Garden* is a book that I believe to be still unsurpassed in the field of children's fiction, and it is obviously a book that is profoundly concerned with time. The book itself and Philippa Pearce's own comments are better and fuller guides than I can be, and I will only remark

on one or two of the perplexities. Old Mrs Bartholomew, who is also Hatty, has, as we learn at the end, been dreaming of the past and dreaming Tom into it; Tom understands now

why the weather in the garden had always been perfect; why Time in the garden had sometimes jumped far ahead, and sometimes gone backwards. It had all depended upon what Mrs Bartholomew had chosen to remember in her dreams. Yet perhaps Mrs Bartholomew was not solely responsible for the garden's being there, night after night, these last weeks... [Tom] had longed for someone to play with and for somewhere to play; and that great longing, beating about unhappily in the big house, must have made its entry into Mrs Bartholomew's dreaming mind and had brought back to her the little Hatty of long ago. Mrs Bartholomew had gone back in Time to when she was a girl, wanting to play in the garden; and Tom had been able to go back with her, to that same garden.

So if you relied on that passage only, you could conclude that there hasn't been any time travel at all; that what has happened is a kind of extra-sensory perception between Tom's dreaming mind and Mrs Bartholomew's, and that between them they have created the fiction of Tom's visits to the garden. That would still, I think, be a beautiful conception; but Philippa doesn't actually allow you to go away with it, because it is also clear that Hatty when she was a child did see Tom; for instance, she learned from him how to climb a particular tree and carved both their marks on it.

Above all, there's the matter of the skates, which Hatty leaves under the floorboards for Tom, at his request; which he finds now and takes with him into the past. Those skates are real — insistently, brightly, sharply real; and they are insistently a closed loop. They could not be in the house now if Tom had not really gone into the past, and they raise once more the question of free will and the question of going back and changing things. Philippa Pearce knew all about this, and I think she wrote the book as it is in order to leave scope for the reader to think around the matter; she left it open rather than closed. Incidentally, I would say — I have said — that the deep-lying theme of the book is not travel in time but rather the four-dimensional wholeness of life. In the child the old person is implicit; in the old person the child remains.

The Ghost of Thomas Kempe is another glorious book, marvelously funny, and serious too. Nearly all Penelope Lively's fiction, both adult and children's, is concerned with time and with what time does to people. In *Thomas Kempe* there are two time levels. There's the popping-up of the old rogue in the present day; and that is a fairly simple case of time capsule. Thomas Kempe has been walled up for centuries — in suspended animation, and effectively out of time — and now he's emerged. As with all time capsules, this avoids the logical and philosophical problems; a forward traveller in a time capsule is outside time and not affecting anything. He can start affecting things now with a clean sheet, so to speak. The other time scale is that on which the young hero James gets to know the Victorian boy Arnold through the diary of Arnold's aunt. Here the diary is in effect James's time capsule. The nicest detail in the book is when old Mrs Verity remembers Arnold — whom James has got to know through the diary as a small boy and kindred spirit — as a dignified elderly gentleman who visited the village school during her childhood. This brings the past into direct touch with the present, and recalls Penelope's remark that "the span of a lifetime is something to be wondered at and thought about.'

Jane Langton's *The Diamond in the Window* may seem a long way removed from post-Einsteinian thinking, especially since its intellectual propellant is transcendentalism, the heyday of which was a hundred and fifty years ago. Yet I think it does relate to our theme, for a feature of this century's thinking is that we live in a world no longer solid and stable but fluid and elusive, in which it no longer seems very fanciful to suppose that we might disturb the thin skin of appearance to break into another time, another place, a parallel world, a world gone by or still to come, a world where the rules and boundaries we are familiar with no longer run. This sense of the thinness, the frailty of the transparent envelope of daily reality seems to me to be very strong in *The Diamond in the Window*. And the nub of transcendentalism as I

understand it is in Ralph Waldo Emerson's *Essay on Nature*, in which he said, "Nature is the incarnation of thought. The world is the mind precipitated." This gives you as clear a licence as anyone could wish to throw off the bonds of simple naturalism.

The basic pattern of *The Diamond in the Window* is that of a treasure hunt, which is a familiar staple of children's fiction, though the treasures are highly unusual, being transcendental gems of human wisdom. It is also a story in which three people have been spirited out of our world and have to be found in another one which can only be entered in dream. This other world can be described as a world parallel to ours. The notion of the parallel world is one that intrigues science-fiction writers and has appeared in books on the children's list by John Christopher and John Gordon among others; it is at its most interesting when the parallel world and our own interact, as they do in *The Diamond in the Window*. Ned and Nora, the children who disappeared years ago, are trapped and encapsulated in the parallel world, from which they are eventually rescued — now older and, mysteriously, properly dressed for our own world and the present day when they get back. I think maybe the author owed us an explanation of that last bit.

This is a book that simply fizzes with ideas. Some are very old ones but still potent. One is reminded for instance of the ancient belief that the soul is out of the body during dreaming and is at risk of being *caught* out, away from base. That is a risk that, if I read the book correctly, is faced by Eddy and Eleanor. There is also a belief, common in myth and folklore, that a person's life can be secreted in some place or object, and that the person cannot then be killed except by destruction of the object. There is certainly a relationship in this book between the death, far away, of the wicked uncle and the broken spring of the sinister Jack-in-the-Box. There are more speculative paths of thought that can be approached from that wild and wonderful Concord house that figures in *The Diamond in the Window* and other books. One interesting feature is the mirror-maze that shows Eleanor and Eddy alternative future selves; the intriguing thought of one's mysterious future grown-up self is a surprisingly rare occurrence in children's books, though it does appear twice in Penelope Lively: in *The House in Norham Gardens* and *A Stitch in Time*. However, I hate to labor points about *The Diamond in the Window* which is a marvelously funny, ingenious and engaging book, though occasionally preposterous, and is the last one in the world to be solemn about.

You may well think that *The Xanadu Manuscript* (in the United States *The Visitors*) is out of its class in present company. I was quite pleased however to have it in the reading-list, for the non-literary reason that it would offer a glimpse of Cambridge to people who had never been here; its locations can all in fact be found on the ground quite easily. I wrote it because time travel has always intrigued me and I thought it would be fun to reverse the usual process and have somebody from the future arriving here in the present, rather than people from the present departing into future or past. Cambridge seemed a natural choice of setting, since for people coming and going in time you need permanent open spaces; they can't risk landing in the middle of a brick building. I also had in mind that novels set in the future tend to presuppose either a cataclysm or a totalitarian tyranny, and I thought: why not suppose a nice clean civilized future in which none of the horrendous things so often predicted have happened, with people to whom our world would seem a dirty, lively, colorful old place? And I liked the thought of a love story in which the problem of the lovers would be not a social or racial or political divide, but a one hundred and fifty-year gap in time.

I was well aware of the logical difficulty — that if people are to come here from the year 2149, then everything they do here will change the future from which they come. I dealt with this by having them carry out a procedure called restoring which puts everything back as if nothing had happened. All that is left is a fading memory in the mind of the narrator. This may not be a satisfactory solution to the problem; but then, there *isn't* a satisfactory solution that I know of. Time travel is a notion; look at it too closely and it dissolves.

The last of my five books for discussion is the one that belongs most clearly and insistently to the age of relativity. I mean Alan Garner's *Red Shift*, and I am going to discuss it not in all possible aspects, which would take a long time, but in that particular aspect. In its foreground, as you all know, is the love affair of Tom and Jan, and on the first page the author lays down a marker. It's in the opening dialogue between the two:

Jan hung her arms over the motorway fence. Cars went by like brush marks. "Where are they going? They look so serious."

"Well," said Tom, "let's work it out. That one there is travelling south at, say, one hundred and twenty kilometers per hour, on a continental shelf drifting east at about five centimeters per year—"

"I might have guessed—" [says Jan.]

"—on a planet rotating at about nine hundred and ninety kilometers per hour. . . at a mean orbital velocity of thirty kilometers per second . . . in a solar system travelling at a mean galactic velocity of twenty-five kilometers per second, in a galaxy that probably has a random motion . . . of about one hundred kilometers per second, in a universe that appears to be expanding at about one hundred and sixteen kilometers per second per megaparsec."

Jan scooped up more earth [to put down his neck.]

"The short answer's Birmingham," he said, and ducked.

Pure relativity. The title *Red Shift* is itself a marker: it refers to the displacement of the spectral lines of galaxies and distant stars toward the red end of the spectrum, which implies that the galaxies are receding and is the main evidence for the expanding universe.

There are two other strands to the story, involving obvious alter egos of the brilliant but unstable Tom, set one in post-Roman Britain and one in the seventeenth century, in the same cluster of significant places; and the narration moves between them — very disconcertingly on a first reading — without warning and without any formal division; one instant you're in one story and the next instant you're in another. The strands are interwoven by the recurrence not only of places but of characters, incidents and things, especially the stone axe that keeps reappearing; then there are forward perceptions in the two strands with earlier settings, and there are conscious anachronisms: words from *King Lear* in the story of Roman legionaries, and the legionaries themselves speaking the language of GIs, and so on. The underlying notion, I think, is that events in different times could in a sense be simultaneous, just as events in different places can be simultaneous. Present-day Tom transposes with post-Roman Macey and seventeenth-century Thomas not through a series of time-shifts but because they're all there at the *same* time. It is not in fact conceivable in relativity theory that events separated by time could be simultaneous in the same place. That doesn't matter; fiction can thrive on notions just as well as on provable scientific theories; the point to be made is that we are in a post-Einsteinian world, and only in such a world could such a narrative shape have been devised.

Incidentally, the title *Red Shift* is itself a crucial part of the book; this isn't a book that could perfectly well have been called something else. It is a powerful and all-pervasive metaphor; it has of course its obvious con

notations of blood and violence, and with reference to Tom I think the concept of the expanding universe, the ever-retreating galaxies, is a metaphor for the disintegration of a personality.

I should finish by putting this discussion into perspective. I myself find fascinating the effects which different views of time have had on the writing of fiction. But I do not think that fiction can or should be *about* time theory. Ultimately it would be thin stuff if it were.

A view about time may excite a writer, as may a view about politics or art or the environment; it may be an enabler, a generator, or it may merely be part of an unconscious background, but it cannot be the heart of the matter.

I have said more than once before, and will say it again: serious fiction is about the human heart, human relationships, the human predicament. What travels in time is what travels the entire world of fiction; and it is, both in writer and reader, the human imagination.

Authorities consulted

Cornford, F.M. *Plato's Cosmology* London, Kegan Paul 1937

Einstein, A. *The Theory of Relativity* London, Methuen 1920

Encyclopedia Britannica (15th edition) Sections on Time, Astrology, St Augustine Chicago 1985

Encyclopedia of Science Fiction (ed P. Nicholls) Sections on Alternate Worlds, Faster than Light, Fourth Dimension, Parallel Worlds, Perception, Time Paradox, Time Travel London, Granada 1979

Gish, Nancy C. *Time in the Poetry of T.S.Eliot* London, Macmillan 1981

Hartland, E.S. *The Science of Fairy Tales* London, W.Scott 1890

Hawking, S.W. *A Brief History of Time* London, Bantam 1988

de Romilly, Jacqueline *Time in Greek Tragedy* Ithaca, Cornell U.P. 1968

Scholes, R. & Rabkin, E.S. *Science Fiction* New York, O.U.P. 1977

Sorabji, R. *Time, Creation and the Continuum* London, Duckworth 1983

Whitrow *The Natural Philosophy of Time* O.U.P. 1980

SUSAN COOPER

Long ago and far away

YOU LOOK DOWN from the aeroplane, flying over Britain, and — if you are lucky, and there is no cloud or fog — you see a patchwork, a map of the past. It is the story of a people, written upon the land: a long dialogue between people and place. In one form or another, men have lived here continuously for more than a million years. They have not molded the country as the glaciers did, grinding down the peaks and carving out the lakes, but they have scribbled on the land. And the story can best be read from a long way away. A long way up. Looking down from a height of three miles or so, you see their earthworks, their hillforts, their standing stones in mysterious circles and avenues; the pattern of their farming, both before and after enclosure. You see their old ways and their modern roads; the spreading tentacles of their villages and towns. And always, not more than 100 miles from any part of these islands, you see the other dominant part of the place, on whose shifting surface nobody can write. The sea.

If you are English, Scottish, Welsh or Irish — or, like most of us, a mongrel mixture — born and brought up on this long-occupied land, you acquire by a kind of osmosis a sense of the continuum of place and time. It's more than a sense of place — anyone can have that, from a childhood or a chunk of years spent in a particular spot. It's a sort of fluid awareness; a freedom from the shrieking demands of Now, the present moment. Yes, our twentieth-century way of life is geared to the demands of the present, with the television set the ultimate tyrant, tamed only a little by the amber-exuding VCR. But no child is wholly wrapped in the present who has grown up seeing a Norman castle — or a Cambridge college — from his bedroom window, or walking over the slope of a neolithic hill fort on his way to school; knowing that a farmer up the road can still plough up bits of a Roman pavement, or a London developer dig up an Elizabethan theatre (and then bury it again under a concrete block). Here — now and in England — place implies time. The past is omni-present, so that small Kay in John Masefield's book *The Midnight Folk* sees a mark on a door which 200 years earlier had been a plague cross, and knows that the rector found Henry VIII arrowheads when cutting up firewood, and that old Mr Colway in Naseby dug Civil War bullets out of ancient trees.

This sense of the continuum is a treasure which most of us don't know we possess. Like love, it is most apparent through the size of the aching gap left when it is gone. I had to leave behind my own unthinking awareness of time-place when I went to live in the United States 26 years ago, and so ever since then I have come home to Britain at least once a year for a fix, a transfusion; for the re-assurance of being, at least for a week or two, plugged in.

In America, the sense of man's long relationship with the land can be found only in the south-west, in the moonscape country of New Mexico and Arizona, where Navajo and Zuni, Pueblo and Hopi respect their soil and hold their rocks sacred. Nowhere else is the time of mankind written on the land. New England seems deeply historical to most Americans because men and women have lived there for three hundred years. But those were white men and women; they threw away time, those first settlers, when they arrived in America and began systematically to destroy the way of life of their Indian predecessors.

Most of them came from Britain, and should have known better. In the previous 2,000 years in Britain, during recurring invasions from the Continent, over and over again, in Jung's phrase, the soul of the conquered people had entered that of the conquerors — through the relationship each had with the same land. In America, the American Indian soul didn't have a chance. The white invaders did not follow the old pattern of killing the men, raping and breeding with the women, and following the old uses of the land. Instead they killed the men *and* the women, and raped the land. The Roman Englishman put his road from London to Bath, along valleys and around hills in a smooth sweep, using the old tracks but straightening them out when the land allowed: and it's still there, 800 years later, as the A40. The English American has carved out I-95 from Florida to Maine, chopping through any bit of land in his way, and he's made a road which is a long slice, dedicated to the goal of vanquishing place and time.

But that's a suicidal goal. Continuity is the only thing that can reconcile our tiny lives to their large surroundings.

Alan Garner was writing about continuity in *The Stone Book Quartet*. The four stories are rooted in one place, Garner's part of Cheshire, which is as crucial to the workings of his imagination as Herefordshire was to Masefield's and Wales is to my own. In that place, in these books, time links the generations through trades that endure: building and making, the carving of stone, the working of iron. A clay pipe lost in one generation is discovered centuries later in another; a loom worked by a father lies unused after his death until his son makes it into a sled for his own grandchild. And deep in the rock is a cave where a bull is painted on the stone wall, in the buried dark, and in each generation the eldest child is taken to look at it. There are many footprints underneath it in the dusty ground, from this accumulation of lone brave quests. " 'We've been going a while,' said Father."

That painted bull draws the past into the present, just as the Cheshire dialect of the books draws language through the years like a broom, sweeping away time. Language is organic, it grows and changes and acquires mutations and elisions and shifts of meaning, so that a new edition of the Oxford English Dictionary is saluted for keeping us "up with the times". But the old dialects of the English language, and the old languages of Britain, Welsh and the Gaelic, resist erosion more stubbornly. They have the same dogged permanence as the painted bull — or the stone votive axe which is a funnel for human emotion all through time, and always in one place, in Garner's book *Red Shift*.

But *Red Shift* is about more than continuity, and this is not the moment for it.

For writers with an inclination to tell stories outside the passage of time, it is easier to interweave the present and the past than to play similarly with the future. As Philippa Pearce was reminding us, using George Orwell's *1984*, the future has its own way of disappearing. In 1963, I published a novel called *Mandrake* which was set in the future (and was therefore labeled, inaccurately, as science fiction). The story was a kind of Armageddon warning about the dire results of damaging our environment. But the future it projected was only 17 years ahead. It was set in 1980. So today the warning looks pretty silly, because we're still busy damaging our environment, but 1980 has come and gone and Armageddon didn't come with it. The future became the past, when I wasn't looking.

This is a problem we all face every time we look in the mirror. In the case of this book I don't have to solve it, because fortunately *Mandrake* is out of print.

John Masefield plays with the present and the past in those lovely books *The Midnight Folk* and *The Box Of Delights*. But he never lets place take him outside time as Alan Garner does. He is a magician; he doesn't care for metaphysics. There's an enchanted passage in *The Midnight Folk* in which the portrait of Kay's Great-grandpa Harker comes alive; he holds out his hand and takes Kay into the painting. As its landscape opens around him, Key sees the artist in it, painting; and he sees the earlier version of the house in which he now lives and the portrait now hangs. He sees a few other familiar portraits too, painted in earlier years, hanging in unfamiliar places. The past has become the present. But the change is only temporary. Masefield never lets us forget the present; he puts in reminders.

A black cat, with white throat and paws, which had been ashes for forty years, rubbed up against Great Grandpa Harker's legs, and then, springing on the arm of his chair, watched the long dead sparrows in the plum tree which had been firewood a quarter of a century ago.

Masefield's books may seem to be time-haunted, but the true center of their haunting is magic. The old man Cole Hawlings appears to Kay in *The Box of Delights,* with his little dog and his magic box which will move you fast or slow, make you small or large, or take you back into the past or forward again to the present. "I do date from pagan times," he says, and he foretells the future, and disappears, sometimes, into the past. He is, however, a linear fellow. He turns out to be one Ramon Lully who a long time ago invented an elixir to keep him alive in the future, and wanted to do a swap with Master Arnold of Todi who'd invented a box to take him back into the past. Ramon Cole ends up with the box after Master Arnold goes too far back into the past and gets lost there. Through time to the present, he carries the haunting warning that The Wolves Are Running, and its echoes linger in the air even after the wolf villains get their comeuppance.

But then Masefield cops out — an extraordinary narrative aberration — and announces that the whole book has been nothing but Kay's dream. This is the act of a man so firmly rooted in Time, and the realities of life and death, that after bringing an illusion brilliantly to life, he chooses to kill it stone dead. "Only a dream!" I remember being outraged when I first read — or more accurately, heard — the end of *The Box of Delights*; the only unreal part of the book, I thought, was the last page, on which Kay woke up, and Masefield tried to pretend that the Box of Delights had never existed at all.

John Masefield put his toe outside Time, and then went back into it. When I was a young writer I stayed in the mainstream of linear time too: *Over Sea Under Stone* is a

relatively uncomplicated adventure story about the pursuit in the present of an object hidden in the past. Nobody leaves the present moment. My three unremarkable and singularly dated children, by Arthur Ransome out of E Nesbit, find a manuscript containing a map which records the hiding, centuries before, of a chalice, a grail, which is called "the last trust of the old world" hidden "until the day comes".

"The darkness draws towards Cornwall," says the writer of the old manuscript, "and the long ships creep to our shore," and he must hide the grail.

So therefore I trust it to this land, over sea and under stone, and I mark here the signs by which the proper man in the proper place may know where it lies, the signs that wax and wane but do not die. The secret of its charge I may not write, but carry unspoken to my grave. Yet the man who finds the grail and has other words from me will know, by both, the secret for himself. And for him is the charge, the promise and the proof, and in his day the Pendragon shall come again. And that day shall see a new Logres, with evil cast out; when the old world shall appear no more than a dream.

(*Appear* no more than a dream. Not *be* no more than a dream.)

The story which comes out of all this is quite simple, in terms of time. There's even an image in the book expressing its shape, without intending to:

Straight as an arrow the long white road of the moon's reflection stretched towards them across the surface of the sea, like a path from the past and a path to the future...

Everyone in this room has done a great deal of reading for this institute, and I dare day a lot of the piles of books had Eliot's *Four Quartets* at one end and Stephen Hawking's *A Brief History Of Time* at the other. My pile also had to include my own five-book sequence *The Dark Is Rising,* and I read these five, continuously and in order, for the first time since I published the last of them twelve years ago. This was a very odd sensation. For the first time I saw what I had been doing. I suppose I was in fact discovering what my unconscious had done. This is something Jill touched on, and Leon Garfield; something every author knows about. Very often, in all the arts, the thing we make is not necessarily the thing we thought we were making — and I don't just mean the occasional disaster, or the everlasting disappointing gap between the idea and its realization. The imagination takes over from the conscious mind. In *The Dark Is Rising* I thought I'd been telling five stories — about a quest, and about good and evil — all five linked into one, as the movements of a symphony blend into a whole. I hadn't noticed that in the last four of the five books I had at the same time been trying all the while, over and over, to write a definition of Time.

The organizers of our institute are brighter than I am, and I think they had noticed this.

The first book of *The Dark Is Rising* sequence, *Over Sea Under Stone,* deals with linear time — like *The Midnight Folk* and *The Box Of Delights,* though in a much less luminous and magical fashion. These books follow what Stephen Hawking calls the psychological arrow of time: "the direction in which we feel time passes, the direction in which we remember the past but not the future". The same is true of Alan Garner's early books, *The Weirdstone Of Brisingamen* and *The Moon Of Gomrath.* They tell magical stories, growing out of Alderley Edge in Cheshire, and they run between "the long ago of the world'" and the present. There's one moment of breakthrough on the Even of Gomrath, "one of the four nights of the year when Time and Forever mingle". But really these books are not concerned with time, but with what Garner calls, in a lovely phrase, "the world of magic, that lies as near and unknown to us as the back of a shadow".

Then some time in the 1960s, neither of us knowing the other's work, Alan Garner and I both moved in the same direction as writers and began playing with time. Or maybe time began playing with us. We are very different authors, but we started to express the same preoccupation. At least so it seems to me now, looking back. Alan wrote *The Owl Service* (which I'd like to talk about a bit later on), and I wrote the second of my sequence books, *The Dark Is Rising.* Until this point I hadn't actually known there was going to be a sequence. In that book, Will Stanton walks

out of his sleeping present-day house into the snow-covered countryside of a time centuries earlier — and finds that people are expecting him. This happens on page 195 of a 780-page sequence of novels, and it's the moment when the author too walks out of a door, of sorts, from real time to — something else.

There's a lot of walking through doors in *The Dark Is Rising.* Doors are almost as important to the book as snowfalls and rainstorms and claps of thunder. (I remember my editor Margaret McElderry looking at the manuscript and saying gently, "Susan, perhaps this book has a little too much weather.") I took out a few clouds and crashes, but the doors remained. I hadn't multiplied them on purpose; I think the image simply took over because my imagination was so intent on leaving the world it had inhabited before and going through into another kind of preoccupation, another world. Will Stanton finds himself on a hillside facing two immense carved wooden doors, standing closed, alone, surreal; and when he pushes them open, "the light and the day and the world changed, so that he forgot utterly what they had been." The doors, his master Merriman tells him later, are for the Old Ones of the universe "our great gateway into Time" — which is to say, out of Time as we, you and I, know it.

"We of the Circle are planted only loosely within Time," says Merriman. "The doors are a way through it, in any direction we may choose. For all times co-exist, and the future can sometimes affect the past, even though the past is a road that leads to the future ... But men cannot understand this."

No. Men can't — except perhaps Mr Eliot. I couldn't. But I went on trying to, as I wrote. "It is a mystery," says Hawkin, in *The Dark Is Rising,* to Will. "The Old Ones can travel in time as they choose. You are not bound by the laws of the universe as we know them." So, an Old One brings Hawkin forward in time from his own thirteenth century to the nineteenth century, and in the nineteenth he betrays the Light and is sent back to the thirteenth to become the Walker, doomed to carry one of the great Signs until Will, who had watched his betrayal in the nineteenth century, is born into the tenth century to take over this six hundred-year-old burden ...

If you can stand the whirling of the roundabout, this complexity takes you to a stillness that is outside any fixed concept of time — and also outside religion. In *The Dark Is Rising*, the force of the Dark attacks a group of the Old Ones while they are in a church, and is driven back by the Signs, each of which is a cross within a circle. The rector of the church says: well, of course. A cross. One of the Old Ones points out that these crosses were made long before Christianity, long before Christ. The rector says, "But not before God." Will says:

"There's not really any before or after, is there? Everything that matters is outside Time, and comes from there and can go there."

"You mean infinity," says the rector.

"Not altogether," said the Old One that was Will. "I mean the part of all of us, and of all the things we think and believe, that has nothing to do with yesterday, to today or tomorrow, because it belongs at a different kind of level. Yesterday is still there, on that level. Tomorrow is there too. You can visit either of them. And all Gods are there, and all the things they have every stood for. And," he added sadly, "the opposite too."

"Outside Time." These books speak of outside and inside as if there were two parts to Time. In *Greenwitch* Merriman says of a creature of the Dark, destroyed by his own ambition, "The Wild Magic has taken him to outer Time, from which he may never properly come back." In *The Dark Is Rising*, Will hears Merriman speak into his mind "from somewhere outside Time." In the final book *Silver On The Tree*, if Will does not reclaim the six Signs, "the High Magic which guards them will take them outside Time." There is always this double image: the moving river which is linear time, the time in which human beings are conscious of time, and the infinite plain which it crosses, from any point of which any point of the moving river can be reached. Or not reached, if some prohibition stands in the way.

This plain is the continuum of place/time. The image is imperfect, but then images usually are. Like most writers, I make a picture to communicate anything I can't properly explain; and the pictures are not only

never perfect, they're never original either. And in the long run, in this cosmology, there aren't even any pictures. Merriman says in *Silver On The Tree* that eventually all those of the Light will go out of Time: "as I shall go before long, and as one day long hence Will will go too." And at the climax of the confrontation between Dark and Light, the Lords of the Dark "fall backwards out of Time, and disappear."

No image, no picture. Just — out. Into mystery.

Partway into my notes on re-reading *Silver On The Tree*, I wrote, "It makes me giddy, the way this book flickers in and out of Time, interweaving past and present and future." That interweaving is the thing I am trying to define this evening. It isn't easy. There was one point when I thought I'd like to scrap the whole idea of giving a lecture, and just read the Four Quartets aloud instead. (Then I reflected that by the time Wednesday evening arrived, someone else would be sure to have done that already.) Leaving aside definition: my novels interweave time in story. I can't do that in the abstract, and nor, I think, can Alan Garner; we have to do it through place.

My places are a piece of the Thames Valley and the Chiltern Hills, a piece of Southern Cornwall, and more than either a piece of mid-Wales, around Cader Idris, on the southern edge of Snowdonia. (I was there last week, and part of me is always there.) In that magnificent book *The Owl Service*, Alan Garner switches from his native Cheshire to a different valley in Wales which becomes a whirlpool of time: a container for the power of the story from the Mabinogion of Lleu, Blodeuwedd and Gronw Pebyr, which happened once in myth and here, in this valley and this book, is always happening.

You could say, I suppose, that *The Owl Service* is the story, on a most extraordinary scale, of the laying of a ghost. But what is a ghost but an echo of time, in place? Someone in the book suggests to Gwyn that the myth haunts the valley.

"Not haunted," said Gwyn after a while. "More like — still happening."

And later on, Roger says in exasperation, "You'd

think it was the only thing that's ever happened in this valley!"

"That is right," says Huw.

"I don't know where I am," says Alison. "Yesterday, today, tomorrow — they don't mean anything. I feel they're here at the same time, waiting."

Yesterday, today and tomorrow, waiting. Their focus is Huw Halfbacon, unchanging as the stone by the river; magician and laborer, ancient and enduring, waiting like a salmon in this pool of time. I use the image of a pool for Alan's book, and I find I used it once in *Silver On The Tree*, too. "We will strive at our separate tasks across the centuries," says Merriman to Will, "through the waves of time, touching and parting, parting and touching in the pool that whirls forever."

And "the pool" always means a particular part of what Merriman calls "this long-worked land so many centuries on the anvil." In *The Owl Service* it's as if the valley is a magnet for all parts of time. "My Mam hates the place," says Gwyn, "but she can't get rid of it, see?'

We all have places we can't get rid of, loved or hated; places which bring the past into the present. When I was little, walking to school through Buckinghamshire countryside which is the setting for *The Dark Is Rising*, we used to pass the top of a dark, wooded little track which was known locally as Tramps' Alley. The name was accurate; once in a while it was refuge for shambling old wanderers with five tattered overcoats, newspaper in their shoes and trousers held up with string. We were strictly warned to keep clear of them.

I sent Will down Tramps' Alley in *The Dark Is Rising*, and he did indeed encounter a tramp — the Walker — and after that a number of traumatic events which almost cost him one of the great Signs. His master Merriman told him severely that he had been saved from disaster only by the fact that this little lane happened to be one of the ancient routes of the Light: an Old Way. And my pen stopped still, writing that, because I suddenly remembered the proper name of Tramps' Alley. "Don't call it that," our parents used to say fastidiously, "You know its real name is Oldway Lane."

Thirty years later, long after my family had moved to Wales and after I'd gone to live in America, I was driving once from London to Wales when I found I'd missed the turning from the M4 that would take me to the A40, my road home. I turned north at random, and pulled into a sideroad to check where I was on the map. And I found I was right on top of the once green countryside of *The Dark Is Rising*, covered largely now by stretches of concrete and macadam, and when I looked up at the street sign of the little road where I'd stopped, lined with tidy houses, it said, "Oldway Lane."

Place and time. Time and place. For the aborigines of Australia, the Ancestors dreamed place into existence, and to learn about place is to remember that dreaming, calling back time. The boundaries of things blur. Place seems so definite when you look round this room; time so precise when you look at your watch; but look more closely and those boundaries blur too. If you look as closely as a theoretical physicist, you can end up with Stephen Hawking's proposal (in *A Brief History Of Time*) of a universe having no boundary or edge, no beginning or end: infinite space, infinite time. It's not too different from the endless plain of time in *The Dark Is Rising* books, the haunted recurrence of *The Owl Service*, the passion reverberating through the centuries in *Red Shift*.

Alan Garner's *Red Shift* is a brilliant, dense book and I would not presume to try to unravel its evocation of Time. I am a writer, not a critic or teacher, and I have enough trouble unraveling my own. But it seems to me that this novel is more profoundly concerned with the continuum of place and time than any other which will be mentioned here this week. It doesn't talk about time; everything is in the patterning of the story. We flicker in and out of Roman time, Civil War time, present time; the future stretches before the first of these; the past lies behind the third; the second has both past and future, it echoes to and fro. Within Garner's piece of Cheshire, all three coexist, and fierce emotion runs through the continuum, erupting in violent death or in the violence of loving.

The thunderbolt, the votive axe through

which Macey is possessed, Macey who was seven when the Romans came, will be found by Civil War Thomas and built by Thomas and Madge into the chimney of the house in whose ruin present-day Tom and Jan will find it. Sounds and events echo backwards. Orion hangs over them all, turning. And the galaxies retreat through the red end of the spectrum: "the further they go, the faster they leave. The sky's emptying."

So is the ferocity of emotion. Pip loves Brian, says the first line of the graffiti Tom and Jan find on a wall. Then underneath it another line: "not really now not any more."

"Everywhere's been good or bad for somebody at some time," says Jan, "so there's no point in moping about Pip and bloody Brian, whoever they were."

Not really now not any more.

Alan Garner said once, at one of these institutes, "We have to tell stories, to unriddle the world."

None of us is going to unriddle time, but we shall go on trying. (And only be undefeated because we *have* gone on trying...) None of us, not even Stephen Hawking, is going to resolve definitively the question of the real relationship between time and space, the real origin and fate of the universe.

" 'Real' is a hard word," says my minstrel, Gwion, in *Silver On The Tree*. "Almost as hard as 'true' or 'now' ".

He says something else too that is not unrelated to the theme of *Red Shift*, though without its passionate bitterness. In fact, with the opposite.

"For ever and ever, we say when we are young, and in our prayers. Twice, we say it. For ever and ever ... so that a thing may be for ever, a life or a love or a quest, and yet begin again, and be for ever just as before. And any ending that may seem to come is not truly an ending, but an illusion. For time does not die, Time has neither beginning nor end, and so nothing can end or die that has once had a place in Time."

"And the end and the beginning were always there," said Mr Eliot, "before the beginning and after the end, and all is always now."

Now and in England. In *The Dark Is Rising*, in England, the moment of the opening of the Old Ones' doors through Time is marked always for Will Stanton by the sound of a delicate, elusive music: "a sweet beckoning sound that was the space betwen waking and dreaming, yesterday and tomorrow, memory and imagining." Music was the only image I could find for the demonstration of a mystery. It still is. Music is after all made of time, and carries it down the centuries in a chain of renewal – like the seasons, and the turning year, and all other patterns of life, death, new life. Music is an echo, like all life, spreading out over the continuum like the widening ripples in a pool. When Jack draws you into music at the end of this institute, and you sing, think of the echo, that carries our mystery from the blue end of the spectrum to the red, all through the rainbow of time, ut beyond the univere.

Diane Paolitto reminded us that in the early years, fo all children, "calendar time still lies somewhere in the past, enshrouded in mystery."

To be reconciled to the nature of time, perhaps we need to rediscover that early, imprecise perception. When we are children, we have a tranquil acceptance of mystery which is driven out of us later on, by curiosity and education and experience. But it is possible to find one's way back. With affection and respect, I disagree totally with Penelope Lively's conviction about the "absolute impossibility of recovering a child's vision." There are ways, imperfect, partial, fleeting, of looking again at a mystery through the eyes we used to have. Children are not different animals. They are us, wearing a heavy jacket of time.

There's one other image in *The Dark Is Rising* that I would toss into the pool. I put it into the novel, as I did so many others, without really knowing then what I was about. The Book of Gramarye, (the old word for magic and mystery) the book which has in it all the wisdom of the world and of the Old Ones, lies waiting for Will Stanton. Where? Of all places: inside a clock. Its protection is the swing of the pendulum, the passing of time. And when Will has learned its contents, when Gramarye has been released into the world, that pendulum which is Time destroys the book, in "a soundless explosion, a blinding flash of dark light, a great roar of energy that could not be seen or heard."

One day, that's what Time will do to the earth. But the galaxy will rush on, across the plain, across the pool.

Traveling, Gramarye, the mystery, will keep it going.

ELEANOR CAMERON

The pleasures and problems of time fantasy

I'VE OFTEN THOUGHT how like an elegantly played game of chess a fine time fantasy can be. In chess, each pair of pieces and the pawns must always make their own kinds of move and no other. But out of brilliant combinations of these moves come completely original games, full of astonishments brought about by a lively mingling of incisive thinking and imaginative foresight. It was, in a minor way, this characteristic of time fantasy that led to my fascination with it. But going back to what I once wrote at the beginning of a study of time fantasy, which took the genre almost to the end of the sixties, I remind myself that it wasn't simply this kind of intellectual challenge that drew me to it. Not at all! It was supremely the idea of time itself, embodying a wonder and a mystery that so many have felt.

As I recorded in *The Green and Burning Tree*, (1969):

"I will wager," I said to myself some years ago, just as if it were fresh to the mind of man, "that Time is not a thread at all, but a globe, and the fact that we experience it as thread only must have something to do with our 'doors of perception.'"

So that you will know where I'm headed, I must enumerate the three different kinds of time fantasy as determined by what they have the ability to involve in a way no other genre of fiction can do. First, there is the kind that incorporates *legend* into the working out of the story in an intrinsic as opposed to an incidental way or as background, bringing the novel's contemporary characters into close touch with the legendary ones, so that legend is not simply a subject the child has studied but is all woven into the vivid life of the story. One thinks of William Mayne's *Earthfasts*,

having to do with the legend of Arthur; of Alan Garner's *The Owl Service*, having to do with the Welsh legend of Blodeuwedd, a tale out of that great collection of Welsh legends, the *Mabinogion*; and of Susan Cooper's *The Dark is Rising* series, also rooted in the *Mabinogion*; of Ursula Le Guin's *The Beginning Place*, rising out of her extremely dim view of our plastic, technological civilization; of Joy Chant's *Red Moon and Black Mountain*; and of William Mayne's so very strange *A Game of Dark* — these last four moving from present reality to currently created legendary lands and back again. All but *Earthfasts* are, of course, high fantasy as well as time fantasy, high fantasy being those tales in which it is the hero's purpose to save his people.

Second, there is a kind of time fantasy that explores the past, bringing *history* into the child reader's mind both directly and by way of osmosis. It is a way that certain children of this computer age are willing to accept because another dimension enters in, an overtone, a thrilling sense of the unspoken, the evoked, not in the nature of realistic novels. I should think that the concepts and techniques of the two genres of novels, realism and time fantasy involving history, are most clearly contrasted and revealed in comparing Joan Aiken's excellent *Midnight is a Place* with Jill Paton Walsh's *A Chance Child*, both having to do with the beginnings of the Industrial Revolution in England. How dull that sounds! But Aiken, in her own unique Dickensian fashion, creates an absorbing drama in a straightforward, realistic way, while Paton Walsh takes every advantage of the eeriness her conception offers, so that the reader is haunted after the last page is turned by this tale of a present-day child entering into a close relationship with children of the past and becoming one with them in their time for the rest of his life.

Third, there is a kind of time fantasy that sits *half way between pure fantasy at one end of the spectrum and science fiction at the other.* Time fantasy puts past and present together in a way that science fiction is not, primarily, interested in doing. It is far more drawn to life on other planets or in a future on earth after nuclear devastation, or in a relatively near future as in John Rowe Townsend's *The Visitors.* The kind of time fantasy I refer to in this third category incorporates scientific terms and ideas and sometimes psychological ones as in Alan Garner's *Elidor* and William Mayne's *Earthfasts,* both writers making central use as well of a knowledge of magnetic fields. Yet these novels are indubitably time *fantasy.* And it is intriguing to me to observe that, after years of traditional time fantasy, these two writers should have chanced to come forth in the very same year with novels incorporating the same facets of the world of science. In both, the introduction of scientific aspects is handled so subtly and gradually that one is not at first aware of how a knowledge of scientific phenomena is influencing the story. In my own case, with *Beyond Silence,* I was certain in the beginning that what I was writing was time fantasy, though gradually it became clear to me that it could be interpreted as a novel of psychological trauma. And after publication, when friends and reviewers and one critic had a chance to comment, its underlying qualities of both psychological trauma *and* science fiction were pointed out, though many disagreed and held out for one or the other. These qualities or characteristics simply did not come into question in the case of *The Court of the Stone Children.*

3— Now because there would seem to be, apparently, a number of opinions as to just how time fantasy is to be thought about, I must speak of this for a moment. I have always looked upon it simply as the kind of fantasy that takes one or more characters into an age other than our own or into several

others as in E. Nesbit's *The Story of the Amulet.*

But I was baffled to find *The Court of the Stone Children,* a story which brings a child of the French Revolution into the present, discussed under the heading "The New Fantasy" in a subsection entitled "Enchanted Realism" in Sheila Egoff's *Thursday's Child.* And there is no mention of time fantasy as a subject in Egoff's index, nor indeed anywhere else, so that I can only suppose she doesn't recognize the genre. Furthermore, at a conference having fantasy as its subject, *Court* was discussed at the meeting on "Inner Space," and I could make no sense of why certain fantasies had been placed in the section in which I found them. So that it was brought strongly home to me not only how we as individuals feel about and react to certain fantasies, but how we think about them and define them to ourselves. I haven't an idea of what was meant by Inner Space in this particular instance, nor why my time fantasy, along with others unlike it basically, belonged in that category. Or possibly I should have remembered Walter de la Mare's words,

"Carroll's Wonderland is a (queer little) universe of the mind resembling Einstein's in that it is a finite infinity endlessly explorable though never to be explored."

4

In any memorable novel, one has the sense that interpenetrating all is place: that which is the expression of a deep, wide, firm awareness emanating from the tale that makes us know — whether this be an actual place or an imagined one — that it is intimately and vividly real to the writer's five senses and not simply cooked up or sketched in here and there to provide some sort of background for magical happenings. It is that passionate awareness illustrated by Lucy Boston's sensitivity to Green Knowe and Alison Uttley's to her beloved Thackers in *A Traveller in Time.*

As for time fantasy with legend as matrix, having both traditional and consciously created legendary lands as place, I can see very clearly that what were once rich and delectable challenges to the author's giftedness as to the creation of names, practices, and situations evoked out of differences in cultures, such challenges could become problems because of past usages incorporated again and again in published fantasies. For instance, it has always struck me what a hold the tiny territory of Wales, enclosing relatively few square miles, has on the writer of legend-based time fantasy, so that it has become almost *the* place for that genre of fantasy which time and again turns out to be high fantasy, with the young hero of it the savior of *a* people, if not his own.

We all know it is due partly to the irresistible image of Arthur and partly to the nature of the Celts, as so handsomely revealed in Joy Chant's *The High Kings: Arthur's Celtic Ancestors* and Peter Dickinson's *Merlin Dreams*, both full of absolutely stunning illustrations accompanying Chant's searching text and Dickinson's splendid stories, which are Merlin's dreams. Then there is the extraordinary nature of the Celts. As Joy Chant sees them, though the Celts were illiterate, they "were members of the most verbally alive culture there has ever been and had skills of ear and mind lost to literate people." Their bards, poet-priests, were, as she says, "keepers of the soul of the people," and that soul has had, since early times, a continuing, over-the-shoulder awareness of the dual nature of reality, of unity in disunity, of the simultaneity of life and death, and of time as an eternal moment rather than as something with a separate past and future.

For me, the sense of Celtic place is a most memorable quality in all of these legend-based time fantasies: in Cooper's *The Dark is Rising* series, Garner's *The Owl Service* and Bond's *A String in the Harp*, revealing their author's devoted attention to details of the Welsh countryside, the character of the people, and the way the Welsh speak and think and feel, as though these writers have a genuine love of the land and its unique qualities. Indeed, it would seem that this specificity of detail can only be born of a deep love of (or perhaps I should say, intense reaction to) the place one is writing about, and the Welsh must have felt this in Cooper's case, as well as an admiration for the legendlike sweep of her sequence, in giving her an award for it.

About naming, a subject that follows close

on the heels of place: in Bond's and Cooper's and Garner's novels we are in the world of the Welsh past, the world of the bard Taliesin in Bond's case, and the *Mabinogion* in Cooper's and Garner's novels (at those points where its people enter the present), and there need be no created names.

But as for created worlds, only in time fantasy would Hugh and Irene of contemporary America walk in from the freeway to mountains in Le Guin's *The Beginning Place* and find themselves in a land called Tembreabrezi, a place which for Irene becomes her "ain country" and whose ground she kisses for very love of it. Here they are in the midst of men and women named Aduvan and Verti and Lord Horn, Trijiat and Dou Sark, Palizot and Sofir. Oliver and Penelope and Christopher in Joy Chant's *Red Moon and Black Mountain*, out for a bicycle ride in contemporary England, find themselves in the place of the Hurnoi tribesmen, in Kentor lands, on the Northern Plains, in the realm of the Kendrinh and the land of the Vendarei. Oliver himself, he finds, has become O'li-vanh, and I am fascinated by Chant's spelling of various Hunoi names, making wide use of apostrophes and h's so that I know that could I hear them, I would hear them differently than I would, quite possibly, be able to speak them, as if I had been attempting amateurishly to speak a foreign tongue.

This was brought sharply home to me when I heard the tape of Le Guin's songs for her astonishing novel *Always Coming Home*. These are songs which she had composed both in our tongue and in the language of the Kesh, a people who "might be going to have lived a long, long time from now in Northern California." And when Todd Barton sings them, I am realizing how utterly clumsy and unbeautiful has been my own pronunciation, though I would never have dreamed, before I heard him say the words, just how they *could* be said! Surely *Always Coming Home*, taking place in mid-California a thousand or so years hence, is one of the supreme examples (or may I say *the* supreme example?) of a wholly created world down to the last acute accent, which is used widely over certain letters in

Kesh words. Le Guin has written in "A First Note" that

the difficulty of translation from a language that doesn't yet exist is considerable, but there's no need to exaggerate it...The fact that it hasn't yet been written, the mere absence of a text to translate, doesn't make all that much difference. What was and what may be lie, like children whose faces we cannot see, in the arms of silence. All we ever have is here, now.

And concerning this whole subject of creation, of naming, Le Guin has other interesting things to say because she has done so much of it.

About the attitude that colored her work, an attitude handed on to her by her anthropologist father, she writes that certain elements must be "a curiosity about people different from one's own kind; interest in artifacts; interest in languages; delight in the idiosyncracies of various cultures; a sense that time is long yet that human history is very short — and therefore a kinship across seas and countries; a love of strangeness, a love of exactness." Exactness, yes! Which we feel so strongly in the Earthsea books as well as in *Always Coming Home* as to the nature and naming of animals and plants and foods and customs and dress and languages and the looks of different peoples and the names of islands and ports. Which reminds us of Henry James's conviction that the supreme virtue of a novel worth considering is its truth of detail, its air of reality, its "solidity of specification." Think of all those musical, unheard of, yet satisfying names that slip with such naturalness from the tongue! Say aloud to yourself "Tembreabrezi." And the sense of both strangeness and naturalness is, I think, one of the tests of good fantasy; this evoked sense of absolute rightness.

Which brings me to my next mingling of pleasures and problems. This is the repetition, the echoing of certain names, details, techniques, personalities, resolutions, and constructions that we find in time fantasies, echoings and repetitions seeming increasingly to be handed down within the genre, which truly tests the freshness of each new fantasy. For instance, in Meredith Ann Pierce's *A Gathering of Gargoyles* (not time fantasy but

simply high fantasy, and the problem holds for both), we see how Pierce's Orm and Pendar echo from Le Guin's Orm Embar and Pendor, and the precognitive riddling rhyme, which structures Pierce's book, is of the kind found first in Cooper's sequence and then in Jane Louise Curry's *The Watchers*, and in her *The Wolves of Aam* and *The Shadow Dancers*. Because the Eternal Moment is always the powerfully felt presence in any time fantasy, it follows that there will almost invariably be a fate laid down for the young protagonist in those mingled with high fantasy. We are reminded of that sequence in Ingmar Bergman's film "Wild Strawberries" in which the elderly protagonist dreams of his own funeral carriage moving along a warped and deserted street where a giant watch hangs overhead, its hands pointing to some doomed moment. For it is exactly this premonitory sense of dream, in which events seem insanely warped yet exude a sense of dreadful logic, that is best not only in *Elidor* but in so many time fantasies. It is there, in that instant when the children are, through apparently their own decisions, led to that fateful crossroads of incidents which ejects them from our plane of existence into that other which has awaited them since the days of the starved fool. It is there when Roland discovers the empty fingers of Helen's recently lost mitten clutched in layers of smooth-growing turf and, underneath, the cuff frozen in ancient quartz, a situation possible only in time fantasy. It is there when the children are shown an age-old parchment on which the fool had foretold their coming and painted their small pictures in figures of medieval beauty. Here, in these last two details, are the first hints of Garner's captivation by the idea of the timeless moment, which comes to fuller fruition in *The Owl Service*.

Will, of course, in *The Dark is Rising* sequence, is seen by the Old Ones as a person to be taken into that company of rare few which includes Will's uncle Merriman Lyon and King Arthur. Cooper writes in *The Grey King* that "movement through Time...held no difficulty for an Old One," and in *Silver on the Tree*, in a conversation between Uncle Merry and Arthur, Merriman foresees that Arthur will be victorious at Mount Badon. For Lyon is one who knows from his own experience that "All times coexist and the future can sometimes affect the past, even though the past is a road that leads to the future."

In all three of the following time fantasies which are also high fantasy, the young protagonists have also been awaited; Donald in the legendary world of William Mayne's *A Game of Dark*, Hugh in Le Guin's *The Beginning Place*, and Oliver in Chant's *Red Moon and Black Mountain*. There are no parchments with the young protagonists' likenesses painted on them in medieval beauty. But it is known, as a legend or racial awareness is known, that these young people will come at some unspecified time and slay the marauding dragons in the first two novels, and lead the Hurnoi tribesmen to victory over the evil power Fendarl in *Red Moon*.

Concerning structure, symbolism and evocations, the likenesses in these respects between William Mayne's *A Game of Dark* and Ursula Le Guin's *The Beginning Place* are so astonishing that I want to parallel them briefly. Consider these facts: Mayne gives us a boy who turns from a life that has become insufferably oppressive and made almost unbearable by the continual reproaches of a mother who has no least understanding of her son's unhappiness nor of the sense of worthlessness he is haunted by.

But now Donald begins finding himself, time and again, without warning, in a no-color legendary land where it turns out that he must kill a dragon, called the Worm. The people of this other place take it for granted that there is only one way to kill the Worm, but when Donald finally succeeds in this completely alien task, he succeeds because he *is* totally alien, alien to that mindless, unquestioning tradition among these medieval people who "know" *because* it is tradition, that there is only one, decent, honorable, acceptable way to kill a dragon. And Donald, in his turn, because their way is hopeless, knows that there is no other possibility but to kill it in his own outrageous fashion, whether he himself is killed or not, disgraced or not, and thrown out

of the village for succeeding in doing what has to be done for the villagers' sake.

Now, traditionally, a dragon has been called a Worm, and here, in Mayne's novel, the identity of the creature carries a phallic connotation, connected with his father's wretched illness, which fills Donald with revulsion and despair just as the villagers are filled with revulsion and despair by the slime and stench and mercilessness of the Worm.

Let us then take the case of Le Guin's Hugh, a young man who, precisely like Mayne's Donald, turns from a life that has become insufferably oppressive and made almost unbearable by the continual reproaches of a mother who has no least understanding of her son's unhappiness, nor of the sense of worthlessness he is haunted by. "'I haven't got anything,' says Hugh, 'and I'm not anything.'" He is a checker in a supermarket and has no one to love, or to be loved by. Like Mayne's Donald, Hugh, when he hikes in from the freeway to the Beginning Place and climbs upward, finds himself in a colorless legendary land, Timbreabrezi, where it is known that he must kill a dragon. He, too, like Donald, it turns out, must kill it in an unorthodox fashion, for he, of course, has never killed a dragon in his life. Both Donald and Hugh find maturation and release in the killing of their dragons, who differ in this respect:

Donald's dragon, the Worm, a phallic and therefore masculine image, can be identified with his inability to love his father, while Hugh's dragon can be either a he or a she according to who is perceiving it, as "he" by Hugh and as "she" by Irene, the young woman who leads him to it. So that we realize that these two are seeing it as some unconscious restriction within themselves that must be recognized and resolved. Hugh and Irene, who have met at the Beginning Place, are both oppressed by guilt, the inability to love, just as Mayne's Donald was, by a terrible sense of placelessness in a technological world, of belonging nowhere and of having no one to love as they desire to love. And it is only when Hugh discovers a sense of himself, respect for himself, that both Hugh and Irene find release in discovering love for each other on the long journey home to what we call reality. Very clearly, these "other places" in the novels are refuges in their protagonists' unconscious from stress and guilt and an acute inability to deal with an unbearable situation. The weather is always colorless in the world of the unconscious. We are not aware of weather changes. In the legendary land, it is always twilight, the twilight of the unconscious.

It is one of the closest parallels of both structure and symbolism I have come across in the world of time fantasy, indeed in children's literature. But does it matter in the least? I shall speak of this a bit later.

I come now to a conception inevitably repeated out of sheer necessity in time fantasy, the protagonist's transition from present to past, and sometimes, but rarely, into the future. In *The Green and Burning Tree* I called objects, which have either subtle or obvious parts to play in the passage between ages, time or theme objects: visible, physical concentrates of time magic working in suggestive and sometimes symbolic ways. We think of the little antique bobbin boy in Alison Uttley's *A Traveller in Time*, the grandfather clock in the hall in Philippa Pearce's *Tom's Midnight Garden*, upon whose face Tom sees written the words "Time No Longer." There is the time candle in *Earthfasts* with its cold, spinning flame which the wind does not affect — a candle that casts no light, whose length is not consumed when it lies in the cold, drenching grass, that is perfectly self-contained and enduring and that nothing can change. There is Taliesin's harp key in Nancy Bond's *A String in the Harp*, with which Peter feels the most sensitive, intimate, and responsive relationship, and which enables him to behold what no one else can. We remember the apparently harmless and meaningless shield — a tamburan of New Guinea — with its strange designs and colors that become more distinct and ominous and brilliant as tension mounts in Penelope Lively's *The House in Norham Gardens*. There is the mysterious diamond in the window, to the children strangely compelling and powerful, in Jane Langton's fantasy of that name, and there is Tom

Inskip's box of drawings from Edwardian times in K M Peyton's *A Pattern of Roses*, a box which Tim in the present treasures and thinks about, recognizing the scenes that Tom has drawn. And then there are those objects which are actual carriers, such as the barge that takes poor Creep into the past in Jill Paton Walsh's *A Chance Child*, the two stone chairs in Lucy Boston's *The Stones of Green Knowe*, and the boarding school bed in Penelope Farmer's *Charlotte Sometimes*.

Now these last three examples of theme objects which are concrete rather than symbolic or evoking, bring me to an interesting point regarding them. The first time fantasies I ever read — E. Nesbit's *The Story of the Amulet*, Lucy Boston's *The Children of Green Knowe* and *Treasure* (or *Chimneys* in England) *of Green Knowe*, Pearce's *Tom's Midnight Garden*, and Uttley's *A Traveller in Time* — make no use of actual, physical carriers. And so possibly I was imprinted with a certain uncomplex, smoothly instantaneous passage. Neither Le Guin in *The Beginning Place* nor Mayne in *A Game of Dark* felt any need for physical means of passage, as we have seen.

What interests me, therefore, is that in contrast to Boston's stone chairs and Farmer's boarding school bed, I felt no unease or dissatisfaction whatever with Jill Paton Walsh's barge into which Creep climbs and is floated, almost as if the barge has a will of its own, down the canal and under the bridge into a past age. In contrast, the trouble for me is that there seems no particular structural, symbolic, or evoking need for either the stone chairs in Boston's novel, one of which carries Roger far too neatly to whatever age he wishes, or the boarding school bed in Farmer's novel. But Walsh's barge turns out to be an integral part of the story.

And this discussion of means of passage brings me to the subject of tricks in time fantasy brought to mind because of one writer's reaction to *A Chance Child*. When she handed the book back to me after I had lent it with interest to know what she thought, she said only, "Up to the old tricks, I see. It would have been far more effective if Walsh had just told the story straight as a historical novel. I can't imagine why all the fancy business of Creep's going back in time to the days of child labor. Why not just have put him there in the first place?"

Well, I felt it would have been perfectly useless to try to explain my strong response to the novel just as it is to one with such a flat-footed, matter-of-fact attitude. And I realize that there are those who enjoy and understand memorable time fantasy, who see why the materials of certain ideas work better as time fantasy than they would as a straight novel, and that there are those who prefer a certain kind of factual logic and common sense to work all the way through in realistic fashion.

But to my way of thinking, in this particular case, for Walsh to have told the story straight, with Creep in the first chapter a child of the Industrial Revolution in England, would have wiped out completely the special, cutting edge that her handling has created. It is an edge provided by Creep's particular situation in the present linked with the past, by the intensity of Christopher's search for his small, brutally treated bastard brother, and by the shock of his finding Creep's moss-covered name carved in the stone of a canal bridge and crossed by an iron bar, deeply notched and grooved. How long has that bar been there, Christopher asks of a workman. "Oh, maybe a hundred and fifty years..." It is like that eery moment, already discussed, in Alan Garner's *Elidor* when Roland discovers his sister Helen's recently lost mitten.

And there is that other moment that only time fantasy woven in with history can offer — that moment, after Creep's inability to laugh, inability to eat, and his invisibility to all but children in the Other Time, when an enraged mother in the cotton mill beats one of the terrible masters with a billy roller, and everyone, *including Creep*, begins laughing, sending up huzzahs, and breaking out into great gales of mirth. Then

Blackie ran to Creep, and put her arm around his shoulder. Creep suddenly wailed aloud, with his two hands pressed to his belly. "Oh, Blackie, I'm so hungry! I'm clemmed to death!"

So Creep becomes vulnerable again because

he has returned to humanity and will work out his human life in the past and be fulfilled in a way he might never have been in the present, nor could have been in his invulnerable ghostliness.

Finally, there is the moment when Christopher later finds a verse hidden behind bushes, cut below Creep's name:

Time as it is cannot stay,
Nor as it was cannot be.
Dissolving and passing away
Are the world, the ages, and me.

"'What does it mean?' asked Pauline...'What he said he meant by it,'" says Christopher, who has been searching through the old records, "'was that those are his words to us, and so Farewell.'" And all of this hauntingly poetic overtone would have been lost entirely if *A Chance Child* had not been time fantasy. And it is the same with K M Peyton's *A Pattern of Roses* and Penelope Lively's *The House in Norham Gardens* and Philippa Pearce's *Tom's Midnight Garden*, all of which could be told straight. Yet how could one tear these conceptions apart and redo them with the same quality of overtone? A different overtone, of course, but not *that* one.

Now you will remember that the writer who disliked *A Chance Child* used the word *tricks*. And it could be that some — perhaps many — people dislike time fantasy because they believe it has to do with tricks. For in a review of Betty Levin's *The Keeping Room* John Cech says, "The author could have made this novel into a time fantasy or a literal ghost story, but her plot is more convincing because she has chosen to play it straight without tricks. The uncanny penetration of historical events into our own present is believable and all the more mysterious because it is realistically presented." I agree wholly with his words "uncanny penetration" and "believable." But I wonder if Cech thought that Walsh, for instance, would have judged *A Chance Child* to present an unrealistic picture of the beginnings of the Industrial Revolution in England *because* it is time fantasy and is unconvincing generally because of the eerie finding of Creep's name carved in stone over a century ago? But there are different kinds of reality! One of the paradoxes lying within the nature of fantasy is the fact that though it contains assumptions no sane person would be willing to admit and though it assaults and breaks the scientific laws of our world, all fantasy that lives and continues to live possesses a strange, private, yet quite powerful and convincing reality of its own.

In any case, there would seem to be a certain misapprehension here, at least according to my own experience. One does not begin to be aware of a certain novelistic conception and then coolly decide which genre it should be written as — historical fiction, ghost story, or time fantasy. For me it comes inarguably as *itself* and one would seem incapable of recognizing otherwise unless one were a paster-upper, a mechanical fitter-together of parts into a certain intellectually decided shape. I could not have *chosen* that either *Court* or *Silence* be straight historical novels, ghost tales, or anything but time fantasy — they had been that from the beginning. However, could Cech be right — in a way? Betty Levin tells me that *The Keeping Room* started out as a time fantasy but turned into a contemporary novel reaching back into the past. And it was only as it unfolded under her hands that she could no longer see it as time fantasy. Perhaps, then, you could say that she had *chosen*? But it seems to me that the material itself, by some mysterious process having to do with the writer's sensitivity, revealed its true nature, its own kind of reality. Now if you call that choosing, then John Cech is right. But one could say that it is not so much a matter of choice as of enlightenment, given by the material itself and how it is most satisfyingly to reveal itself. It seems to me that one feels one's way. Says the poet Eric Barker,

> I go by touching where I have to go,
> Obedient to my own illumined hand.
> I part the darkness and I follow slow.

 To go back to what I asked concerning the close parallels of structure and symbolism between *A Game of Dark* and *The Beginning Place*, "But does it matter in the least?" which could be asked of basic parallels in many works of fiction in the whole world of literature: if you can say of a book that, aesthetically speaking, it is a living thing because of the various influences it exerts, then the air it breathes and that sustains it is its creator's private vision. The essence of private vision is the deepest mystery of all. Technically, it has to do with theme; certainly it makes itself felt through conviction and point of view. It is of course secreted in none of these elements alone but in all of them combined in such a way as to defeat a wholly satisfactory summing up. It is an expression, emerging either consciously or unconsciously, out of the writer's deepest attitudes and convictions about life. Jill Paton Walsh is aware of its presence and the necessity for a continued striving to fulfill it, for she has said in connection with her own work, "What the author writes will often fall far short of his vision of the book, but that must not be through failure of will power and devotion."

To my mind, it is the power of private vision that makes the similarity between the basic construct of one time fantasy and another, in certain aspects, of no importance whatever. We have noticed that Donald in *A Game of Dark*, Hugh in *The Beginning Place*, and Oliver in *Red Moon and Black Mountain* all feel sickeningly incapable of carrying out the task laid upon them, of fulfilling the role of hero. And Will in *The Dark is Rising* sequence cannot help thinking of himself again and again, despite Uncle Merry's knowledge of him, as a perfectly ordinary English school boy. If we are to consider dream laced into the structure of the novel, no two fantasies could be more unlike than Jane Langton's *The Diamond in the Window* and Penelope Lively's *The House in Norham Gardens*, in both of which dreams play such essential parts that neither could exist without them. Tim in *A Pattern of Roses*, Peter in *A String in the Harp*, and Clare in *Norham Gardens*, are all aware of the past, the pattern of it they are concerned with, but take no part in the resolution of events in the past except that Peter finally throws Taliesen's harp key into the lake to save it from being taken into public hands. At times a letter, as in *Beyond*

Silence, a journal as in *The Court of the Stone Children*, public records of the past as in *A Chance Child*, or an old person telling of what happened in childhood as in *Tom's Midnight Garden* are essential to our and the protagonist's understanding of what lies behind the convolution of events. Surely, we think, all the possible variations have been played out and there can be only a reshaping of the forms we know so well.

But there is no end to originality, to the power of a unique point of view in giving us something new and treasurable. I was reminded of an astonishingly different understanding, born into the child through tribal tradition — this to do with time — by some words in Barry Lopez's remarkable *Arctic Dreams: Imagination and Desire in a Northern Landscape*. He says that Hopi is a language that

has only limited tenses...makes no reference to time as an entity distinct from space...It is a language that projects a world of movement and changing relationships, a 'continuous fabric' of time and space... All else being equal, a Hopi child would have little difficulty comprehending the theory of relativity in his own language, while an American child could more easily master history. A Hopi could be confounded by the idea that time flowed from the past into the present.

Lopez then quotes Benjamin Lee Whorf who cautioned that all observers "are not led by the same physical evidence to the same picture of the universe."

It is the men and women who are most sensitively attuned to the mysterious phenomena of life and time, of possibly quite different pictures, and who have the ability to express richly and clearly all they discern, who will give us the impressive time fantasies of the future.

There are so many paths to follow, unexpected crossings, extraordinary possibilities, not having to do primarily with tricks but with a subtle elegance of perception. And because of the peculiar qualities of time fantasy, who knows what strange wonders still lie waiting in the dark to surprise and delight us, to set our minds and imaginations moving towards entirely fresh ways of seeing?

BETTY LEVIN: SEMINAR

Past and future - Time's eye

And do not call it fixity
Where past and future are gathered
— T.S. Eliot

SOME OF US HAVE become so time-conscious during the past months that time allusions leap at us daily from newsprint and TV screen. Terms we keep encountering include traditions; time-honored; new; memories (usually in conjunction with making them); and history (which we are supposed to experience, and which is sometimes referred to as live history). Often these terms are bandied about in bewildering combinations. For example: "New traditions for your microwave," or about a battery, "A legend with a warranty that lasts six years into the future." In Boston there is a shop called The Nostalgia Factory, where you will find not only the picturesque but advertisements of banned products like DDT and asbestos. For a price. On the other hand there is in America a national organization that calls itself the Anti-Nostalgia Association for the Establishment of Time. It exists to promote contemporary concepts and values and to promote the future over the past.

The founders and spokespeople for the Anti-Nostalgia Association might be distressed to learn that their position is time-honored and in the great tradition of eighteenth and nineteenth century American thinkers. Beginning with Thomas Jefferson, who espoused what he called "the sovereignty of the present generation," Americans were exhorted to sever all ties with the past. An 1842 article stated "the whole essay of our national life and legislation has been a prolonged protest against the dominion of antiquity in any form whatever." De

> **BOOKS FOR DISCUSSION:**
> Lucy M. Boston *The Children of Green Knowe*
> Gregory Maguire *I Feel Like the Morning Star*
> Jan Mark *The Ennead*
> Ruth Park *Playing Beatie Bow*
> Rosemary Sutcliff *Warrior Scarlet*

Tocqueville observed that in America, "the tie that united one generation to another is relaxed or broken; every man there loses all traces of the ideas of his forefathers or takes no heed of them." And a New York canal builder declared, "Did we live amidst ruins and scenes indicating present decay we might be as little inclined as others to look forward. But we delight in the promised sunshine of the future, and leave to those who are conscious that they have passed their grand climacteric to console themselves with the splendors of the past."

Emerson took a stand for the present. He maintained "The reverence for the deeds of our ancestors is a treacherous sentiment... Give me insight into today, and you may have the antique and future worlds." Of the Concord writers, Thoreau went the farthest in disavowing the past. To him the historical past was degenerate. In contrast primitive nature was strong, savage, pure, and free.
A reverence for nature masked a growing ambivalence. When Hawthorn wished "the whole past might be swept away and the burdensome Parthenon burnt into lime," and yet admitted that he found it difficult to write

without a historical framework; when he decried (during his term as American consul in Liverpool) his fellow countrymen's habit of seeking connections with the past, speaking of "this diseased American appetite for English soil," and yet confessed that he himself would like "to find a gravestone in one of those old churchyards with my name on it," American attitudes had begun to change.

The change gained momentum after the Civil War. New economic pressures and political scandal, advances in technology and urban development, and the influx of immigrants whose languages and customs seemed so foreign made the present somewhat disconcerting, the past rather appealing. By the time America celebrated her Centennial, many of her leaders and writers were looking back through time in search of national and personal roots.

The past was synonymous with the simple rural or village life of previous generations. "I confine myself," wrote Mark Twain, "... to the boy-life out on the Mississippi because that had a peculiar charm for me." Congratulating Thomas Bailey Aldrich on his book, *The Story of a Bad Boy* Twain said,

By the time I had finished it at three in the morning, it had worked its spell ... the bringing back of one's youth, almost the only time worth living over again, the only period whose memories are wholly pathetic — pathetic because we see now that we were in heaven then and there was no one able to make us know it.

Here in this clear statement about nostalgia as the basis for fiction for and about children we have the complete turnaround — an attempt to recover the immediate, preferable past.

The great flowering of children's literature in nineteenth century America was rooted in this kind of nostalgia.

But was it nostalgia for the real past or an imagined one? Twain, for instance, remarked that in his schooldays he had no "aversion to slavery. No one arraigned it in my hearing ... There was nothing about the slavery of the Hannibal region to arouse one's dozing humane instinct to activity." Yet he recalled seeing a dozen black men and women chained to one another awaiting shipment to the southern slave market, "the saddest faces I have ever seen." Still, he had no aversion to slavery. It does seem to follow that when he wrote *Huckleberry Finn* he created the past of his childhood more than he recalled it.

Moreover, while his literary sensibility led him to celebrate the simple virtues of a simple life, he lived his own life in that huge, opulent house in Hartford, Connecticut that he had built with gothic turrets, a balcony like a pilothouse, and an interior crammed with expensive and elaborate furnishings.

Margaret Sidney, author of the popular *Five Little Peppers* series, captured the imaginations of several generations with her brand of unabashed nostalgia, a reverential and saccharine portrayal of a poor, small-town family. She who grew up the advantaged daughter of a successful architect wrote about the simple, struggling childhood of her imagination.

The fictional Peppers abandoned the fictional little brown house the moment they landed in the lap of luxury, and although they visited it afterward to recapture the flavor of their happy past, most of the first book in the series and all the sequels show the children growing up with every material comfort wealth can buy. Yet it is that simple, impoverished existence, albeit briefly shown, that Sidney's admiring readers usually remember about *The Five Little Peppers*.

Howard Pyle, whose writing and illustration for children celebrate traditional medieval styles and themes, was aware of the imaginary basis for his love of the Middle Ages. Writing to a friend who lived in the Cotswolds, Pyle said,

I doubt whether I shall ever cross the ocean to see those things which seem so beautiful and dreamlike in my imagination and which if I saw might break the bubble of fancy and leave nothing behind but bitter soap-suds... by the by, *do* you see them, or do you only carry motives of them around in your 'nut' the same as I do the old German castles?

At just about the same time (1890s) Mark Twain, who was living abroad and a guest in many fine houses and courts, admitted,

Scoffing democrats as we are, we do dearly love to be noticed by a duke, and when we are noticed by a monarch, we have softening of the brain for the rest of our lives.

And let's not forget that while he placed Tom and Huck in an idealized recent past, he set a Connecticut Yankee in King Arthur's court.

Small wonder that when Frances Hodgson Burnett wrote *Little Lord Fauntleroy,* the story of the young hero's transformation from impoverishment in New York to vast wealth and position as an English lord achieved unprecedented popularity. American readers, young and old, were already steeped in rags-to-riches formulae, but this book contained the added virtue of plugging the hero into the revered socket of established wealth and tradition.

So the English connection was reaffirmed, the past restored.

Already the climate in England favored the past as a suitable subject for children's literature. By the turn of the century E. Nesbit would be offering child readers talismans of antiquity and a role model who was an Egyptologist. The time was ripe for Kenneth Grahame to declare, "In England we may choose from a dozen different centuries to live in; and who would select the twentieth?"

Just in time for Kipling's *Puck of Pook's Hill* and its sequel, *Rewards and Fairies.* What a different kind of seizin' of Old England Puck hands to Una and Dan from the kind Little Lord Fauntleroy inherits. Americans who sought a deeper past than that which America's brief history could provide were ready to claim their cultural inheritance. Kipling's vision, both localized and vast, allowed his readers to travel with Una and Dan into a past that was at once mythic and historic, grounded and fluid, permanent and vanished.

Some of his readers were so captivated that they grew up to write children's books that extended and altered the imaginary journey into the past, or else brought it into the present and future. Kipling had depicted the fleetingness as well as the sweep of time:

Cities and Thrones and Powers
Stand in Time's Eye
Almost as long as flowers,
Which daily die;

But, as new buds put forth
To glad new men,
Out of the spent and unconsidered Earth
The cities rise again.

In "On the Great Wall" Kipling set his landscape in time's eye:

The farther north you go, the emptier are the roads. At last you fetch clear of the forests and climb bare hills, where wolves howl in the ruins of our cities that have been... In the naked hills beyond the naked houses ... you see puffs of black smoke from the mines. The hard road goes on and on ... past altars to Legions and Generals forgotten, and broken statues of Gods and Heroes, and thousands of graves where the mountain foxes and hares peep at you...

We can imagine Rosemary Sutcliff reading these words, entranced. Not only the description, not just the temporal vision, but the feeling on that frontier, the saving friendship between Parnesius and Pertinax. Think of what she created in *The Eagle of the Ninth,* her depiction of life at the edge of the civilized world, her intense memorable characterizations. Think of William Mayne's *Earthfasts,* what he calls "the evident landscape," and what he shows beneath it, history and legend combined, including the grave of the once and future king. In *The Grey King* Susan Cooper sets her Sleepers under a different mountain, but the grit and scree are as evident, and so is the magic of time unfixed.

Since the talismans of continuity that Kipling employed are traditional, it isn't surprising to find them in Sutcliff and Mayne, Garner and Cooper. An iron ring, a sword or knife, a stone or a stone circle, a cold flame or one that flickers without burning — each is suffused with what Heidegger called "presencing," the continual manifestation of things in and through time.

In *Red Shift* a single object is seen in different pasts. In *The Dark is Rising* the links that are forged and connected join the past with the future. In *Earthfasts* the old things are shaken loose, the Jingle Stones walking, the extinct wild pigs erupting into the present and running amok through the market square, the baffled drummer boy trying to reconcile the future century that confronts him with his own expected time, and the stunning apparition of King Arthur, a chieftain of the Dark Ages awakened from his long sleep and driven by his destiny. First a shadowy presence, then an armed horseman, determined and deadly, he nearly prevails against the imperative of history. "'Futurus sum,'" he pronounces. But his time has not yet come. He must return to his sleep beneath the earth, though his presence will remain in the reader's mind. For Mayne's Arthur is not only then; he is to come.

Rosemary Sutcliff's *Warrior Scarlet* is a novel that defies classification. To call it historical fiction is to suggest that its setting and action are based on recoverable information about life in Bronze Age Britain. But it isn't so much a re-creation as a subcreation, as Tolkien employed that word to describe the creation of a secondary world that compels primary belief. Unlike Kipling's magnificent mythic story from *Rewards and Fairies,* "The Knife and the Naked Chalk," *Warrior Scarlet* is so intensely human and so rich and lifelike in detail that while it does compel belief in that prehistoric setting, it also transcends its time. No character moves through time like Arthur or the drummer boy in *Earthfasts.* Drem and the others are fixed in time's eye; it is the story's emotional power that gives it its immediacy and universality.

Its affinities with the Kipling story are arresting: the tribal imperative, the stunning impact of new technology. And there is also the practical and symbolic use of oak, ash, and thorn. In "The Knife and the Naked Chalk," the flint man gives up his eye in order to bring to his people the weapon that can kill the wolves that prey on their sheep and threaten their continued existence. But the loss of his eye is nothing compared with what he loses when his people avoid his shadow and sing to him — and of him — the song of Tyr. He is doomed to be worshipped as a god, to lose his human status.

Now Tyr is a son of Odin, the Norse god who put out his own eye to gain the power of the word — of poetry, magic wisdom. Odin's son, Tyr, fought the archetypal beast, the wolf Fenris, overcoming him only by sacrificing his right hand. Think again about Sutcliff's Talore

the hunter, Talore One-Arm. But Drem is not a god. He is a boy with a crippled arm, even though his task — the slaying of a wolf — resonates with mythic significance.

The life of the flint people and Drem's Sun People share conditions that must have existed for eons. Stone Age tribes, eclipsed by the more advanced Bronze Age peoples, must have become indeed half-people during and after that transition. When Drem sees his future with the half-people, despite his regard for the shepherd Doli he envisions himself condemned to a shadow existence.

Talore, on the other hand, inspires Drem to hope, to believe that he can take his place in his tribe. Talore is godlike to Drem and godlike in image. In Celtic mythology a king of the people of the goddess Danu lost his arm in battle. Because physical perfection was a kingly attribute and requirement, he had to give up his sovereignty. But the silversmith, also a deity, crafted a silver arm for him, enabling him to reclaim his kingship. One of the gifts of this king was his power to restore the slain to life. And so does Talore, raising Drem out of despondency and estrangement.

Yet Sutcliff's treatment of Drem's banishment and despair and his struggle to be restored to life among his people is related in human rather than mythic terms. While Talore does stand in relation to Drem as the Celtic king must have done with those he revived, Drem's future is not entirely resolved. He will never wholly belong to either culture, Sutcliff makes this clear when Drem inquires about Doli's burial place and is rebuffed, and again when another warrior mocks him: "Even the great Drem One-Arm cannot hunt in two worlds at once."

It is her vision of dual and successive periods that gives this book such marvelous dimensions. The final scene at the Beltane fires and the making of the new fire for the hearths looks ahead as well as back into the distant past. And the iron dagger introduced into the tribe recalls the immense shift for the flint people when metal entered their stone world. The priest in *Warrior Scarlet,* with prophetic sight, envisions the future:

We are the Sun People, and it is in my heart that bronze

is of the Sun, and the cold iron only of the earth. As the little people are the people of the blue flint, so we are the people of the shining bronze; our day is the day of bronze as theirs was the day of flint; and in a world where iron rules, we shall rule no longer. Aiee Aiee! It will be a cold gray world, and the kings and the heroes will be dead.

To offset this chilling vision Sutcliff includes the other side of change — Drem joining with Blai, one of the Dark People. The reader finishes with a sense that it is only in myth that change is so abrupt and final, while the truth is that time takes time. Change is transition and fusion; the sun will not be instantly and utterly eclipsed by the cold gray iron.

Can Sutcliff's vision of life as it might have been lived nearly three thousand years ago have anything in common with Jan Mark's vision of life in a somewhat remote future? Are the writers' tasks so different, one from the other? Not, I think, when each timescape is so removed from our own that objective documentation is scant or entirely absent. Not when the authors employ similar themes and subjects. It may be coincidental that the young heroes of *Warrior Scarlet* and *The Ennead* are physically impaired, but it is significant that in each the handicap delineates a bitter state of mind that is at least as crippling as the physical deformity.

Like Sutcliff, Jan Mark puts the deformity to literal and symbolic use without overwhelming the characterization. Where Drem feels unnoticed by his fellow tribesmen and comes to see himself as a ghostly nonentity, Isaac lives in similar isolation and estrangement, although his response to it is different from Drem's. Each youth is believable within the context provided, and in an almost uncanny way both contexts are imbued with the same kinds of societal rigidity spawned in part by external pressures that threaten its survival.

These books share other elements. By setting all the conditions of time and place in her prologue, Mark frees the story from sci-fi clutter, so that she can begin at once with Isaac at his coming of age, as Sutcliff has done with Drem. While Mark sees Isaac's predicament largely in political terms, she

makes sure that we see him as at once human and mythic. Early on we recognize that his story echoes familiar legends — Prometheus, Job, Israel in Egypt.

But Mark's story of Isaac and Eleanor (and Moshe) is about human aspirations and self-knowledge, and — most especially with Isaac - about the education of the heart. While its time and place come from an imaginative source different from Sutcliff's, *The Ennead*, like *Warrior Scarlet*, is informed by specific ideas about its time/place context. Mark has said:

When I wrote the story, I was really thinking of Rhodesia as it was then. It became Zimbabwe subsequently. Which was a colonial government which had seceded from the parent nation in order to pursue its own way of life in direct contravention of the wishes of its neighbors. And this is what happened on the planet I was writing about. [Its inhabitants, who had left Earth because it could no longer support life, had moved] remorselessly through the system rendering one planet after another derelict. They were coming to the end of their resources. But wherever they went, however bad life was where they lived, there was always something worse to go back to.

Mark named the nine planets after the nine Muses, goddesses of culture, and their star after their mother.

So there were these nine planets circling a star called Memory, and housing people who had no memory of anything, no religion, no art, no literature, no culture at all.

Except for Moshe and Mr. Peasmarsh. Mr. Peasmarsh, who came from Earth, spoke a "dying language, full of strange pictures," and recommended to Isaac that he find a Bible or someone who knew it to learn what Cain said to the Boss when he asked him where Abel had gone.

Moshe is to Isaac what Doli of the Half-People was to Drem, for he can impart a sense of the past, a sense of story, making it possible for Isaac to begin to place himself in a context beyond his own immediate predicament. Moshe tells the story of the Golem to show people that they live enslaved by fear, the name Erato written on their foreheads. But they are unable to understand this analogy because they do not know what a story is. They cannot make the connection with a legend about a Golem who obeys without thinking until one day he resists, after which the rabbi, seeing how dangerous he may become, erases the shem from his forehead and makes him fall down dead. Only Isaac and Eleanor gather the seeds of Moshe's humanism and nurture them, are nurtured by them. Even though Moshe is silenced, he is not yet utterly erased.

Although Ann Schlee's *The Vandal* tells a coming of age story too and draws on mythic and historical memory in the development of the hero, this book conveys a different time sense from either *Warrior Scarlet* or *The Ennead*. And this is so in spite of many recognizable references and some similar fictional devices. The ritual fire harking back to the pagan fires of Samhain, at the opposite end of the Celtic year from Beltane; the traditional chants or songs connecting children with children down the ages; the grandmother's piercing cry for seeds; the timeworn paths that concrete cannot obliterate.

Paul is susceptible to the past. This makes him different, a societal risk; it makes life awkward and ultimately insupportable. For Paul there is no evident landscape to give him his time-bearings, to lend insight into what has gone before and to guide him toward his future. The inhabitants of his world live entirely in a vapid present. Lacking a past, they cannot conceive of a future. When awareness ignites in Paul, when it is fostered by his deliberate pursuit of knowledge, by his determined sedition, he comes face to face with the consequences of being different — first banishment in a kind of limbo, next estrangement from his family, then exile. He endures these consequences for the sake of a future which will be connected with the recovered past.

In this book the past is seen as a generating force, erupting like a volcano through centuries of earthcrust and surging through Paul as it does through the youngest children. It seems conceptually closer to books like *Earthfasts*, where the past is contained in and released through a particular place and its relics.

Even relics out of place may carry the past

through time, as Eleanor Cameron shows us in *The Court of the Stone Children*. A kind of energy resides in the unresolved pasts of the stone children, awaiting the right time, the right person to act for them in the present. So too the attic toys in Jane Langton's *The Diamond in the Window*, not only the sinister Jack-in-the-box but the playthings of an earlier generation which bring Eleanor and Eddy closer to the lost children. The stone children, however, are not ghosts like Penelope Lively's Thomas Kempe; they are — in relation to the heroine — more like the tribespeople of New Guinea in *The House in Norham Gardens*. Again the word presencing comes to mind, even though the time gone by or the future shown is closer to our own present than the past of *Warrior Scarlet* and the future of *The Ennead*.

But place or objects imbued with the past may not be revealed to the child or children without the mediating offices of an older person. In *The Court of the Stone Children* Mrs. Threlkeld and Mrs. Staynes provide historical connection, and in *The Diamond in the Window* Uncle Freddy and Aunt Lily are living representatives of the recent past. Like Puck, Kipling's Old One; like Merriman, Susan Cooper's Old One; like Doli the shepherd and Moshe, they are messengers or witnesses, transmitters of the story that Nina and Eleanor and Eddy and the other young protagonists will bring with them into adulthood. Just as Una and Dan harken to Puck's call: "Fast! Hold fast all I give you," they will hold fast the story and pass it on to those who come after them.

Until Lucy Boston's *Green Knowe*, perhaps no fictional house was so enlivened by history as Thackers in Alison Uttley's *A Traveller in Time*. Uttley and Boston have spoken almost with one voice about the houses they wrote into their fiction. Uttley's family had owned hers for hundreds of years. "I was devoted to my home," she wrote, "and most of my books have taken this house for the scene of the action." Lucy Boston, who acquired hers before the Second World War and spent many years lovingly uncovering its periods, has said, "All my water is drawn from one well. I am obsessed by my house ... the house that all the books describe."

Although each house — in reality and in fiction — reveals the accretions and alterations of time, *A Traveller in Time* and *The Children of Green Knowe* connect a particular past with the present, so that the details and sense of place combine in each to convey both specific times and their continuing presence. Uttley provides explicit signposts:

The walls of Thackers quickened by them, the place itself alive with the memory of things once seen and heard, for such grief was of eternity and outside time.

She includes simple landmarks like Uncle Barnabas' use of traditional place-names — the River Derwent called by him the Darrand. She includes a talisman, the little mannikin that exists in the present when Aunt Tissie gives it to Penelope, and in the past, when Jude presents it to her. Jude himself is special, because while he is not all there in his own time, he is capable of moving out of his time (in his mind). The mannikin may not be necessary for Penelope's ability to travel through time, but it is important material integument, binding the past to the future.

Penelope's increasing involvement in Thackers' Elizabethan tragedy establishes a tension between then and now. As her sense of belonging to the place grows stronger, her amnesia works forward as well as backward. When she decorates the marchpane Thackers as it will be in centuries to come, she is so firmly fixed in its Elizabethan period that she is unaware of the foreknowledge that has informed her act.

In this book prophetic sight, or a knowledge of history, is both a gift and a curse. Penelope cannot put back the clock; her beloved's future is in her past. All that she has is the love that makes her "forget past and future in the clear present which I shared with him."

The children of Green Knowe are less substantial than those Elizabethan characters. Nor do they command such intense feeling in Tolly. Except when they appear in their own separate stories, they are seen out of their own time and in Tolly's. Yet the sense is there of the walls being quickened by them, the

house alive with their memory. And of course it contains their portrait and their possessions.

Mrs. Oldknow does everything in her power to draw Tolly close to them. After seeing some of their things he asks whether sometimes there are other children here.

Mrs. Oldknow looked at him as if she would like to know everything about him before she answered.
"Yes," she said "Sometimes."
"Who are they?"
"You'll see when they come, if they come."
"When do they come?"
"When they like. Now let's unpack."

This kind of teasing taste is designed to stimulate the appetite, and Mrs. Oldknow has a few other tricks up her sleeve as well. She knows Tolly can't be possessed by the house until he feels that he possesses it. So when he asks whether the flames in the fireplace are theirs, she is quick to share them with him, the blue flames his, the orange ones hers. This paves the way for his real question: "Is it my house? — I mean partly?" "Of course it is — partly, as you say." And she is telling him that the house will be his for only a part of its time, that it belongs to those who lived in it in every century of its history, and to those who will come after him.

Even as she gives him a sense of past and future and his place in the continuum, she realizes that he needs time to absorb it all. Like Puck with Dan and Una, she lets him see with his own eyes and hear with his own ears and conjure the child ghosts with his own imagination. At the same time she is always alert to the chance to nudge him along in the right direction, as when she speaks of the children in the painting in the present tense. Tolly picks this up at once. Toby has a real sword not because he was going to become a soldier, but because "he's going to be a soldier."

In addition to Mrs. Oldknow's bewitching nudges, there are the same kind of details as in *A Traveller in Time*, details found in a place with a history and conservative setting.

So gradually the children emerge for Tolly like photographs in developing fluid, less substantial than the Babbington family was for Penelope. While Boston leaves room to interpret the children's presence as a projection of Tolly's lonely, lively imagination, we choose to believe that they are travelers in time, leaving their footprint and the echo of their laughter in the present-day Green Knowe.

For Tolly they are real, though not quite palpable, like the voice he and Mrs. Oldknow hear singing to the baby in an earlier time.

And they recede as his need for them diminishes. As emanations of the house, their home and his, the children of Green Knowe have given him a sense of his place in the continuum. They have helped to heal the wounds of his rootlessness and abandonment. Healed, he is ready for tomorrow — for a living friend, a real puppy, school. Even so, the reader can tell through Mrs. Oldknow that the vital present will not sunder him from the past.

The sense of place in Gregory Maguire's *I feel like the Morning Star* has an opposite effect, sundering its inhabitants — especially those devoid of personal memory — from any integrated sense of before and only a vague and stifled sense of after. Set in the foreseeable future, the book presents an imaginable extension of a world we already know. And what a long way it is from "the promised sunshine of the future" those nineteenth century thinkers set their sights on.

The most profound and dismal feature of the underground colony is its featurelessness. It lacks not only an evident landscape but a timescape as well. The pacified elders, themselves victimized and colluding with the system that victimizes them, seem to possess just enough of the past to want to shun it. Unlike Paul's parents in *The Vandal* and all those tractable citizens who nightly erase their memories, the adults of Pioneer Colony manifest differing degrees of obedient mindset. The equivalent of Mrs. Willmay in Maguire's book is Dora Prite, who carries her past intact, and with it her unrelenting anger. Where Mrs. Willmay struggles to maintain selfhood, Dora contains her grief and rage, wrapping herself in silence.

The closest Sorb or Mart or Ella can come to a sense of time-to-come beyond the circumscribed calendar marking their predictable world, is in private dreams where shards of memory usually scatter but sometimes coalesce. For Sorb, who hears his name called, or nearly hears it, it feels like being haunted. But the children in Ella's care are her dream of the future.

Escape and liberation require more than technical skill — hope, memory, and a willingness to listen to whatever voice calls. Dora Prite, casting off her bitter silence, gives voice to her own outrage and shares her history with the young people. "Once you can love," she tells Ella, "you can learn to act." Her voice joins with the ghostly voice inside Sorb and all the voices that echo through time.

So it is these young people, in possession of their own brief pasts — albeit in shambles — who lead the children into the unknowable future. When Dora Prite sings them out of the most dangerous gallery, she gives them more than momentary cover. Her singing is also a gift to the gifted, to Ella especially, Ella who is herself already a giver.

The Gift is central to the experience Beatie and Abigail share in Ruth Park's *Playing Beatie Bow*. Granny is both mentor and nurturer. She stands for the past, for tradition, for Power in the present, and for Sight into the future. In all of these states she is also the transmitter, the human connection for Beatie and Abigail. At the same time, she is old; the Gift in her is waning. It is this loss of Power that becomes the fulcrum of the story, because she cannot allow Abigail to return to her own time until she has fulfilled her role as The Stranger.

Park's brilliant achievement in this book is in the slowly shifting time-view. She begins in Abigail's present, our present. The first encounters with Beatie are strange and dreamlike. It takes the unfolding human predicament to bring Abigail and the reader into full acceptance of the Rocks in Sydney a century earlier. In time that acceptance allows Abigail and the reader to peer out of the nineteenth century into the twentieth, to see it as Beatie has, an uncanny and mystifying vision of the future The time shift is so commandingly executed that the span of a century is altogether believable.

Notice how the Gift is associated with illness, with fever. Remember Penelope's recuperative state when she comes to Thackers. Consider Jude, who is not all there and Isaac, who is spastic and twisted, Drem with his useless arm, Sorb after being subjected to the lisopress, and Tolly arriving at Green Knowe wan and frail.

The terms by which we describe those who are sickly or who behave abnormally are: they are not themselves; they are not all there. In Orkney legend and custom a sick child is in mortal peril; it can be snatched away by the folk of Elfland, a changeling left in its place. The Orcadians call such a child, who is not all there, "in the hill." Although it is an old tradition, it was still very real for many nineteenth century Orcadians.

And so, for a while, the gifted, still-wasted child Beatie possesses the Gift she dreads — Sight and foresight. Like Sorb she has come away hearing her name called — out of her time, as it turns out, by the children playing Beatie Bow. Terrified of what she cannot comprehend until Abigail convinces her about the time, she is none the less eagerly curious about the future she has glimpsed and will not live to see.

As Beatie and Granny share their time with Abigail, so does she begin to share hers with them. Nor is it hard for her to believe what she learns from these Orkney immigrants. Listening to Beatie describe the vision of herself grown, with no wedding ring, a heavy book in her adult hands, Abigail takes the first voluntary step toward participation in this past; she begins to fulfill Granny's prophecy. Estranged in her own family, Abigail is the Stranger who will make the Gift grow strong again in the Tallisker family.

Abigail's simultaneous perception of past and future seems akin to Granny's recollection of her power in the old days, "when past and future were spread out before me like a field of flowers." But Abigail's perception of time keeps shifting. Looking for the nineteenth century dwelling in twentieth century Sydney, she is amazed and terrified that "all signs of

the family's life could have so completely vanished, as if they had never been... And the same thing would happen to her and her parents." Yet later, confronted by the unalterable past — the ship lost with all hands in 1874 and her inability to warn Judah — she sees time as something that "could stretch and twist all in a second and turn into some other aspect of itself." Her final discovery about Judah's death and Gibbie's survival, her realization that she has fulfilled the prophecy by saving that sickly monster of a boy so that he could continue the Bow family and the gift, leads to reconciliation and acceptance.

The theory she had had ... that time was a great black vortex down which everything disappeared — no longer made sense to her. She saw now that it was a great river, always moving, always changing, but with the same water flowing between its banks from source to sea.

What Ruth Park and these other writers have done for children of the NOW generation is to show them how to catch that flowing water in their hands — not to stop it, but to slow it for an instant and let it trickle through the fingers, to catch the light of the moment before it rejoins the river.

Whether we are so enamored of the past that we deserve the Anti-Nostalgia Association for the Preservation of Time, or whether we have cast our fearful or rapacious eye on the future alone, there is no question that for many of our children the present is all they encompass. To show them that Cities and Thrones and Powers Stand in time's eye almost as long as flowers, which daily die, is to provide them with a vision of past and future of which — like it or not — they are a part.

The past may be the dawn of civilization and it may be yesterday. The future may be light-centuries from now and it may be tomorrow. The closer and more recognizable the past or future, the more we are likely to scrutinize the fictional construct for authenticity. The more remote the time, the greater the imaginative latitude. Yet the demands on writer and readers remain those associated with all literary experience. The difference these writers may make is that they pass the timescapes they envision on to children.

In the ancient Celtic world, where time was fluid and full of mystery, the poet was believed to be endowed with Sight. He not only recorded and interpreted the history of his people, he composed the stories that connected them with the Otherworld. Our language and literature spring in part from that mythic source, as well as from the Germanic tradition in which the Word — poetry and power — was seen as one gift.

In each of the books considered here the young protagonist moves from a static or fixed state that limits perceptions and response to an awareness of change, to a more fluid state that makes it possible to move, substantively or imaginatively, out of a self-centered present. Often there is an older character with a story to tell or a history to relate, who imparts some crucial understanding. Even if it is only a glimmer, it may help the young protagonist to connect with the past and look to the future — to see with time's eye. There is, first and foremost, Puck, and then Doli, Aunt Tissie, Moshe, Mrs. Oldknow, Dora, Granny — each with the Gift to hand on.

It seems to me that this is what their creators are doing as well — all of them, from Kipling to Park.

They are fulfilling their bardic function so that young readers, along with their heroes and heroines, may be unsettled, enlivened, and gifted too.

NEIL PHILIP

Dreamtime

In 1895 an old Wiltshire man told John U. Powell:

I've heard 'em say that Adam were made and then put up again' a wold hurdle to dry.[1]

And when Adam came into consciousness, he woke into the eternal present. The expulsion from Eden was, we might say, the fall into history. Every time a child is born, the same play is re-enacted. The child is born into an eternal present. But sooner or later, the awareness of history, of a before-time, begins.

Alongside the myth of the Fall, there persists a belief in the recoverability of that primal innocence. This potent myth, which the historian of religions Mircea Eliade has called 'the myth of eternal return,'[2] informs much children's literature.

We think of history as a straight line, from the beginning to now, one event after another. But we know that this is not wholly true. Most of us have in part the ability which Thomas Hardy had to an extraordinary degree, 'for burying an emotion in my heart or brain for forty years, and exhuming it at the end of that time as fresh as when interred.'[3]

So most human cultures have a second view of time, as a loop or circle — time as, in Eliade's words, 'the moving image of unmoving eternity' — and seek access at certain moments to a primal reality, which the aboriginal peoples of Australia call 'dreamtime', to the innocence of Eden. The point of intersection of these two views of time — the line and the loop — is the point on which much of our children's literature focusses, attempting, in the terms of the crucial pun in Alan Garner's *Red Shift*, to equate momentum with memento.[5]

A key work here is Philippa Pearce's *Tom's Midnight Garden*, in which these two times, line and loop, interdepend so subtly. At their point of intersection, at the moment of equilibrium, there is a gate for Tom into the eternal garden — but there is a home for him in linear time too:

Tom felt a tightness round his ribs, as though he were being squeezed apart there. He wanted two different sets of things so badly: he wanted his mother and father and Peter and home — he really did want them, badly; and on the other hand, he wanted the garden.[6]

Not many books achieve the delicate balance of *Tom's Midnight Garden*, but I would suggest that its central concerns recur in many children's novels — fantasies, historical novels, adventure stories — and echo through all aspects of their structure and expression, from the use of tense to order a narrative to the notion of the recovery of a pure, transparent language in which to speak to the child.

In her book *The Case of Peter Pan* Jacqueline Rose sees children's writers as seeking 'to retrieve a form of language or expression which would be uncontaminated by the intrusion of the verbal sign'.[7] And she demonstrates that the innocence of the word, like the innocence of the child, is a convenient fiction.

For us, of course, the myth of unsullied innocent childhood is yet another version of the myth of eternal return, and one which is full of dangers. Yet nevertheless the idea of each child as the first human, born in the present tense, with an innocent eye, does give the historical novelist for children a unique vantage point into the past, a way of intersecting linear history, using the historical present to explore the eternal present.

One of the key differences between literature for adults and for children, it seems to me, is that in a children's book we are engaged in a discovery *with* the characters, where in a book for adults we would be engaged in a discovery *of* them. In adult fiction, the author keeps the reader constantly revising his apprehension of earlier scenes by the release of information which was previously available to the narrator but withheld from the reader. But in, for instance, Leon Garfield's *Jack Holborn*, there is a sense in which the narrator, Jack, does not know, until he discovers it in the course of narrating his adventures, that Lord Sheringham is Captain Rogers's twin. He structures his story without benefit of hindsight.

This sharing in the narrator's discoveries, rather than wising up to the narrator's ploys, is one explanation of the powerful appeal for children's writers of first-person narrative; the device allows them to embody a naive narrative voice in complex fictions which, like Garfield's, explore in action rather than analysis life's perplexity. It is a trick which only works for stories — such as *Jack Holborn* — in which the narrator's discoveries confirm rather than overturn the attitudes of the childish self; in a book such as Peter Dickinson's *The Seventh Raven* the ingenuous first-person narrative seems just that, a trick. The fact that ex-political hostage Doll speaks throughout as the person she was *before* the shattering events she relates implies that they have really made little difference to her. Dickinson was trying in that book to explore the politics of violence while remaining within children's understanding of human motives and emotions. To maintain an objective third-person narrative stance while preserving the reader's gradual introduction to those politics might have required a too damaging simplification of affairs; but it would have allowed Doll to demonstrate rather than assert the change which her confrontation with violence effects in her.

Third-person narrative for children generally concentrates on a naive protagonist, for instance Mary Lennox in *The Secret Garden*; the problem then is to prevent the narrative tone from becoming either too knowing or too gauche. The point at which an author allows the central character — whether narrator or protagonist — to have secrets from the reader is the point at which fiction for children meets fiction for adults.

Just as the child protagonists are innocent of history, so too the child readers will approach a novel about, say, the slave trade, such as Peter Carter's *The Sentinels*, or the scandal of the mid-Victorian baby-farms such as Ann Schlee's *Ask Me No Questions*, in quite a different frame of mind from the adult reader. This ability to bring history to life as a fresh immediate experience unmarred by previous knowledge and judgment, to introduce both the protagonist and the reader into the living heartbeat of a past time, is the unique privilege of the children's writer.

And at the best, such writers can penetrate the mystery of time, to the moment where in Richard Jefferies's words:

Time has never existed, and never will; it is a purely artificial arrangement. It is eternity now, it always was eternity, and always will be. By no possible means could I get into time if I tried.... When all the stars have revolved they only produce Now again.[8]

In Alan Garner's *The Stone Book*, Mary's father takes her to the top of a church tower and shows her her world in a moment of pure joy and wonder:

'There,' he said. 'You'll remember this day, my girl. For the rest of your life.'
'I already have,' said Mary.[9]

1 John U. Powell: *Folk-lore Notes From South-West Wilts* (Folk-Lore XII, 1901)
2 Mircea Eliade: *The Myth of Eternal Return* (London 1955)
3 Florence Emily Hardy: *The Life of Thomas Hardy 1840-1928* (Macmillan Press: Basingstoke & London 1962) p.378, quoting Hardy's Journal of October/November 1917
4 Mircea Eliade: *The Sacred and the Profane* (New York 1961) p.109
5 Alan Garner: *Red Shift* (Macmillan Publishing Co.: New York 1973) p. 102
6 Philippa Pearce: *Tom's Midnight Garden* (1st ed. 1958; Puffin Books: Harmondsworth 1976) p.150
7 Jacqueline Rose: *The Case of Peter Pan or The Impossibility of Children's Fiction* (Macmillan Press: London & Basingstoke 1984) p.46
8 Richard Jefferies: *The Story of My Heart* (1st ed. 1883; Quartet Books: London, Melbourne & New York 1979) p.52
9 Alan Garner: *The Stone Book Quartet* (with an Afterword by Neil Philip, Dell Publishing: New York 1988) p. 23

Pictures on the page

IT'S A GREAT HONOR to be invited away from my drawing board to meet you all here today. I think the best contribution I can make is to offer a few brief observations about my job as an author/illustrator or, if you prefer it, my particular vehicle for time-travel, and then try to illuminate this further by showing some slides. I hope I will put this into perspective against the tradition from which I draw my inspiration. I find the illustrators I most admire all worked for children, not only as picture-book designers but adapting their skills to a variety of texts, working in what one might call the English tradition. It's a certain line, a way of drawing or of seeing things which goes back to Rowlandson and long before that. There have always been strong connections in this country between art and literature, so it's a narrative tradition which comes very naturally to us, and still persists in spite of big-business imperatives and the pressure to sell co-editions world-wide. I stress the word drawing because although we all work in color these days it's still the skill in draughtsmanship which holds the story, the structure beneath the paint. It combines with the text, not just as part of the design of a page but as a part of the emotional response which a story-teller seeks to create in his reader.

Since I first started doing the rounds of publishers with my folio, years ago in the fifties, my job has moved more and more in the direction of younger children, towards doing my own picture books. I've no complaints about this. It's one of the most demanding and exacting of activities imaginable and it goes on getting more and more exciting. For me it's not a question of näivism,

or, to coin a dreadful cliché, of trying to 're-enter the world of childhood'. This would be highly embarrassing and I'm pretty sure children wouldn't want us there even if we could. It's more a matter of essaying the essential ease and accessibility of style, to try to hone down a complicated technique to an onion-like whole; very simple in shape but containing many layers within.

In earlier times all European artists were required to develop narrative skills which were needed to communicate the stories of the Bible to a largely unlettered populace. Now in the late twentieth century illustrators are much concerned with the same kind of challenge; to involve someone who cannot yet read in a story through their pleasure in the imagery. It is a great mistake to assume that a non-reader's aesthetic responses are necessarily crude or undeveloped; far from it. Our visual memories are probably better before the age of six or seven than at any other time of our lives. In this first introduction to fiction the words carry the thread, but the characterization, the setting, much of the humor and drama of the plot is there to be discovered in the pictures. A delightful and satisfying dialogue emerges, a shared experience the importance of which I certainly don't need to emphasize in this knowledgeable company.

So as picture books are such an enormous subject, one which I find myself talking about a great deal, (and in a good many places) I am jumping at the opportunity to open up some discussion about that other part of an illustrator's job, that of interpretive illustration. The skill of illustrating other people's stories, particularly those for older children, has been somewhat in eclipse for a whole package of reasons. The decline in public library book-buying power, and now a more recent threat to our school library service because of changes in educational funding, has resulted in publishers having to look more towards trade outlets, where eye-catching full-color picture books are naturally going to be the strong sellers. (Older children are still reading, I'm sure of it, but where they get their books is something of a mystery.) We have been landed with a divided market in which small children get large-format colored books, slightly older ones get short text books with a few line drawings (there have been some good developments in this field with some fine writers rising to the challenge and encouragement for the skill of black-and-white line drawing.) Older children tend to get no pictures at all; an unnecessarily rigid demarcation.

Interpretive illustration requires rather a different mental process to doing a picture book. You receive the story in manuscript form, immerse yourself in it, try to get the feel of what the author is after, and give it a visual dimension in a supportive way. It's rather like acting, except that you are a whole troupe of actors, stage designer and director all rolled into one. It's enormous fun. If it's a fairy-tale your opportunity for time travel is unlimited. You can research the period; clothes, cooking pots, houses, weaponry are all grist to your mill. You find out that authors, when engaged in writing and concentrating like mad on their plot and characters, unconsciously leave an indelible imprint of themselves which runs through everything they do like the letters in a stick of sugar candy, and you have to read this too. A good illustrator's presence in a book is always going to be a strong one – who can imagine Alice without thinking of Tenniel, or Winnie the Pooh without Ernest Shepard? – but he must always strive to serve the text. The ideal aim, after all, is give both author and reader not what they want exactly, but what they never dreamed they could have.

When I was offered an opportunity to illustrate Frances Hodgson Burnett's *The Secret Garden* it was not just an exciting prospect. It fulfilled a long-held aspiration. I read it as a child, in a green cloth-bound edition with illustrations by Charles Robinson. I read it to my own children (in the same edition, which I had kept.) It still makes me

Mary, Dickon and Colin: drawing by Shirley Hughes from *The Secret Garden* (Gollancz, 1988)

cry. Coming to it as an illustrator made the focus change. I had completely accepted the background in which it was set in the Charles Robinson illustrations, a kind of baroque mansion somewhere in South-east England. But I wanted to take it back firmly, with the text, to Yorkshire, — a tough bare moorland landscape with the wind whistling and wuthering across it, a Tudor house, low-panelled rooms and galleries and stone mullioned windows. But the story calls for some very realistic characterization. There are Mary and Colin, two selfish little pigs of children at the outset, trapped in that fatal combination of having been utterly indulged but never loved, but who learn affection and respect for other people, and bloom like the tangled briars, so triumphantly at the end.

A counterpoint with the Sleeping Beauty theme occurred. The image of a young girl in a rose garden spiked about with a hedge of thorns is a powerful one, and ages old. So I did find the over-grown roses creeping into the imagery. Children may not mark this kind of symbolism consciously but they take it on board all right. I had a very good time researching the house and garden, sitting around with my sketch-book in National Trust houses among the crumbling urns and fountains, walled gardens and collapsing greenhouses. In the end, of course, you go home and make it all up.

The Secret Garden is a novel in which the grown-up characters are as interesting as the children. I revealed the sad and mysterious Mr. Craven very gradually, his face covered or turned away in the first sequences. As I so much want this story to be read by today's children I was determined that there would be a picture on every other spread — something of a challenge as it's a longish text. I relied heavily on the in-house design and editorial skills at Gollancz, which were superb. But I laid it out myself, endlessly juggling the spaces allowed for illustration in each chapter so that I could draw the bits I wanted. We knew we had to keep production costs down, so I accepted the further challenge of having color plates wrapped round the sections, which is much less costly than having them tipped in,

but meant that I had to illustrate whatever occurred in the text at that juncture. I never could put up with a color plate which doesn't coincide with the action (being asked to 'See p. 182' always filled me with indignation as a child.)

After much pleasurable labor, many meetings, bikings to and fro of galleys and an enormous quantity of gum, we emerged with a slap-up edition with sixteen color plates, seventy-odd black-and-white illustrations and endpapers all for under ten pounds, which I call good publishing. I enjoyed every minute of it, though I did sometimes wish that I could talk to the author. There were some burning questions about the story which had never occurred to me until I started to illustrate it, which sadly will never be answered.

Now I have aspirations towards *A Little Princess*, a Cinderella story if ever there was one.

COMMENTARY ON THE SLIDES

Dogger

This is an icon from my own past. He belonged to one of my children. I came upon him one day at the back of a cupboard where he had been living in quiet retirement for many years. I was glad to see him again, but he reminded me of that searing situation experienced in almost every family when that all-important object of affection goes missing at bedtime, and all hell breaks loose trying to find it. The text for a picture book isn't always easy to write; it often takes more time than a much longer piece. But this one just seemed to write itself. Ideas float about like icebergs, largely below the surface of the mind, until something seems to trigger them urgently into view. As I am an illustrator they translate themselves very readily into pictures. Picture - book plots, like films' are unthinkable without the visual element, so you reach for a pencil or felt pen to get down some roughs at a very early stage.

Alfie and Annie Rose

Having a good story in mind naturally stimulates the desire to draw, and for me characterization grows out of this ... Just as authors find their characters taking on a life of their own and influencing the plot, this happens to me when I start to draw. When I first did this quick sketch of Alfie, a four-year -old hero of mine running up the street ahead of his mum, who came trundling behind with his baby sister Annie Rose and the shopping, I knew that he was positively pink in the face to get into the action. Rough sketches done at this stage, drawn very rapidly, often have a vitality and lack of self-consciousness which is sometimes hard to recapture when you come to doing the more finished color illustrations the second time round.

'Alfie' from the first rough draft of *Alfie Gets in First* by Shirley Hughes

Scenes from everyday life: Double spreads from *'Out and About'*

When I am illustrating every-day life today I am still drawing on my own recall of childhood, of course. But it is very necessary to keep up with close observations of a fleeting attitude, a figure in motion, the way people (especially children) group together when absorbed in a game or conversation. I lurk about a good deal, armed with a sketchbook, in parks and sand-pits. Even in swimming pools and supermarkets, though this can be hazardous!

How differently these young parents and children would move, sit or stand if they were wearing tightly laced stays, long petticoats, waistcoats and hard hats!

When I was an art student, long ago, we were expected to give a lot of rigorous attention to life drawing. We sat in front of antique statuary (I had a lot of trouble with Laocoon wrestling with the snake), then graduated to the life-room and did examinations in anatomy. Although I sometimes found this tedious, in retrospect I am very grateful that we were put through this kind of discipline. It does help to give imaginary characters a convincing fluency. But characters drawn in the pages of a book are not a matter of mere anatomical accuracy (many brilliant illustrators have managed without this.) They are protagonists in a drama. You make them up out of your head and they must be charged with the necessary emotional involvement to carry the story along and make the reader want to turn the page and see what happens next.

Up and Up

A story told entirely without words represents a kind of mount Everest to any illustrator. As with a mime or an old silent two-reeler comedy the movement, facial expression and gestures have to tell the story. Mine is about flying, not the sort you do in an airplane, but in dreams. Most of the younger children I talk to have vivid memories of this experience.

My small Icarus flies over a landscape which bears a strong resemblance to that of my childhood. I wanted the opening sequence in the endpapers to show the whole town, so, like a bird, the reader sees it all from above until alighting on the beginning of the action. The perspective all had to be rigged, of course, to give the dizzying sense of height. I couldn't have used an aerial photograph even had this landscape still existed (which it doesn't). Part of my motive for doing this book was to break down the competitive thing which builds up around reading (who has got to book 5 and who is left struggling with book 2, and so forth.) The response from children has exceeded my wildest hopes. They write telling me the story, and a great deal about their own experience of life into the bargain.

Some heroes of my time (and a bit before): E.H. Shepard

When I first laid eyes on A.A. Milne's 'Winnie the Pooh' as a small child I clearly remembered being as fascinated by the layout — the way those little line drawings were nonchalantly dropped into the text — as by the story. I have often wondered since if somebody at Methuen decided to set the page in this way, or if it was Shepard's idea or perhaps Milne himself was consulted? One feels that it was inevitable.

I think that there's a danger that Ernest Shepard's towering talent as an illustrator can be taken for granted because he was so prolific and so superbly professional. He could, quite simply, draw *anything* with felicitous charm. No barrier was put in the path of this prodigious draftsman. He was encouraged to draw and trained from an early age and draw he did, producing a staggering body of work over his long lifetime.

It is not really as the visual originator of that unforgettable little boy in a smock, or the bear with very little brain that I admire him, but for his line, his handling of light and shade, the way he can set his figures in a landscape; this one, for instance, from *The House at Pooh Corner*, with the wind fairly whistling through the branches of the Ashdown Forest.

This was the era when all the best professional illustrators with a family to keep depended upon the monthly cheque from *Punch* magazine, for which Shepard did drawing after drawing. This one, illustrating Milne's poem 'Jonathan Jo,' came out in *Punch* in May 1924, which pre-dates the book, 'When we were very young'. The jokes he illustrated seem now singularly un-funny (did the artists invent them too? I hope not!) He now had an opportunity for some lovely full page poem illustrations. He pot-boiled of course, — what true professional doesn't? —

but at a consistently high standard, one that most of us can only dream of as our best.

I think it is in his interpretation of *The Wind in the Willows* that he shows the full range of his artistry. Anthropomorphic animals are always a tricky subject for any illustrator, and many very distinguished ones, including Rackham and Burningham, have done this story, but no other, for me, has got so near the heart of it as Shepard with his deceptively slight line drawings.

Like all great children's classics the book has many resonances. It is a pre-first-world-war Arcadia, with the river bank, the countryside around, still wrapped in an un-suburbanised rural idyll, and the wild wood and all that it stands for. It's also memorably about the desire to escape, to run off and be a gypsy or a wayfarer, which all children need to do in their imagination, and the equally strong pull toward the warmth and security of home, and having a snug little place of your own all kitted out as you would like it.

Shepard's pictures seem instinctively to express all this. But there are many practical problems for an illustrator, being required to characterize these little animals not only in their own homes but also in the world of men. Just look at how cunningly Shepard gets round this by rigging his perspective to make the pictures of Mr. Toad, escaping from prison disguised as a washerwoman, completely convincing.

Will Heath Robinson

Heath Robinson has to be mentioned as one of our great classic illustrators before he turned to comic magazine invention, drawing those lunatic machines for which he is justly famous. (So much so that I believe he is to become the next super-star with a theme park devoted entirely to his maverick imagination). But he did superb work as a serious illustrator, here, for instance, illustrating 'A Midsummer Night's Dream' with a rapturous use of black-and-white. His color plates for his own idiosyncratic book 'Bill the Minder' fascinated me so much as a child I never wanted to read the text. I felt sure it would never live up to my idea of what the story ought to be.

William Nicholson

William Nicholson is one of my great heroes, both a fine painter (you can see some splendid examples in the Fitzwilliam Museum, here in Cambridge) and graphic designer; he saw no artificial barriers between the two. His posters, in partnership with James Pride under the name of the Beggarstaff Brothers, were unique in a way that one could claim paralleled the work of Lautrec. And he was a fine picture book artist. This is a self-portrait from his Alphabet. 'A is for Artist': a woodcut which translates his consummate mastery of form and characterization into the simplest possible areas of solid black. If I was asked to choose a handful of near-perfect picture books his 'Clever Bill' would certainly have to be included. Hand lithographed in this case, to be commercially reproduced later, word and image are deftly turned together like a phrase of music, completely satisfying at the conclusion. It comes as no surprise that his son Ben became one of our most impeccable abstract painters.

Edward Ardizzone

In spite of his name (he was half Scottish and half Italian) a perfect exponent of the English line. Unlike Shepard he had to fight to fulfill his destiny as an illustrator and worked as a clerk in the Eastern Telegraph Company for six years or so before he got any formal art training. By trial and error he forged for himself that unique style, impeccably organized areas of light and shade which always relate beautifully to the page. He taught himself by copying Daumier, whose influence can be clearly seen.

Once arrived at, his style fitted him like a suit of beautiful old clothes, one in which he was absolutely at home but which adapted itself to an astonishingly wide range of texts, from fairy tales to Dickens and Bunyan. As a war artist in Italy, often going behind the lines on a bicycle, he brought his illustrator's eye to bear not only on the horror and violence of war but on the moments of ennui and waiting, so well expressed in this typical sketch of 'Troops in the Castle of San Arcangelo'.

He is best remembered for his own beautifully written picture books, the heroic adventures of Little Tim and his friend Ginger, done in color wash and line with deceptive simplicity and ease, the tonal values used with absolute accuracy.

Just as some people are born with perfect pitch, Ardizzone seems to have been naturally blessed by a perfect sense of tone. He could dash a few lines onto the surface of the paper with his 'dip and scratch' nib, and establish with perfect economy the depth of vision from foreground to background which he wants us to see. He often likened the page of a book to the proscenium in a theatre; open the book and up goes the curtain. But it is on an atmospheric and detailed world, one to be entered and lingered in at leisure.

His dumpy little children (seen here in *The Little Bookroom* by Eleanor Farjeon) *Nurse Matilda* by Christiana Brand, or in perfect rapport with the children's poems by his old friend James Reeves in *The Blackbird in the Lilac* or in Clive King's *Stig of the Dump* are always touching. His work is full of genuine sentiment but never, ever, sentimentality. A tight-rope which we all walk, but he performed it so sure-footedly, and with such modesty and affection, that there can hardly be an illustrator working today who doesn't feel his wide-ranging influence and salute him.

Carrying on the line: Charles Keeping

Keeping is equally well known for his black-and-white work as well as his picture books. His technique springs from his skill as a printmaker. He was totally uncompromising in his address to children. *Charley, Charlotte and the Golden Canary* expresses his feelings about the destruction of the old East End of London where he grew up. His visual excitement in bricks and mortar is complemented by that image of power and freedom the leaping horse, which figures so often in his drawings.

Quentin Blake's

sprightly ease of style is unique in spite of much imitation. But don't be fooled by this seemingly insouciant line, skidding across the page like a loose-limbed vaudeville turn. It conceals a very thoughtful approach to his many texts, and on the tightrope between cartooning and illustration he always comes down firmly on the latter.

John Lawrence

uses line and wash in a way which sets him firmly in the British tradition of Ardizzone and Anthony Gross. But he also includes in his repertoire an exemplary skill in wood-engraving, that most dangerous and demanding of illustrating techniques; slow, infinitely painstaking (no process white over your mistakes, one tiny slip of the knife is irreparable), used to stunning effect in his illustrations for '*The Canterbury Tales*' and many other texts.

Victor Ambrus

though trained in Hungary, is a most dashing exponent of British history. He is at his best with figures in action. They surge across the page. He describes muscular galloping horses, glinting armor, sea battles and grave warrior faces in a free-flowing line with well-placed massings of solid black brush work. All appears effortless and strong, the hallmark of an artist in full control of his chosen medium.

Fritz Wegner

has a formidable talent which is all too easy to take for granted. He has a witty eye for comic detail and uses color wash with as much skill as he does black-and-white line. But he also has a strongly romantic side which makes him an ideal interpreter of fairy tales.

Charlotte Voake

is a young illustrator at the beginning of her career with a gently relaxed water-color technique which conceals a sharp wit and invention. In her Nursery Rhyme collection *Over the Moon* the style is at once traditional but very much her own.

Patrick Benson

is another young illustrator working brilliantly in a hatched pen and wash technique. In the 'Hob' stories by William Mayne he has tackled a most demanding interpretation, setting it not quite in reality but not yet never-never land, using a small format to great effect with formal plates offset by a commentary of little drawings dropped into the text. A tour-de-force of professionalism in one who still has his career before him.

Time Thirst

THE TROUBLE WITH living in time is that each of us gets only one small chunk, and we're not allowed to choose which chunk.

If you think of the passing centuries as a series of linked sausages, then each child gets only a single sausage, or part of a sausage. It's too bad.

This accounts, I think, for our time thirst, our eagerness to know about all those centuries in which we cannot live, before we came into the world or after we die.

We are like children at a grown-up party. We sit on the stairs in our pajamas and look on. We haven't been invited to the years before we were born, and therefore we have an urge to stare into the darkness beyond our cribs into times past, to see what it was like when Grandmother was a girl.

Books can satisfy that thirst, ordinary books about the past, books without fantastic journeys from one time into another. In her true stories about her own childhood, Laura Ingalls Wilder permits us to look back at the American frontier before it was macadamized and covered with shopping malls.[1]

The television series *Upstairs, Downstairs* does the same thing, opening windows on the parlors and kitchens of the generations before we were born. Peering through those windows we are enchanted to watch Mrs Bridges prepare a meal for the king without a microwave oven, and Mr Hudson polish the silver, or shout into an antique telephone.

In my grandfather's house in Illinois there

were old copies of the young people's magazine *St Nicholas*, displaying a similar world. Gentleman-ly boys and ladylike girls sat on wide front porches with their lordly fathers and queenly mothers.[2] There was an atmosphere of intense respectability. I used to sit on the rug and leaf through the pages, soaking up the ambience of my father's childhood forty years earlier. The houses were different, the clothes were different, but the children were the same — playful, eager, sometimes obedient, sometimes naughty, and they too left their homework until the very last minute.

They are all very well, stories like these, books set in the past, books written in the past. But sometimes our time thirst is so great, we aren't satisfied to look on. We want to go back ourselves, or go forward into the future. We want stories with protagonists who make fantastic time-journeys.

And there are authors a-plenty who invent clever ways to do it. H.G. Wells didn't bother to explain his time machine.[3] He left minor details like that up to its fictional inventor. It was simply a gadget bristling with gears and belts and pulleys. You jumped into the saddle, pulled the ivory levers, and you were off.

Other writers have tried harder to work out a plausible system. In Jack Finney's *Time and Again* a present-day New Yorker named Simon Morley goes back to the city of 1882 by a method that is a simplified version of the theory of relativity.

...a man ought somehow to be able to step out of that boat onto the shore. And walk back to one of the bends behind us.

It's a pretty notion. But how exactly does one get out of the boat?

By painstaking effort, Simon, the would-be time-traveller, is surrounded by a carefully re-created physical setting. He is installed in the Dakota, an old apartment building on Central Park, elaborately fitted out with the furnishings, the gas lights, and the cooking equipment of the 1880's. He is dressed in the proper clothing. The New York *Evening Sun* of January, 1882, is delivered every day. He lives and breathes in an artificial nineteenth-century environment. And at last, after weeks of dreaming himself into it, the pretense becomes reality. Taking a walk in the falling snow in Central Park, he sees a sleigh skimming along the street. He has stepped out of the boat and gone back to the year 1882 in the city of New York.

This fancy that time is a river appears again in *A Chance Child* by Jill Paton Walsh[5]. Poor mistreated young Creep is carried back into the cruel circumstances of England's industrial past in a ruined canal boat. Silently it carries him downstream, coming to rest at places along the shore where children are working in underground mines, or dodging among the dangerous machinery of textile mills, or laboring in foundries among showers of sparks and burning coals. This time the engine that powers the time-travelling craft is their common wretchedness.

A boat is again the vehicle of transport

"...we're like people in a boat without oars drifting along a winding river. Around us we see only the present. We can't see the past, back in the bends and curves behind us. But it's there..."

in *Storm Without Rain* by Jan Adkins.[6] A boy whose grandfather owns a boatyard on Buzzard's Bay returns to the time when his grandfather was a boy, and works beside him in the same boatyard. Much care is taken in this book with descriptions of old tools and methods of woodworking, increasing the magical sense that the boy has actually gone back in time. The explanations of how the transition was managed are ingenious.

I ran the plane halfway down the plank.....my hands were beginning to learn the even pressure that peeled away a single long curl...I pulled out the curl to make a long spiral, a helix. I bent the helix this way and that. I could make one curl touch another...Was I looking at a model of time?[7]

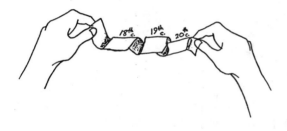

What if some days of the year are like the same days of every other year - like muggy summer days with the same sou-wester and the same haze and the same bright glare and the same heat. Bend the spiral. See how they touch? A year apart they touch, maybe on the same day, and if the spiral were long, if it went forever and bent back and forth, the years might touch.[8]

It's another pretty notion, one that will permit the reader to suspend disbelief, at least until the last page.

In Betty Levin's time-travel book about Iron Age Ireland, *The Sword of Culann*[9], there are no persuasive analogies and explanatory metaphors. Her modern children make their backward journey by the powerful magic of Celtic belief in two special times of the year called Semain and Beltane. These are mysterious cracks in the calendar when there is a backing and forthing between the real world and the world of the spirits.

At such times it is dangerous to leave the house. If the baby is not watched, it may be stolen away. Semain and Beltane are natural moments when Claudia and Evan can slip

through the crack and find themselves in the past, then slip forward again at the end of the story into their own time.

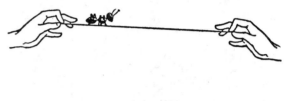

Madeleine L'Engle has no trouble explaining how the children in her *A Wrinkle in Time*[10] traverse vast distances in time and space. Instead of travelling in a straight line from here to there like ants on a string, one simply "wrinkles" the string by folding it into a loop in order to move at once from the beginning to the end. The diagram makes it perfectly clear. There's nothing to it. It's called *tesseracting*.

The late Jorge Luis Borges has envisioned the most extraordinary pattern of movement across the broad face of time. In his story, "The Garden of Forking Paths"[11], he plays with the notion that there is

an infinite series of times...a growing, dizzying net of divergent, convergent and parallel times...We do not exist in a majority of these times; in some you exist, and not I; in others I, and not you...Time forks perpetually toward innumerable futures. In one of them I am your enemy.

Of course there is a little problem with this idea of perpetually forking paths, all existing at the same time. It's called the conservation of energy, or the First Law of Thermo-dynamics. Any scientist would realise at once that the speculation was fatally flawed; but few writers are scientists. And the concept is an intriguing one that lingers in the memory.

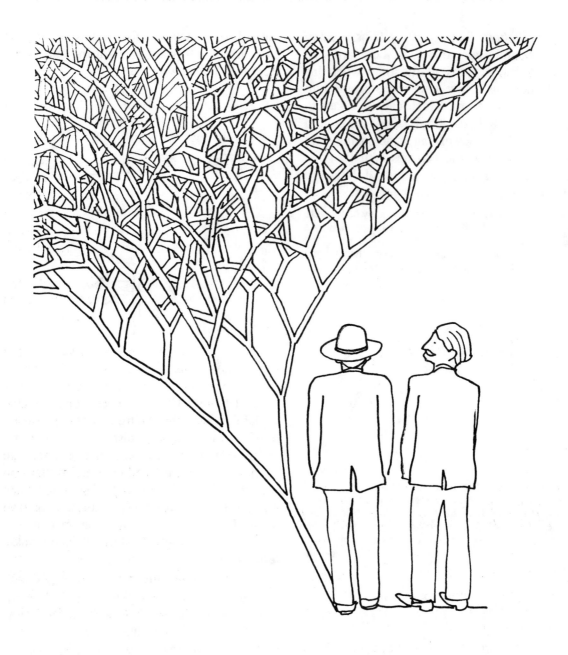

What are all those other paths along which we might be simultaneously careering?

These are only a scattering of the multitude of explanations in time-travel books of how the trick is done. Some are satisfying, some are not. Very few face up to a very important logical difficulty: what is the consequence to the orderly sequence of history of all this rattling back and forth in time? What is the result of the intrusion of living three-dimensional bodies into spaces and times in which they don't belong? Does the intrusion have an effect on the present? Surely it must? Can one really make a lighthearted visit to some past era, then skip carelessly back again without having joggled the entire course of events?

A few hardy souls have dealt with the problem.

To Alison Uttley, in her *Traveller in Time*[12], the past is irrevocable and cannot be changed, even by a time traveler who wishes to set wrong things right. When young Penelope finds herself back in the age of the Tudors in the old manor house where the story begins, she watches helplessly an attempt to save the life of Mary, Queen of Scots, and can do nothing to interfere, to make it succeed. History is history, and you can't budge it. Thus the present is not affected by Penelope's sojourn in the past.

But shouldn't it be? Wouldn't a foreign body inserted into an earlier time by definition change things, here and now?

No one has considered the matter with more care than Jack Finney, in his *Time and Again*, the book in which a contemporary New Yorker goes back to the city of 1882. At one point in the story one of his characters presents the "twig-in-the-river" theory.

> ... if time is a river, it's infinitely bigger than even a Mississippi at full raging flood. While you ... are the very tiniest of twigs dropped into that torrent ... A twig tossed into that enormous and incredibly powerful current, into the inconceivable momentum of that vast Mississippi of events, will not and *cannot* affect it *one goddam bit!*[13]

But of course he is wrong. And Finney makes the most of it, exploring the ramifications of messing around with the past so thoroughly, they are worth recounting.

It is discovered that in actual history an advisor to President Cleveland talked him out of buying the island of Cuba. If there had been no such advisor, Cleveland might have bought Cuba, and the whole history of our relations with that island would have been different.

Therefore, why not go back in time and change things so that the advisor was never born at all? Arrange things so that his mother and father never met in the first place, never married, never produced a son? In fact, why not go back in time and fix up a lot of other things that have gone wrong, and tidy up a lot of loose ends?

You can see the larger danger that arises from Simon Morley's inquisitive excursion back into the year 1882. Before long the Central Intelligence Agency might follow him and begin barging around clumsily, interfering and destroying, fouling up history, ignorantly knocking everything askew — with incalculable results.

But Simon wakes up to the danger. He protests.

> ... Who's given this new little breed of men ... the power

of God to control the lives and futures of the rest of us? Most of them we never heard of, and we sure as hell didn't elect them! ... Even if you're right about Cuba ... look what it leads to. It leads directly to bigger and bigger changes, with a handful of military minds rewriting the past, present, and future according to *their* ideas of what's best for the rest of the entire human race. No, sir, gentlemen; I refuse.[14]

And then he saves the world from this peril by going back into the year 1882 once again in order to interfere in the lives of the mother and father of the inventor of this method of travelling in time. He prevents their meeting. The inventor will never be born. The danger is averted forever.

The most classic exposition of the consequences of interference with the past is a famous short story by Ray Bradbury, "A Sound of Thunder".

Here too there is a time machine, one that takes men on safari into prehistoric time to shoot dinosaurs. They are warned that they must not disturb the ancient environment. They must not step off the metal path laid down by the time machine.

But in spite of the warning someone stumbles off the path and takes a few steps on the mossy floor of the jungle. He comes back into the present with a dead butterfly stuck to his shoe.

At once we see the result of his mistake. Everything in the present is subtly different. The honest man who was elected to high office just before the time-safari was NOT elected after all. The votes have gone to the fascist candidate instead.

> He fumbled crazily at the thick slime on his boots. He held up a clod of dirt, trembling, "No, it *can't* be...Not a little thing like *that*! Not a butterfly!"...
> It fell to the floor, an exquisite thing, a small thing that could upset balances and knock down a line of small dominoes and then big dominoes and then gigantic dominoes, all down the years across Time.[15]

Bradbury's story presents the logical extreme. There is no such thing as a twig too tiny to affect the course of the Mississippi, no bit of microcosm so small that it won't affect the macrocosm.

We would-be time travellers must heed this warning: *stay put.* We must stick to our own age.

The twentieth century must be permitted to work itself out by the natural forward circuit of the hands of the clock. Time travel is risky. Let it alone.

But I can't help wondering. How do we know that everything we are experiencing at this very moment, right here and now, is not the result of some blundering trespass into an earlier era, some wrenching distortion of what was supposed to happen?

It sounds silly, I suppose, but how can we be sure this is the *right* present, not a random mistake, the consequence of some time-travelling busybody's appalling meddling in the course of past events?

Never mind. It's all trumpery, of course. There is no such thing as time travel.

At least, let's fervently hope so.

References:

1 Laura Ingalls Wilder, *Little House in the Big Woods*, Harper and Row, 1932, 1953.
2 *The St Nicholas Anthology*, edited by Henry Steele Commager, Random House, 1948.
3 H G Wells, *The Time Machine*.
4 Jack Finney, *Time and Again*, Simon & Schuster, N Y, p 52.
5 Jill Paton Walsh, *A Chance Child*, Farrar, Straus, Giroux, 1978.
6 Jan Adkins, Storm Without Rain.
7 *Storm Without Rain,* p.71
8 *Storm Without Rain,* p.116

9 Betty Levin, *The Sword of Culann*, Macmillan, 1973.
10 Madeleine L'Engle, *A Wrinkle in Time*, 1962.
11 "The Garden of Forking Paths" in *Labyrinths*, by Jorge Luis Borges, p 28, New Directions, 1962, 1964.
12 Alison Uttley, *A Traveller in Time*, Viking, N Y, 1939.
13 *Time and Again*, p.140
14 *Time and Again*, p.389
15 Ray Bradbury, "A Sound of Thunder", in *R is for Rocket;* Doubleday edition, 1962; Bantam 1975 edition, p 68.

Picture Book Time

Those images that yet
Fresh images beget..
— W.B. Yeats

THINKING ABOUT traveling in time, I retain an acute memory of the first of several visits to England's Cambridge more than thirty years ago, when I was struck by the wondrous beauty of the place. But since this university is also legendary as the heart and soul of the country's theoretical science, I felt it my bounden duty this year to read Stephen Hawking's *A Brief History of Time* — which the blurb called "a popular work, written for those who prefer words to equations." I certainly prefer words to equations. It was a valiant struggle, and even though I occasionally found the book exciting and even humorous, the effort, for my nonscientific intellect, was ultimately rather fruitless. Einstein's flat statement that "for us convinced physicists the distinction between past, present and future is an illusion ... There is no more difference between past and future than between left and right. The equations of time look the same forward or backward" — well, this is terribly paradoxical to me.

What I do understand is that all the King's horses and all the King's men cannot put Humpty Dumpty together again after he's fallen and smashed himself. If you've read Hawking, you know the image he uses of the broken cup on the floor. In what he calls imaginary time, as Einstein says, there is no scientific difference between past and future, but Hawking says, there's that little matter of

BOOKS FOR DISCUSSION:
Mitsumasa Anno *Anno's Journey*
John Burningham *Come Away from the Water, Shirley*
Virginia Lee Burton *The Little House*
Barbara Cooney *Miss Rumphius*
M.B. Goffstein *My Noah's Ark*
Russell Hoban *The Rain Door*
Arnold Lobel. *On the Day Peter Stuyvesant Sailed into Town*
Charles Keeping *Willie's Fire Engine*
Jill Paton Walsh/Mary Rayner *Lost and Found*
Cynthia Rylant *When I was Young in the Mountains*
Maurice Sendak *Where the Wild Things Are*
Brinton Turkle *Thy Friend, Obadiah*
Chris Van Allsburg *The Wreck of the Zephyr*
Brian Wildsmith *Professor Noah's Spaceship*.

real time, and there is indeed a very big difference here between forward and backward directions; and the reason the broken cup doesn't go back in time and reassemble itself — or Humpty Dumpty, for that matter — Hawking sanguinely observes, is that this is strictly forbidden by the second law of thermodynamics! All the more power, I say, to Charles Lutwidge Dodgson, the inscrutable mathematician of Oxford, who, always toying with time, did manage to make it reversible, didn't he, when he had Alice grow smaller, as well as larger, just by making her drink something.

I am on much more solid ground with literary rather than physical ramifications of time. We find in human thinking eminently discussable notions — all the way from the Bible and Aristotle and St Augustine and Shakespeare to this year's newest book. You have this week been hurled into the complexities of time — as Shakespeare said, "the whirligig of time brings in his revenges." My own level of comprehension is probably nearer to that old limerick about relativity written long before the jet age by one Arthur Henry Reginald Buller:

> There was a young woman named Bright
> Whose speed was much faster than light
> She set out one day
> In a relative way
> And returned on the previous night.

Seriously, however, it was Einstein who believed that the source of all science as well as of art is the mysterious, for creation must be preceded by imagining — in his words, "the gift of fantasy has meant more to me than my talent for absorbing positive knowledge." Years ago, in fact, I used to admonish parents who revered facts over fancy, "it takes a certain elasticity of mind to comprehend a dragon."

And with William Blake,

> To see a world in a grain of sand
> And a heaven in a wild flower
> Hold infinity in the palm of your hand
> And eternity in an hour.

Would Einstein object? I think not.

Eleanor Farjeon couldn't abide Peter Pan's Tinker Bell, as I cannot; she said that Barrie, who did know something about illusion, knew nothing about magic. Much of Eleanor Farjeon's magical writing has now vanished in the USA — but not without a few traces. Most of you must know that timeless tale of time in a Sussex village, much-loved by storytellers and their listeners, "Elsie Piddock Skips in Her Sleep." It begins when Elsie is three and ends in triumph when she performs her magical skips at the age of 109.

Do you remember in Ingmar Bergman's

Wild Strawberries the nightmarish sequence that contains a moment of utter, demented terror when the disoriented man confronts a large jeweler's clock with its hands missing? And there are the implications of clock time gone askew — from the sinister opening sentence of Orwell's *1984*, "It was a bright, cold day in April and the clocks were striking thirteen" to the portentousness of the wayward grandfather clock in *Tom's Midnight Garden*. "'What a funny watch,' remarked Alice to the March Hare. 'It tells the day of the month and doesn't tell what o'clock it is.'" But Lewis Carroll, who dealt with time with a mad logic and a logical madness, devised an even funnier clock in *Sylvie and Bruno*, called the "Outlandish Watch." Setting the hands back in time also pushed events back to the time now indicated — an anticipation, perhaps, of H G Wells's *Time Machine*? Moreover, pressing a reversal peg on the watch actually started events moving backward — a sort of mirror image of time's linear movement. "'It's a queer sort of memory that only works backwards,' the Queen remarked to Alice. 'What sort of things do *you* remember best?' Alice ventured to ask. 'Oh, things that happened the week after next,' the Queen replied in a careless tone."

A few years ago, we heard Eudora Welty's riveting lectures at Harvard — lectures jam-packed with wall-to-wall humanity. The three, published as *One Writer's Beginnings*, plunged deeply, gracefully, into memory, and she began with clocks.

> In our house on North Congress Street in Jackson, Mississippi, where I was born ... we grew up to the striking of clocks. There was a mission-style oak grandfather clock standing in the hall, which sent its gong-like strokes through the livingroom, diningroom, kitchen and pantry ... Through the night, it could find its way into our ears; sometimes, even on the sleeping porch, midnight could wake us up. My parent's bedroom had a smaller striking clock that answered it. Though the kitchen clock did nothing but show the time, the diningroom clock was a cuckoo clock with weights on long chains, on one of which my baby brother, after climbing on a chair to the top of the china closet, once succeeded in suspending the cat for a moment ... All of us have been time-minded all our lives. This was good at least for a fiction writer, being able to learn so penetratingly, and almost first of all, about chronology. It was one of a good many things I learned almost without knowing it; it would be there when I needed it.

Diana Paolitto has shared with you her specialized knowledge — which I surely cannot claim — of how the child perceives time. Indeed, the very notion of childhood has done its own traveling in time. For childhood finally attained full recognition, it is generally acknowledged, only in the nineteenth century.

Most of us, I daresay, have shared part of our lives with children, and we know how unpredictable their perceptions can be, swinging abruptly from the surprisingly keen to the totally irrational. Henry Wadsworth Longfellow's daughter Alice used to give a prize to Portland schoolchildren for the best essay about her father, and her favorite statement by a child was: "H.W.L., was born in Portland, Maine, while his parents were traveling in Europe."

As adults, our consciousness continually roams back and forth — past, present and future — along a highly personal time line. For the infant, there is obviously neither past nor future nor even present, only *now*, which as a concept comes long before *soon*. I wouldn't begin to know how to chart the surge of the baby's or the young child's perceptions. "When I was a little girl," a three-year-old once began a conversation with me. At some point the child surely begins an apprehension of time as a personal experience as well as a linear movement. Do you know that enchanting English classic, *The Young Visiters*, written by Daisy Ashford at the age of nine? Its opening sentence is "Mr Salteena was an elderly man of 42 and was fond of asking people to stay with him." Are there intimations of relativity in the nursery?

Consider all the references to time with which we unthinkingly litter our conversation and which embed themselves in the child's consciousness, with or without confusion. Walter de la Mare, in his haunting introduction to his anthology *Come Hither*, tells how eager he was, as a boy, to get to a place that was fabled in his family — called East Dene. "But (my mother) smiled a little strangely when I asked her to take me there. 'All in good time, my dear,' she whispered in my ear, 'all in very good time.' What kind of time, I wondered, was *very good* time?"

St Augustine asked, "Quid est tempus? What in discourse do we mention more familiarly or knowingly than time — this great enigma?" Children hear these phrases: Time flies; it takes time; in no time; high time; just in time; on time; at the same time; part-time; keep time; time out; for the time being. And there are the didactic implications familiar to every child in the phrases *waste time* and *no time like the present*, which the poet David McCord acrobatically turned upside down in a poem called "No Present Like the Time."

"No time like the present," they always used to say,
Meaning — Busy! Do You Hear Me? Don't Delay!
Much better in reverse (it doesn't have to rhyme):
Simply, simply, *No present like the time*.

I have not forgotten my title here, "Picture Book Time", nor that beguiling idea from Yeats — "those images that yet, fresh images beget." Herbert Read, an inspired art and literary critic, developed an interesting theory in his book *Icon and Idea*; and he makes what he calls an immensely presumptuous claim that art has been, and still is, the essential instrument in the development of human consciousness and that its significance lies in the fact that it is the particular activity by which man tries to bring the visible world into his consciousness, and is actually forced to the attempt by his very nature. Such an activity is not fortuitous but necessary; and its products are absolutely essential to the human mind. Herbert Read goes on to include the literary arts, too, as the transmutation of the world into word. Then he goes back to the prehistoric epoch, so-called because it left no written records, which might indeed extend backwards beyond the invention of language. And almost contradicting St John's Gospel, he says,

Before the word was the image, and the first recorded attempts of man to define the real are pictorial attempts, images scratched or pecked or painted on the surfaces of rocks or caves ... We can grope backwards ... and reconstruct, with careful observance of the fragmentary evidence, the first dawn of a specifically human consciousness: a consciousness not yet aware of causality but aware of synchronicity — able, that is to say, to make a mental connection between events that are separate in location. *To make a connection*, however irrational or illogical it may seem to our sense of reason — that was the first step in civilization ... But the connection could only be made — rendered visible, realized and represented — by a sign, which is an image that can be separated from the immediate perception and stored in the memory. The sign came into existence to establish synchronicity, in the dumb desire to make one event correspond to another.

For me, all this is an exciting footnote in the study of picture books. Yet, paradoxically, another footnote: Rudolf Arnheim in *Film As Art* made a statement already quoted by Paul Heins.

As far as content goes, the word has the range of all the other media together; it can describe the things of this world as immobile or as constantly changing; with inimitable ease it can leap from one place to the other, from one moment to the next; it presents not only the world of our outer senses but also the entire realm of the soul, the imagination, the emotion, the will.

As good a place to start my slides as any, this one is from the famous is *Orbis Sensualium Pictus,* meaning the visible world, with one of its subtitles being, "A nomenclature and pictures of all the chief things that are in the world." The book was written by a famous seventeenth-century educator, John Amos Comenius, a Moravian bishop, and first published in 1658.

It was called by the ninth edition of the *Encyclopedia Britannica* the first picture book ever made for children and is an educational classic of enormous influence, having been the most popular textbook in Europe for over a century and used even in this country for well over 200 years. It was a kind of elementary encyclopedia; here you see a page in both Latin and English, the original having been printed in Latin and High Dutch, showing and briefly explaining various time-pieces — a sundial, a clock, an hour-glass.

from *Orbus Pictus*

Now these are some nursery rhymes, all about clocks and time, as illustrated by Martin and Alice Provensen; we have "A Diller, a Dollar"; "Hickory, Dickory dock"; Wee Willie Winkie running through the town in his nightgown at eight o'clock; and "Bell horses, bell horses, what time of day?"

Of nursery rhymes, Pamela Travers has said that they are the shortest stories, and:

the generations cannot help meeting in them since the material comes out of antiquity and tradition. The lessons they propound go back to the drying of the Flood. They carry in their minuscule pockets the origins of all the novels and dramas in literature.

For example,

Solomon Grundy
Born on a Monday
Christened on Tuesday
Married on Wednesday
Took ill on Thursday
Worse on Friday
Died on Saturday
Buried on Sunday
And that was the end of Solomon Grundy.

Travers asks, "Isn't it a newspaper in little, a scenario for a Dickens novel? Could Tolstoy have done better? Did Shakespeare know of it when he wrote on the seven ages of man?"

When I began to come to grips with the significance of time in stories told both verbally and visually, I knew that I would not find many analogies in picture books to the remarkable novels on our reading list, with all their emotional richness, narrative complexity, and leaps of the imagination. I also soon realized that the folk tale in picture-book clothing would not do for my purpose here, because despite a profusion of artwork, the illustrated folk tale is not usually a picture book in the strict sense, but rather an illustrated folk tale. For the true picture book is written with pictures as much as with words; thus, it becomes an immediate dramatic experience, which is why it is linked more to film than to other kinds of books.

And while illustrations for a folk tale can be a decorative display or even works of art in themselves, they are not really a *sine qua non.*

A renaissance of folk tales, with their earthy wisdom and vision of humanity, as texts for picture books began about twenty-five years ago. Of course, back in the last century we had the genius of Caldecott, who not only used traditional material but injected such meaning into the spare texts that he surely is the originator of that art form, the true picture book. And we have the modern work of Marcia Brown (I think she does approach the true picture book with the beautiful pages of *Once a Mouse*) as well as of Warwick Hutton, Trina S Hyman, Margot Zemach, Sendak, Uri Shulevitz, Erik Blegvad, Nancy Ekholm Burkert, Barbara Cooney, among others. But some illustrators have rushed in headlong where humility, wit, scholarship, good taste and vitality of imagination should have led the way.

Moreover, a quest for authenticity here has often brought unchildlike exoticism into the picture book, and the elevation of the decorative and the painterly effects over the needs of narrative often results in a consumer product aimed at adults rather than a means of communication with children. Scarcely anything in the public domain — legend, song, fable, myth, fairy tale — has been left unpictured between the covers of a book. And again and again the question has been asked, what does all this eye-catching visual display do to a child's imaginings, the child's own image-making? Yet partly because so many contemporary books are weighty with graphic display and rather frothy in narrative content, the attention of artists, critics, and purchasers seems to center on folk tales. So I owe you some comment on their relation to the subject of time.

Fairy tales, I think, actually stand outside linear time; the Opies say, "they are the space fiction of the past. They describe events that took place when a different range of possibilities operated in the unidentified long-ago." In fact, the unspecified period of their setting — their very timelessness — is probably what makes them so believable. It was Perrault's work that added to our oral tradition the phrase "Once upon a time." The original seventeenth-century French was "il estoit une fois," but the word *upon* was added by Robert Samber, who made the first English translation. And so it came about that the

phrase was given embellishments — grace notes, it you will — for example, "Once upon a time, and a very good time it was, though it was neither in my time, nor in your time, nor in anybody else's time."

There is a sense of the relativity of time in fairy tales, or an interlocking of time between the Otherworld and the human domain. A rescue from fairyland sometimes occurs after a year and a day, the dominating idea in William Mayne's absolute gem of a story, *A Year and a Day*. The Sleeping Beauty was put to sleep for one hundred years; Cinderella's magic ceased to function at midnight, an example of so-called barrier time. John Rowe Townsend very thoroughly covered other aspects of the subject as E. S. Hartland writes about it in *The Science of Fairy Tales*, so I can omit some of the statements I originally had here. Let me only add that a Japanese version of the "Rip Van Winkle" theme can be found in the tale of Urashima, who takes a sea-maiden for his bride and finds fairyland under the sea; the story was made into a beautiful picture book by Taro Yashima. And the hundreds of tales of the Buddha's reincarnations surely deal with time, as do the countless creation myths of the North American Indians.

Now, having mentioned some supremely successful illustrators of picture-book folk tales, I want to back up a bit and speak of another entirely unconventional book in which time does play an ancillary role. A story like "Hansel and Gretel," which is so strong and significant, is a perfect example of the eternal plot that entertains on one level and that probably becomes embedded in our unconscious minds as a prototype of the fear of desertion and death and the final attainment of love and security. This story is strong enough to submit to temporal changes in the telling, not in words but in altered pictorial concepts that quite legitimately reveal new truths and ever deeper meanings.

A few years ago Anthony Browne made "Hansel and Gretel" into a new picture book for somewhat older readers and deliberating gave it *not* a timeless fairy tale setting but a transposition into our own time, showing the

From *Hansel and Gretel* by Anthony Browne

peculiarly late-twentieth-century aspect of urban dreariness and deprivation. Since children have fewer preconceived notions about such matters, the modern setting should not disturb them in the least. The intensely realistic pictures are loaded with clues and symbolic images. Here is the poor woodcutter and his wife with their two children, after a terrible famine came and they could find nothing to eat. Note the accouterments: the TV, the beer bottle on the mantel, the framed Holman Hunt on the wall, and the despair of the characters. And the next picture, the mirror that draws us into the situation, the boy without his pillow case, and the contemporary trappings of feminine vanity on the bureau, even the Oil of Olay! And here is the most powerful, most pervasive, and most brilliant symbol in the book — the first use of the ominous black triangle, resembling a witch's conical hat. No matter what we think about illustrating folk tales, the practice will go on, but at least we can ask, if not the *why*, then at least the *how*, of the illustration. Instead of the saccarine, sentimental, or deadly dull and diluted; instead of the artist's self-indulgent grandiose art-gallery paintings that overpower essence and ethos and meaning, the artist's creative imagination should totally penetrate and encompass the story.

Susan Cooper once pointed out that the poetic imagination is not limited to creating verse; nor is a poem dreamy but rather precise and tough, *as the best children's books have to be*. She means, she says, that the story is tough, the language precise, and the whole work clothed in imagery. Now, Susan was not talking about picture books, but her words surely apply to the good ones, and we ignore such requirements of the picture book form to our ultimate peril. Glamorous illustrations cannot be the salvation of a weak text — nor the other way around.

As a preface to historical time in picture books, here is a book that has been called the most beautiful picture book ever made. It is Boutet de Monvel's *Joan of Arc*, not only the masterpiece of this great often-imitated illustrator's successful career but a triumph at the turn of the century of French lithography. Slides cannot do justice to the immediacy of the clamor or battle, the magnificence of the patterned, textured clothing and the emotional impact of the tragedy of the martyred Joan.

So we come to the first book on my printed list. With *Obadiah* we have the simple past; the point of the story is the boy's friendship with the pigeon, not with the historical background, even though his Quaker setting is of importance. (It's of even more importance in the first story about this boy, *Obadiah the Bold*, because he wants to be a pirate, and his mother says, "But Quakers are never pirates!") For children, too, there are two pasts: our own, on which we instinctively draw to understand the immediate, confronting present; and the past of others gained from hearing or reading — in other words, personal and collective memory. Nevertheless, for children, in most cases, I think it's safe to say that the most important aspect of time in story is the straight sequential narrative; and that time is not a philosophical question but a matter of sheer duration. Children would, I think, agree with the king in *Alice*, who said gravely, "Begin at the beginning, and then go on till you come to the end; then stop." We must remember that the story itself signifies a progression that takes place over time -a process of unfolding. And there is a certain suspense in *Obadiah* in the unfolding of the action. Uri Shulevitz, artist and teacher,

From *Thy Friend, Obadiah*, by Brinton Turkle

actually claims, with a good deal of authority, that the action of a picture book follows linear continuity, preserving the natural time sequence of events without subplots or digressions or flashbacks or other retrospective devices. Thus, in the use of time patterns, here, then, is a major difference between the picture book and other fiction. But more about these time patterns later on, because daring and successful innovations have crept in, especially in picture books for somewhat older children.

With *On the Day Peter Stuyvesant Sailed into Town*, the historical background is crucial to the whole thing. This is not, strictly speaking, fiction at all, but a lovely humorous view of New York history and of a notoriously irascible man. Coming from Holland, Stuyvesant found the colony of New Amsterdam a perfect mess.

> The governor slipped in the mud and the mire
> And he said, "Things are not all well here.
> I am standing in garbage right up to my knees
> And the air has a very bad smell here."

Apart from this foreboding of a future time, the book actually ends with a prophetic dream. In Eleanor Cameron's *Court of the Stone Children*, Gil says, "Prophetic dreams and the curious working of time go together." Well, here we have it in reductio ad absurdam. the last verse of the book is:

> That night Peter Stuyvesant heard a strange sound
> Underneath a round moon brightly gleaming
> It swept past his door, a great tumble and roar
> But old Stuyvesant knew he was dreaming.

And then there's the last witty, wonder-filled, wordless page.

In *Lost and Found*, a settlement appears at various eras — from the Stone Age to the contemporary now — as one child after another is sent on an errand with an object to be given to a grandparent. An arrowhead lost by the first child is found in the Middle Ages by the second, who is carrying a jug of cream; centuries later, a boy finds the jug but loses a sixpence, which a contemporary girl finds as she takes a gift to her granny. "Place implies time," said Susan Cooper in her lecture. The very repetition here is comforting, reassuring,

in a picture book. We have layers of time here, the present in the future of the past, a circularity of time linking the present with time past, which are both present in time future — all familiar concepts to you by now but rarely found in picture books. And, incidentally, a unique example in picture books of Paul's accordion-squeezing, in the enormous time span. Penelope Lively's *A Stitch in Time* deals novelistically with the past penetrating the present, a book that centers on time, continuity, and memory. Maria thinks, "Places are like clocks. They've got all the time in them there's ever been, everything that's happened. They go on and on, with things that have happened hidden in them, if you can find them, like the fossils you find, if you break the rock." And in *The House in Norham Gardens*, Penelope Lively says, through Clare, "Places are very odd — the way they manage to be both now and then, both at once."

In Virginia Lee Burton's 1942 picture book, the little house sits through seasonal changes; anthropomorphic, she wonders about the light of the city and how it could be to live there. The scenery changes; time passes; sprawling developments come; then apartment buildings, then skyscrapers. She is nearly obscured; and the lights are so bright she can no longer see the stars. Eventually, of course, the great-great grandaughter of the man who built her so well comes and recognizes her; the little house is trundled away to the country once more. *The Little House* is another example of the accordion compression of time. A few years ago, the writer Ann Tyler wrote about this book in the New York Times, telling how she received it as a birthday present when she was four and how she has never stopped reading its rhythmic prose "with phrases repeated till they took on the inevitability of a melody." Let me excerpt some of what she wrote.

I believe the book spoke to me about something I hadn't yet consciously considered: the passage of time. And it introduced me to the feeling of nostalgia — the realization of the losses that the passage of time can bring ... Children begin as creatures of the moment. And doesn't growing up mean that dawning knowledge that all moments are joined, each moment linked inexorably to the one that follows? It's not that I hadn't yet experienced time. (Time passes so slowly for children, they experience it more than adults do.) But I'd experienced it unreflectively, and changes came as sudden jolts in my existence. So here was this story that spelled out for me all the successive stages ... Like a child, the little house has her periods of restlessness. And like a child, she finds even longed-for changes both exciting and saddening.

But the book is also about altering the pastoral environment — about the evils, and admittedly not about the necessity, of urban development. The book is a gentle ecological tour de force, coming long before we began to pound into young heads our guilt over our own destruction of the planet. But perhaps its non-strident accents can prepare the way for stronger meat to come. Is it ludicrously simplistic to be reminded here of Patricia Wrightson's Nargun, that stirring to life of a cold, primordial stonelike creature from the time of the creation of the world? "Sudden and savage came his cry"..."full of all time and darkness behind the stars," working his mischief on the people who ravage the land.

Here is a book, Cynthia Rylant's *When I Was Young in the Mountains*, in which personal memory simply and straightforwardly, with undeniable nostalgia, re-creates a vanished time, a vanished way of life. Again, here is the pastoral, back-to-nature yearning, slightly romanticized and linked to the movement of the 1960s. If it is a bit sweet, so are many memories of a serene childhood; it casts a golden light over the past. Beautifully illustrated by Diane Goode, the book is made of scraps torn from family history. As Eudora Welty observes, "the [human] memory is a living thing — it too is in transit. But during its moment, all that is remembered joins, and lives — the old and the young, the past and the present, the living and the dead."

My Noah's Ark makes very subtle use of time even though it is, on the surface, a long-remembered story, which centers on one specific object, and the telling goes back and forth between the child's experience and the woman's; thus, the use of time alternates between flashback and sequential time; each picture is a moment in a long span of implied time. It's all a reduction, a distillation of experience; there is little tension, yet the story

From *My Noah's Ark* by M.B. Goffstein

is not at all static. During the careful unfolding process in which only the absolute essential details are selected and shown, the character of the woman — seen only through her connection with the toy ark — is clearly revealed. The text is gentle, spare, understated, as Goffstein's texts always are; and with no dependence at all on color, the little masterpiece is actually an epigrammatic form of art and text.

Shirley Hughes played straight into my hands with one chapter of her new book *The Big Alfie and Annie Rose Storybook*. You recall that I mentioned a few minutes ago that at some point, young children begin to develop an appreciation of time as personal experience as well as linear movement. Here we have a lovely example. Of course, the retrospective part of the book is neither nostalgic nor romanticized — how could it be, from Shirley Hughes? No, it's perfectly straightforward family history told with an endearing honesty. Grandma comes to stay, bringing along a three-generational family photograph album. Moreover, Grandma is in this episode the main character — not relegated to the supporting cast. Time is stretched back and forth as Grandma tells the children the stories behind the photographs. Shirley Hughes has said that she thinks in pictures, and her books are thus like silent motion pictures.

In *Miss Rumphius*, a fictional biography unique in picture books, we find again, not the simple historical past but a linear tale ending contemporaneously. There isn't simply one incident or one phase of a life but the total significance of events over the course of time. Like her grandfather, the girl wants "to go to faraway places, and when I grow old, I too will live beside the sea." But he tells her that there is a third thing she must do — a folkloric element here. "You must do something to make the world more beautiful." So she grew up; she worked; she traveled; and when she grew old, she walked over the countryside, scattering lupin seeds and making the land lush with color. Each goal achieves fruition at a different time in her life — as in *Ecclesiastes*, "to everything there is a season, and a time to every purpose under heaven." And I must say that at seventy-two, Barbara Cooney has made, and continues to make, the children's book world more beautiful.

Mitsumasa Anno took everyone by surprise with the first of his *Journey* books; how he loves to mess about with time and place and present the reader with paradoxes! No time frame is even suggested, so in this marvellous, controlled jumble of time and allusion, there are no anachronisms. We see Europe's art, architecture, music and society in a disguised, unspecified past, with the solitary horseman riding serenely through countryside, village and town with references cunningly tucked away beneath the surface activity. In the slides we have glimpses of Beethoven composing, of Van Gogh's Bridge at Arles, and the Pied Piper taking the children away; we see Sancho Panza and Don Quixote with the huge windmill, while a modern tractor works in a field; and there is Robin Hood, along with Millet's painting "The Gleaners." And much, much more. *Anno's Journey* represents a combination of brilliant imagination and equally brilliant craftsmanship; the visual narrative isn't really fantasy, even though as pictured the journey is impossible. Alice (in *Through the Looking-Glass*,) said to the Queen, "One *can't* believe impossible things." "I daresay you haven't had much practice," said the Queen. "When I was your age, I always did it for half-an-hour a day. Why, sometimes I've believed as many as six impossible things before breakfast."

But now we *are* going to dip into fantasy, and we'll begin with *The Wreck of the Zephyr*. Narrated in flashback, the story is told by an old man — about a boy, proud of his extraordinary skill, who defiantly takes his craft out in a fierce storm and is knocked unconscious. Now, in a secondary world full of realistic details, the boy witnesses boats riding wondrously — not upon the water, but above it, and insists that he is capable of learning the magic art of navigating through air. In the dark of the night, propelled as much by his hubris as by a fair wind, he does manage to glide across the sky — but then the wind shifts and the boat crashes to the ground. Here is the wonderful ambiguity of illusion and reality; here, too, is the severe logic that fantasy must be built upon; there is irony in the ending and the revelation that time — a lifetime — has passed, but no feeling of improbability, no lack of credibility. No pun intended, but this is no mere flight of fancy; the fantasy has the clarity, solidity, and force of the paintings.

A remarkable book not on your list is *One Monday Morning* by Uri Shulevitz. Taking his idea from an old French song, in which a king, a queen and a little prince come to visit a little boy, day after day, never finding him at home, Shulevitz realized that as a story, it would be both boring and frustrating; so he cleverly added a new character every day, thus making it a cumulative tale, which young children love, and ending the whole thing successfully on the Sunday. Calendar time — the days of the week — is the frame for all the delightful imaginings: "On Tuesday morning, the King, the Queen, the little prince and the knight all came to visit me, but I wasn't home". The primary realm of the story is a dreary street of tenement houses, and to deepen the gloom, the story opens on a rainy Monday, but drab reality follows the days into

From *Come Away from the Water, Shirley*

a secondary world of the imagination, as the size and bright color of the royal retinue blot out the dull background. And of course the sun is shining at the end. Incidentally, the book is a superb example of the way a true picture book relies on pictorial material to describe what might otherwise have to be put into words; time, especially is *shown* rather than *stated*, and the perfect balance between artwork and text is achieved here with a kind of childlike grace.

Maurice Sendak's statement was quoted by someone earlier: "We don't remember childhood, we discover it." And if Sendak was a pioneer in directing his sensitivity to an exploration of the often painful inner life of the child in picture books, he is also the great innovator, the touchstone by whom future creators of children's books will be judged — this man who claims not to write for children but to have "a passionate affiliation with childhood." Confining my comments to the aspects of time in the psychic experiences of *Wild Things*, I need only point out that his carefully honed text, which I think he said he worked on for three years, tells us that

the forest grew and grew and grew in his room until his

ceiling hung with vines and the walls became the world all around and an ocean tumbled by with a private boat for Max and he sailed off through night and day and in and out of weeks and almost over a year to where the wild things are.

As you know, the wild rumpus is wholly conveyed with full-page pictures — no margins, no text — a brilliant interlude. And when the odyssey is done in reverse, he

sailed back over a year and in and out of weeks and through a day and into the night of his very own room.

And as every perceptive child knows, the supper was still hot despite the fact that the moon, its phases altered, is ample evidence that time has mysteriously passed. In fact, the encapsulation of time harks back to an aspect of it in folklore — Max is gone only briefly in earthly time, but in psychological time it's almost a year.

If *Wild Things* was a breakthrough in presenting psychological time in a picture book, *Come Away from the Water, Shirley* carries the process a step further in its daring use of synchronicity. The contrast of the facing pages: outer clock time versus inner time; parents' spoken thoughts versus the girl's unspoken thoughts; an uneventful, restful day at the beach for the parents, a fantastic private adventure for the girl. The dual portrayal of time is a stroke of genius, as it shows co-existent layers through which the characters of the fantasy can simultaneously experience more than one time. With Shirley's inscrutable face, who can really tell? The book represents the high point of sophistication and challenge in all our picture books today. And I suppose it could well prove to be an opening wedge into children's fiction that demands more maturity, more conceptual development, more understanding — like Margaret Mahy's *The Haunting* or *Tuck Everlasting*, and eventually on to sterner stuff. I am reminded of something Henry James once said:

Small children have many more perceptions than they have terms to translate them; their vision is at any moment much richer, their apprehension even constantly stronger, than their prompt, their at all producible vocabulary.

Elaine Moss, who was working in an Inner London school at the time the book was new, tried it out with groups of children aged five to eleven. Some of the children never jumped over the book's gutter at all, while some of them loved the story and compared it with *Peter Pan*! Many of them were intrigued with the clues: Shirley never appears on any left-hand page, but "she must have been there, or her mum and dad wouldn't have kept talkin' to her, would they?" In both this book and Sendak's *Wild Things* one actually sees the framework of the basic hero story — the hero leaves home, conquers obstacles or undertakes a quest, and then returns home.

In *Sylvester and the Magic Pebble* we see again the folkloric year — barrier time, if you will, because it's only when the wish is duplicated that poor Sylvester can be released from his cold, stony enchantment. And we know that time passes; if Steig merely said that Sylvester was returned to his parents in about a year, the reader would have no sense of the passing of time; but even through words are not the same as clock time, the reader has enough hints to convey the *feeling* of time passing: his mother weeps, they all look for him, they ask their neighbors, they go to the

From *Sylvester and the Magic Pebble*

police. And "night followed day and day followed night over and over again."

"The seasons change, and finally one warm spring day, the sorrowing parents decide to have a picnic in the country."

Both Russell Hoban's *The Rain Door* and Charles Keeping's *Willie's Fire Engine* represent a transition between two worlds — a bit like John Townsend's slippery time, even though the stories take place within a single day. One stifling hot day Harry follows the old rag-and-bone man and gets through the magic rain door to the junkyard where he keeps his cloud-catching water tank. But the old man is threatened by a lion, so Harry builds a crazy contraption — to scare off the lion (Thunder) so that the horse, naturally called Lightning, can get on with his work. The contraption is build of bones and rags and iron and rope, wire and rusty bolts, gears and wheels and mainsprings, and a horn that shouts, "GAHOOGA!" The illustrator, of course is Quentin Blake.

From a mood of total zaniness, we consider *Willie's Fire Engine*, in which a quiet, yearning little boy is transported through dream from sordid existence into fairy tale hero. I have found that Americans are a bit terrified of Charles Keeping's picture books — brave, original stories and brave, expressionist artwork; many of them were not even published in the United States. He portrayed the drab world of the disadvantaged child, and although the books require rather intense concentration, they interest the older child for their implicit commentary on human issues and dreams. Very different from *One Monday Morning*, this is also a story about the contrast between grim streets and the warmth of romantic fantasy; this, however, is definitely dream time — far different from clock time. As you see, Keeping has always used color as a device for regulating the emotional level of the proceedings.

Professor Noah's Spaceship is pure fantasy, the only picture book here that verges on science fiction — complete with hardware — a story of the future firmly tied to the past. It's the Noah story, cleverly updated with a strong ecological twist. Wildsmith, never a writer, has done a rather prosaic tale based on a thoroughly intriguing idea. The earth is a mess; animal life in grave peril. They observe a huge, wondrous object under construction and find it's Professor Noah's, as he prepares to leave this polluted planet for a better world. As in Genesis, they travel for forty days and forty nights, but in mid-voyage their time-zone guidance system goes askew, and event-ually the dove, sent to reconnoiter, discovers that they have traveled backward through time to the Earth "as it was in the beginning." The slight didacticism is mitigated by the delightful ironic comment at the end. The otter says, "'How lovely it all is; thank goodness for all the rain; there seems to have been some flooding here.'"

Eleanor Cameron, deeply preoccupied with time, prefaced her book of essays with Isaac Singer's words from "Zlateh the Goat."

Literature helps us remember the past with its many moods. To the storyteller, yesterday is still here, as are the years and decades gone by. In stories time does not vanish. For the writer and his readers all creatures go on living forever.'"

Yet I have an additional concern. Aren't we all losing our freshness of vision? We are daily surrounded by a manmade environment of buildings, the vulgarity of advertising and television, packaged goods and tawdry books that lack visual integrity, that are fake and degrading. Such an environment injures us all — children and adults — injures our intellects, our emotions and our sensibilities, which form the basis of our creative powers. But overarching even this idea are the words of Gabriela Mistral, the Nobel-Prize-winning poet of Chile, who has said,

We are guilty of many errors and many faults, but our worst crime is abandoning the children, neglecting the fountain of life. The child cannot wait. Right now is the time his bones are being formed...and his senses are being developed. To him we cannot answer 'Tomorrow'. His name is Today.'"

ROSEMARY SUTCLIFF

History and time

I SUPPOSE WE ALL know that if we go back to the earliest people — lacking all known history, all written records, any kind of calendar, any fixed points to hang memory on — awareness of time must have been so vague that they had very definite need to spill blood into the earth at seed time to bring about the harvest, light great fires at the dark of the year to give strength to the sun and bring life back to the world, because they had no guarantee that without their help any of these things would happen. That would be the state of things until, as a few thousand years went by, wise men took to looking at the skies, and the first calendars - Stonehenge may have been one of them, though not nearly the earliest - came into being. Then of course the whole thing became gradually more formalized and, if not brought under control, at any rate brought to a state where it was possible to think about it, both forward and backward, visualize it and give it symbolic shapes.

According to the theologian O. Culmann in his book *Christ and Time* the symbol of time for primitive Christianity as well as for Biblical Judaism is the upward sloping line, while for Hellenism it is the circle. (In many ancient faiths the snake swallowing its own tail is the symbol of Eternity)

This belief in the cyclical nature of the Universe was based on the concept of the Great Year, which has two distinct interpretations: on one hand it is simply the period needed for sun, moon and planets to get back to exactly the same relative positions as they had held before, in some specific earlier point in time. On the other hand it signified the whole life span of the world from its formation to its destruction and rebirth.

The two interpretations were combined in late antiquity by the Stoics, who believed that when the heavenly bodies returned at fixed intervals of time to the positions they had held at the beginning of the world, everything would return to being exactly as it was in the beginning, and the entire cycle would repeat itself again in every detail. Nemesius, a fourth-century Bishop of Emasa, put it later:

'Socrates and Plato and each individual man will live again with the same friends and fellow citizens. Every city and village and field will be restored just as it was, and this restoration of the universe takes place not once but over and over again. Indeed to eternity without end.'

I think he must have been writing about this as someone else's belief, not as his own, unless of course he was some kind of heretic. Around five hundred years earlier, Virgil said the same thing, but more poetically: 'Now is come the last age of the song of Cumae; the great line of the centuries begins anew... a second Typhis shall then arise, and a second Argo to carry heroes; and again shall great Achilles be sent to Troy.'

Which brings us rather nicely to Homer and the historians and storytellers. Though Homer dealt with allegedly historical subjects, his history was of the 'aristocratic' kind, which is in fact hero myth with maybe a seed of history somewhere in the midst of it. It involves no chronology, no real sense of the passage of time. Despite Odysseus's twenty-year absence, neither he nor Penelope seem any older when he finally gets home. Only poor Argos, the dog. The Apple of Discord, which starts the Trojan war, is thrown down among the guests at the wedding feast of Achilles' parents; the judgement of Paris, the abduction of Helen and the outbreak of the war all follow each other without pause, but by the time the black ships sail for Troy, Achilles, who according to our ideas of time-lapse can't have been *much* more than a twinkle in his father's eye, is a grown warrior. And to confuse the issue still further, seems, before the end of the ten-year siege, to have sons also of fighting age. (I speak of this from bitter experience, being in the midst of trying to produce a retelling of the Siege of Troy for eight to ten-year-olds). For Homer it clearly made no difference that year follows year.

By the time of Herodotus and Thucydides, history had ceased to be a matter of isolated episodes covering the lives and deeds of heroes, and began to depend on continuity of events, institutions, laws. The passage of time had become more relevant. But even so, Herodotus still had much of the minstrel about him and can always be relied on to abandon fact in favor of a good story or even a juicy piece of gossip, whereas Thucydides, a perfectionist with a dry historian's mind, aware of the smoky splendors and general vagueness behind him if he looked back, considered that serious history could be concerned only with the present or the most immediate past, because anything beyond that was in the very nature of things thoroughly unreliable.

But to go back to the Christians and the straight ascending line. For the early Christians the Crucifixion was a unique event. It was not subject to repetition, and so for them time had to be linear and not cyclic. This essentially historical view of time with its emphasis on 'Once and for Always' is the very essence of Christianity, and this is brought out clearly in St. Paul's Epistle to the Hebrews:

'...nor yet that he should offer himself often, as the High Priest entereth into the Holy Place every year with the blood of others; for then must he often have suffered since the foundation of the world. But now once in the end of the world hath he appeared to put away sin by the sacrifice of himself.'

The end of the world was not of course quite so near as St. Paul and the early Christian Church expected. But for men who believed what was in that Epistle there could be no way but straight ahead; and for us, following that teaching, time has been a straight line leading from way behind us to way in front, ever since.

Nevertheless, one of the greatest historical philosophers in the eighteenth century, Giovanibattista Vico, professor of rhetoric in the University of Naples, believed in historic cycles. He interpreted the concept in a more sophisticated way than previous believers had done. He maintained that certain periods of history had a general basic nature which reappeared in certain other periods, so that it was possible to argue by analogy from one such period to another. He drew a parallel between the barbarism of the Christian early Middle Ages in Western Europe and the barbarism of the Homeric Age, pointing out certain common features, such as rule by a warrior aristocracy, a ballad literature (our own Celtic, Bronze and Iron Ages fit in with that), and he called such periods 'Heroic'. He did not think that history is strictly circular, because new things are always being created, and therefore the whole process must move slowly forward. As R.G. Collingwood puts it: 'Not a circle but a spiral; for history never repeats itself, but comes round in each new phase in a form made different by what has gone before. The barbarism of the Western Middle Ages is different from that of Homeric Greece through the influence of Christianity (an influence which doesn't seem to have gentled it much, actually, when one thinks of the brutalities of the Crusades). Vico thought, however, that similar periods tended to reappear in the same order; a Heroic period always followed by what he called a Classical Period, in which thought prevailed over imagination, prose over poetry... I know this works for Homeric Greece. I'm not so sure about the Middle Ages. I can't find a classical period for them until the eighteenth century, which seems to leave rather a lot between.

Vico also believed that 'man is a being who can only be understood historically'. In other words, knowledge of our past is vital to our understanding of ourselves — which makes him a man after my own heart.

Many years ago, when I was sure of myself as only someone scarcely out of their apprenticeship can be, I was talking to an audience of school teachers in the Midlands that are sodden and unkind, when a County Inspector of Education stood up and asked me what was my justification for writing historical novels, which he clearly considered a bastard form, instead of leaving the job to legitimate historians who knew what they were talking about. I looked him straight in the eye and said 'Historians and teachers, you and your kind, can produce the bare bones, all in their right order, but still bare bones; I and my kind can breathe life into them. And history is not bare bones alone, it's a living process.' Looking back I'm rather shaken at my hardihood, but I still think I was right.

There are of course two views of history, the Man's-eye view and the God's-eye view. It is because history books for the young must of necessity take the God's eye view that they can so often and so easily become dull; that, and because they so often break their subject up into small static pictures, each as it were separately framed by the reigns of successive monarchs, instead of treating it as a living and continuous process of which we are part, and of which our descendants, always supposing that we have not blown the world up or destroyed the ozone layer by then, will be a part also. It is enormously important that the young should be given this sense of continuity, of their roots behind them. Because to know and really understand something of where we came from, as Giovanibattista Vico would have agreed, can play a big part in helping us to understand and cope with where we are now and where we are going. All of us, in our own particular stretch of history, stand too close up to be able to follow the whole pattern, and we never know how the story ends, and this is especially true of us today, because we seem to have come to one of Vico's patches which, the last time round, covered the end of the Roman Empire and, if he was right, then the next stage should be the Dark Ages. You couldn't really call St. Dunstan and the glories of Wessex 'The Dark', but the Romans could not know about that. We can hope that we are not going irrevocably into the Dark, but we can't know. We can't know if there is a St. Dunstan or a

Wessex for us; we are in exactly the same boat as the Romans sixteen or seventeen hundred years ago.

That is why children can surely get a truer picture of the past if something that breathes life into the bare bones is given to them over and above the factual side of history. They need the Man's eye view as well as the God's eye view of the past; and that means us, the tellers of tales, the historical novelist. *Not*, I hasten to say, the dealers in Historical Romance, which is quite another matter.

The young have a strong feeling for the primitive and fundamental things of life. That is why myths and legends certainly not meant for children in the first place have been largely taken over by them. It is one reason why children enjoy Westerns, even in these days of science fiction; one reason, come to that, why I enjoy them too. I used to think that there was something shameful in enjoying Westerns once one was past the age of running around with two fingers stuck out, shouting 'Bang, bang, you're dead!'. But then it dawned on me that they are or were the Hero Myths of the Middle West. They seem to come from an earlier, rougher and more splendid time — Homer might not have scorned them — they have all the elements of Heroic Myth; outsize characters, big basic themes — love and hate, comradeship between men, loyalty and divided loyalty, treachery, revenge for slain kinsfolk; the age-old struggle between light and dark, in which the Hero, standing for light, though sometimes of a rather murky kind, always wins, but sometimes at the cost of his own life; the deep sense of ritual, especially the ritual of death. We all know 'High Noon' and all those other walks through empty towns, footsteps echoing in heat-drenched silence, or doom-laden pulse-beat of accompanying music as tension mounts; the hands held carefully away from the six-shooter still in its holster; the Goodies wearing white hats and the Baddies black — that bit of ritual almost as rigidly adhered to as the fact that in Pantomime the Demon King always enters from the left of the stage and the Fairy Godmother from the right.

Myths and Legends, Westerns, my sort of

historical novel, are all alike in dealing with these big basic themes, though in somewhat different ways. As I said, the instinct for this is strong in children. In most adults it has been pushed down, sometimes only a little way, sometimes almost entirely, into the subconscious. But it's always *there*, in the same place as the Australian Aboriginal keeps his dreamtime, in tribal memory and race memory; and it still needs feeding and watering, because without it the soul of man is not quite complete.

So — there is my right to tell my own kind of historical stories. I can't play with time, making intricate patterns of it; I can't handle time slips; I could never have written *Red Shift* or *A Traveller in Time* or *Tom's Midnight Garden*. For me, writing a historical novel entails a one-way trip backwards into some particular point in time and space, and once there bringing it to life as convincingly as possible. The question then arises 'How is it done?' I can't do it from the outside, looking backward, only by making the trip myself, and a very lonely trip it can be, and soaking myself in time and place so that I can tell the story from the inside looking out, through the eyes of people who don't know the outcome of the battle being fought at Hastings over the Downs this afternoon. That is what makes a child write and say, 'It makes me feel as though I was there'.

At one time when I was doing quite a lot of talking for schools, I used to start off by saying to my audience, 'Now I want you to shut your eyes and do some strong imagining for me.

'Those of you who want to be a boy: you are a young Roman soldier on sentry duty on Hadrian's Wall. You're marching slowly up and down the rampart walk, keeping a sharp eye open to the north, because it's always from the north that trouble comes. It came last week — cattle raiders. That was your first taste of action, and you have a gash in your sword-arm to show for it; it's half-healed now, and it itches in the way that healing cuts very often do. The mizzle rain blows in your face, and the watch seems a very long one but you're going to a cockfight in the fortress

ditch later on tonight, and that cheers you up.

'Those of you who want to be a girl needn't go so far back, only as far as London in the Middle Ages. You're a merchant's daughter, and twelve or thirteen years old, and your father has arranged for you to marry another merchant, maybe ten years older than you are. He has gone abroad on business, and you have just had a letter from him and you're excited and pleased because, although your father chose him for you, you do rather like him. You're reading your letter in a patch of sunlight in a room over the warehouse — people mostly lived over the shop or the business in those days — and there's a clove pink in a Venetian glass on the table, its shadow falling across the page, and outside a man wheeling a handcart piled with cabbages pulls to one side while a company of men-at-arms goes jingling by.'

Then after a suitable pause 'All right, come back to here and now.

'Those two were real people. The soldier was a Syrian by birth, he served many years in Britain, married a British girl and settled down, and we have his name, Barates, on a tombstone. 'The merchant's daughter was called Catherine, and the letter still exists. It's a nice letter, gentle, humorous, one can almost see the young merchant smiling to himself as he writes it in an inn chamber by candlelight: 'Grow up as quickly as you can, so that we can be married. Go to my horse and ask him for three of his years, and I will pay them back to him again from my own, with a horse-cake by way of interest, when I come home.''

That usually got the audience tuned in, and in a state of mind to listen to me without too much shuffling.

I do much the same kind of thing on my own account when finding my way into the book of the moment. But of course in that case there are a good few other things to be dealt with first, because it's no good doing too much soaking oneself in time and place without first making reasonably sure that one has got time and place right — well, as right as one can. And that means research, and a lot of it.

But let me make one thing clear: I never start off with the research; I mean I never decide in cool blood that it would be interesting to set the next book in a particular time and place and then start to read up about it. First has to come the Basic Idea, and it is no good my going in search of the Idea, it has to come looking for me. Sometimes it comes from outside, from something read or seen or experienced, once from a little privately published handbook on the Lake District turned out by a friend in spring - cleaning his attic, once from seeing in an Athens museum a dagger with lily flowers inlaid on the blade. Sometimes it comes from inside, like the thought out of nowhere which I had one morning while making toast. 'Yes, but when the Romans were withdrawn from Britain they had been here four hundred years. They had settled and intermarried. Some of them would be virtually British, others would have at the very least a British grandmother. Some of them must have gone wilfully missing to remain in Britain when the galleys sailed.' It was a really dazzling thought, and while its further possibilities were dawning on me I burned the toast; but it resulted in *The Lantern Bearers*.

From the Basic Idea springs the theme; not yet the plot. I'm not terribly good at plots any-way, and tend to have themes instead. At this point I buy a large red exercise book — it has to be red, that's a kind of personal ritual of my own — and start on research. First of all the historical background. At this stage I am dealing with the history of facts, or supposed facts. Theme and plot, if any, often develop with the history in a process somewhat like weaving; and by this stage I am beginning to feel my way into time and place and get the feel of it, the smell of it.

There are two kinds of Truth, the Truth of Fact and the Truth of the Spirit; and it is possible to be meticulous about fact and yet catch no atmosphere of the period at all. Sometimes there's a gap in known facts which can only be filled by the Truth of the Spirit. This of course is dangerous because it can become only invention, and the only possible test is 'Does it smell right?' If it does, then it's

probably the best one can do. Into the red exercise book also go details of daily life. What houses do my people live in, what food do they eat, what weapons do they carry, what songs do they sing? How do they make their marriages? How do they bury their dead?

Details of place, too; the actual lie of the land, flora and fauna, weather and atmospherics, marks of human occupation, taking care that nothing from a later period than the story gets in by mistake.

Details of the people of the story, both historical and fictional, who are now beginning to emerge from the background, their looks and characters and previous history, anything and everything that can help to conjure them into real people with back views as well as front ones, not just cardboard cut-outs wearing Olde Worlde costumes.

Some people believe that human beings change fundamentally as time goes by. I don't - or only on the surface. The men of the first Elizabeth's reign thought no shame to cry in public if they felt like it; the men of my youth had been so trained to think it *not done* that by the time they were sixteen most of them couldn't cry at all except with great pain and difficulty for, say, the death of a wife or a dog. But that doesn't mean that the capacity for grief is any different. I have seen an Etruscan tomb with the figures of a man and a woman lying very calmly on top of it that makes nonsense of the idea that the Ancients did not know love between men and women in the way that we know it. One has to be careful about the samenesses and the differences, all the same.

Usually the book has become urgent and I have started to write it well before the research is finished; and it is at this point that my people and their world really start to develop. All their particulars in the red exercise book are really only blueprint, only theory. I know what somebody looks like; I know that he has blue eyes and speaks with a slight stammer, because I have decreed that he should, nothing to do with him at all. But once the writing starts, he begins to take on a life of his own, and he goes on doing it until the time comes when, if I make him do something out of character, I know it instantly as one knows it of a friend in whose company one has passed a good deal of time. 'I don't believe he would have done that, said that, reacted in that way.' Then I have to set to work to discover how he would in fact have reacted, what choice he would have made. And if that doesn't fit with the story, that's just too bad, adjustments will have to be made. By this stage also of course there is the chance that he will do his own thing when really I wanted him to do something quite different.

By the time the book is finished, I have lived with the characters in it for maybe a year of my time, maybe a year or two or twenty years of theirs, and I feel oddly bereft. But with any luck the Basic Idea of the next book is already with me. If it isn't, I am not at all happy until it arrives, not only for my next supply of bread-and-butter, but also because without a book on the stocks I suffer from a sense of being cut off from some kind of supply line; a sort of loneliness - or rather, aloneness.

At the risk of repeating myself: I spoke a while back of the importance of giving children a sense of continuity in time and history, and some awareness of their roots behind them, to help them understand where they came from and where they are going to. This I think was first given to me by the books my mother read to me when I was a child, and it has mattered deeply and potently to me ever since. And so in the natural way of things I have, over the years, woven a sort of web that here and there runs from one book to another, so that the continuity does not break between book and book. I don't decide on these spider-threads in advance and drag them here and there in any arbitrary way; I simply allow them to grow naturally and surface where they will, and wherever and whenever they surface, I am pleased to see them as one is pleased to see a familiar face one had not particularly expected to see.

Continuity is a very comforting and reassuring thing, in a sense which goes beyond the personal, and far beyond our normal usage of those words — the sense in which the First

World War poets must have been aware of it in the certainty that if they were blown up tomorrow Spring would still come back to the places that they loved, and there would, probably, be honey still for tea.

It's the 'Life Goes On' thing.

I hope you won't think that I'm being ego-centric and over-pleased with myself if I round all this off by reading you a couple of extracts from my own books at points where the spider's threads surface and which give me pleasure as though I had had nothing to do with spinning them myself.

The first is in *Frontier Wolf* set in the mid-fourth century and centering on a Roman frontier post:

Just where the track dipped to the paved ford below the pony's watering pool a tall stone stood up, leaning a little, in the wayside grass. Dark, smooth, with somehow the look about it of having passed through fire; the look too of being very old, older than anything else in that country-side. As they trotted by, Gavrus leaned from his saddle and lightly touched the smooth-worn crest in passing; and Alexion, glancing round for another view of the thing, saw the leader of the escort echo the gesture, and the men behind him... 'Another custom of the Pack, he supposed, and clearly one that you did not ask about. Oh well, there'd be time for finding out about such things later. Too much time maybe. So much time that childish things became important because they helped to fill it up a little. A small cold shiver took him between the shoulders, the kind of shiver out of nowhere that makes men laugh and say that a grey goose is flying over their graves."

And then later in the story:

Alexion, reaching aside by long custom to touch the Lady in passing, felt the stone rain-wet and heart-cold and curiously empty, and knew, though he instantly denied the knowledge in himself, that the Romans would not come back."

The book I have just finished, which is with Bodley Head now, is woven into *The Gododdin*, the seventh century epic of a kamikaze style raid by a company of post-Roman British warriors on a Saxon war host gathering at what is now Catterick Bridge. In the course of training for this raid three of them are holing up in the ruins of the same fort around two hundred and fifty years later, and it seemed obvious that there must be some mention of the stone which Alexion's troopers had called the Lady. So:

We went down to the burn that ran through its steep

gorge below the western rampart, and drank and filled the leather bottle where the water ran clear and deep above the remains of a paved ford. There was an upright stone, I mind, marking the place where an old track from the fort must have entered the water, heading westward; a black stone, dappled with grey and golden lichen. I set my hand on its rounded poll, and got the odd uncanny feel that it was used to the touch of men's hands in passing. But that must have been long and long ago.

One more, drawn from *Knight's Fee*. Early Norman, sited in the Down country near my home; but it concerns also *Warrior Scarlet*, set in the same countryside but in the Bronze Age, and telling the story of a boy with a withered right arm. A few years after writing *Warrior Scarlet*, I came across the mention in an old book of a flint celt that had been dug up on my stretch of the Downs. A tool or weapon shaped something like an axehead to be held in the hand without any haft. They're not uncommon, but this one was special, being shaped for use in the left hand. Obviously it was Drem's, my Bronze Age boy's. It was too late to give it to him in his own book, but I had to get it to him somehow; so I gave it to him in retrospect through *Knight's Fee* which I was writing then.

Two boys, one Norman, one Saxon, up from the valley farm of Dean in the lambing season, to spend a night with the shepherd kind on the High Downs:

They huddled close, for the wind seeped through the hurdles for all the lacing of furze branches. Ship and White Eye and Joyeuse lying nose-on-paws among their feet. Randal sat with his hunched shoulder leaning against Bevis who leaned companionably back, and stared a little sleepily into the fire, where a red hollow like the gaping mouth of a dragon had opened under the crackling thorn branches, and listened to the soft hush of the wind across the thatch. "And all the time the wind blows over" he thought "Ancret's people, and the Saxons, and Harold dead at Hastings over yonder, and now the Normans; and all the while the wind blowing over the Downs, just the same." Half asleep as he was, he was suddenly aware of the new life in the lambing pens, the constant watchful coming and going of shepherds and dogs and lanterns, as something not just happening now, but reaching back and back, and forward and forward, into the very roots of things that were beyond time.

Something of the same mood must have been upon Lewin also, for when he had brought out the meal bag and tipped barley meal into the birchwood bowl, thrusting away the dogs' soft, expectant muzzles, he rose - but he could not stand upright in the little bothy - rooted in the willow basket hanging from the roof, in which he kept his few personal belongings, and brought out something wrapped in a rag of yellow cloth.

"I'll show you a thing," he said to Randal, "sitting here at nights I've had it in my heart to show you, a good while past. Showed it to the young master when he stood no higher than my belt." And as Randal looked up expectantly from the fire, and Bevis watched with the interest alight in his thin eager face, he unfolded the yellow rag and put into the boy's hand a thing not unlike a double axehead made from flint, mealy grey.and tawny with the outer weathering that flint gathers through the years. An axehead, but with no hole to take the haft, nor any flanges for binding it on.

Without quite knowing why he did so, for he was not left handed, Randal put out his left hand for it, and felt his fingers close over it as something infinitely familiar. But he had never seen such an object before.

"What is it?" he demanded.

"What it is called, I do not know, but with such things it is in my mind that men fought the wolf-kind, and maybe each other, very long ago. I have seen others turned up on the Downs, but never one to equal that one. I found it up on Long Down years ago, and kept it, because it was made for a left-handed man even as I."

Randal shifted it to his right hand, and found that it was true. One could use it perfectly well with the right hand, but it did not lie there happily, as in the left.

"Left handed, or one handed." He did not know what made him say that. He leaned forward, looking at it in the light of the fire - and then, maybe because of the strange mood he was in, maybe because he was half asleep, maybe because of that dark thread of the Old Blood that Ancret had recognized, running in his veins, an odd thing happened. Once, in the outer bailey at Arundel, he had watched spell-bound while a wonder-worker who made live pigeons come out of an empty basket, had made a striped pebble picked up from the dirt where the fowls were scratching, grow in his hand without any visible change, into a yellow iris flower. He could see now the shimmering silken fall of the petals, the dark hair-fine intricacy of the veining that sprang from the slender throat, the sheer singing strength of the color. And as the pebble had become a flower, so the thing he held was suddenly warm as though fresh from the knapper's hand ,and the outer crust of the centuries all gone like a little dust, leaving the beautiful dark blue flint in all its newness. It was as though the thing flowered between his hands. He had an extraordinary sense of kinship with the unknown man who had first closed his fingers over that strange weapon, who had perhaps seen the wolves leaping about the lambing folds, as he, Randal, had almost seen them for an instant tonight; an extraordinary feeling of oneness with Dean, of some living bond running back through the blue, living flint, making him part of other men and sheep and wolves, and they a part of him.

KATHERINE PATERSON

The time of my life

WHEN I HEARD that the Institute was going to be about time, the first thing that came to my mind was a verse from an Isaac Watts hymn:

Time, like an ever rolling stream,
Bears all its sons away;
They fly forgotten, as a dream
Dies at the opening day.

Pretty depressing stuff, eh?

Of course, to take one verse out of Watts is something like taking one verse out of the Bible. The hymn is not primarily about the transient quality of human life, it is about the eternal nature of the Creator. If you know the hymn, you know the other verses and you know as well that it is a paraphrase of Psalm 90, the opening verse of which reads: "Lord, thou has been our dwelling place in all generations." In other words, it is a hymn of trust in the Eternal. But when you get right down to it, on the daily basis upon which our lives are lived out, most of us Congregationalists or Presbyterians or members of the Cambridge Punting Club are much more concerned about time than we are about eternity. We're more interested in the meaning of our own lives in time as we measure it on this tiny planet than we are in the mystery of space/time relativity in the universe. "We bring our years to an end," the Psalmist says later in Psalm 90, "we bring our years to an end as a tale that is told." That is the time we're most concerned with — the time in which our own little tale is told.

When Bruno Bettelheim received the National Book Award for *The Uses of Enchantment*, he cast his acceptance speech in the form of a fairy tale. Beginning with "Once upon a time" and telling of the little boy born to the anxious and eager couple in the old country and of his trials when there arose in that a land a cruel and wicked tyrant and of his escape from the tyrant, finding at last a new land across the sea where he lived happily ever after.

Now most of us would not cast our own lives in the form of a fairy tale. Comedy, tragedy, soap opera, perhaps, but not a fairy tale. Still I suspect all of us want to find some coherence in the story of our lives. We love to tell stories which seem to supply that coherence — that seem to say that life is not meaningless, that it has, if not a plot, at least a certain significance. We want to know that, in the vast harmony of the spheres, our little, often incomprehensible lives have sounded a few clear notes that someone else heard.

A psychotherapist that I met recently (perhaps I should insert socially rather than professionally) said that he thought that each of us early on in our lives asks ourselves a question and then proceeds to live out our lives in accordance to the answer we give that basic question.

He gave the example of a man who had been the child of British civil servants in India. India was not thought to be a healthy climate for European babies, so his mother had come to England before his birth, and then when he was six months old, had left him in the care of relatives and returned to India to be with her husband.

Now this man had asked himself the question 'Why did my mother abandon me?'

And the tiny child had said to himself, 'My mother left me because I was bad. I must be perfect, or people I care about and depend on will leave me.' It took him sixty years to realize how much his answer to the riddle of his infancy had damaged his life. But he clung to it because it gave his life meaning, and any meaning, even a negative one, is better than no meaning at all. We are desperate, most of us, that our lives not be simply born away in that ever-rolling stream of time. We want to know that once, once upon a certain time, I lived, and my life mattered. We want our once upon a time to be coherent and meaningful to ourselves and to other people.

So we turn to stories, for stories seem to halt that rolling river. Stories have a shape. They have a beginning that moves meaningfully step by step with cause and effect through time to a consummation, an ending, that makes sense in the light of all that comes before. In a properly told story when you get to the ending you recognize it because it was all there in the beginning, you just didn't know enough then to see it.

The fantasy of fiction is that the writer can interrupt the ever rolling stream of time and give it shape and meaning. Indeed, for the storyteller, time is not so much a stream as a line from which the writer can pluck out a segment and invest it with form and purpose.

This is what we do all the time with memory. We are constantly shaping and reshaping the stories of our own lives. We take it for granted, and we are arrogant enough to fight with our brothers and sisters about whose account of the past is the "true" one, when each of us has made a fiction of the facts, if indeed there ever were any facts to begin with. Yet, however subjective and faulty, however mixed of reality and dreams, memory is the stuff from which we fashion the stories of our lives.

Last fall there was a program on Vermont Educational Television on the human mind, entitled "The Search for Mind." Everybody knows what a brain is, but no one quite knows what the mind is. "The mind is what the brain does," said the narrator, conceding immediately that he had solved none of the mysteries of the mind by that sentence.

And the human mind is a mystery. It cannot be reduced simply to brain cells, chemical reactions, or electrical impulses. The most moving episode on the program dealt with the British musician Clive Wearing. A few years ago this outstanding young artist and director was struck by a strange inflammation of his brain that virtually destroyed his memory. "It's as though he's wearing blinkers," his wife said. "Every moment is an awakening into consciousness." Wearing can't make the connections that every child takes for granted. The imaging of the past and the future with which each one of us composes the narratives of our own lives is not possible for him. He writes constantly in his diary trying to preserve a fleeting moment, but the next moment he will wonder how those words in what seems to be his handwriting got on that page, or indeed where the diary itself came from.

His intellect otherwise is not impaired, which makes his condition even more tragic, and he is often deeply depressed. Yet there are two elements of his former rich life that despite his cruel situation have not deserted him. The first is his love for his wife. Every time he sees her, which may be five minutes since he last saw her, he throws his arms around her and greets her with great joy, welcoming her back into his life as though she has been gone for years. In his strange diary he writes on nearly every page "I love Debby for ever and ever." Even though for Clive Wearing there is no ever.

And the second element of his past life that mysteriously remains is his music. We watch as his wife takes him into a room where there is a piano and a small group of singers. At first he seems confused. He says he doesn't know how to play, but his wife gently urges him to try. He strikes a chord, the singers begin and immediately the face of Clive Wearing is transformed as he sings and directs Mozart's "Ave Verum Corpus."

Somehow love and music have survived his ravaged brain. No one can explain why this can be so when his memory seems otherwise to have been destroyed — when he seems unable otherwise to make connections between past and present and future. But somehow this miraculous survival in his mind and heart of love and music deepens the tragedy of his life, which is that he has no story.

But it also makes us marvel at the basic properties of that which we call mind. In Clive Wearing's damaged brain a mind which knows love and can create beauty survives.

Modern neuroscience, unlike the scientific materialism of a past generation, has come to believe in what we call mind — a human intellect and will that cannot be reduced to brain matter. There are, moreover, certain modern physicists who contend that the universe posits mind — intellect and will — that cannot be reduced to the elements of matter. These physicists have theorized and their observation seems to bear out that matter is finite — that the universe had a beginning, has a middle, and will, indeed, have an end. And behind and before and round and through and beyond the finite universe there is, as a growing number of these scientists affirm, there is an eternal intellect and will — a mind which created all matter out of nothing.

Some of them have been driven to this conclusion by their observation of how the universe seems to work. Do you know the question today's physicists ask of a new theory? They ask, "Is it beautiful?" For experience has taught them that truth is invariably beautiful.

Nor can this beauty be reduced to either chance or necessity.

According to the physicist Henry Margenau:

We do not believe that beauty is only in the eye of the beholder. There are objective features underlying at least some experiences of beauty, such as the frequency ratios of the notes of a major chord, symmetry of geometric forms, or the aesthetic appeal of juxtaposed complementary colors. None of these has survival value, but all are prevalent in nature in a measure hardly compatible with chance. We marvel at the song of the birds, the color scheme of flowers (do insects have a sense of aesthetics?), of birds' feathers, and the incomparable beauty of a fallen maple leaf, its deep red coloring, its blue veins, and its golden edges. Are these qualities useful for survival when the leaf is about to decay?[1]

In his book about the discovery of DNA,

The Double Helix, James Watson says, "So we had lunch, telling each other that a structure this pretty just had to exist."[2]

It sends me back again to the 90th Psalm which says:

Let thy work appear unto the servants,
And thy glory upon their children.
And let the beauty of the Lord our God be upon us.

And what are the properties of beauty to a physicist? There are three — simplicity, harmony, and brilliance.

Now most discussions of modern physics mystify me, and I'm left in a cold sweat simply trying to understand even the most elementary explanations of the theory of relativity, but beauty is a quality I know something about.

I remember a few summers ago, lying on the couch at our summer house reading a new book. When I finished, I said out loud to my husband, "This is a beautiful book."

"What's it about?" he asked.

Instead of answering, I burst into tears. I was amazed at the power of my reaction at the time, but those of you who have read *Sarah, Plain and Tall* will probably understand. It is, indeed, a beautiful book. Tears are the more appropriate response to beauty, but for a moment, let's apply objectively the scientists' test of beauty.

Simplicity. Yes, it is complete in itself, direct, and without superfluous words.

Harmony. You'd have to look a long time to find a book in which the parts — character, setting, plot — so gracefully conform to one another and to the language of the whole.

Brilliance. And here, like the scientists, we are not talking about intellectual cleverness but about clarity — about the light it sheds not only on itself, but beyond itself to other stories and other lives. Don't you keep thinking of it? Don't you compare other books to it? Don't you know the prairie better now? And what it means to care about another person?

It seems to me that beauty so defined is a good test to apply to art of any sort — perhaps, particularly, to the art of children's books. For the stories that have endured, the stories to which we turn as we seek to shape our own lives are all beautiful in this sense.

The stories that have shaped me most are the stories of the Bible. I know this is true, but I often try to figure out how. How has the Bible made me the writer I am?

I think it has something to do with the concept of time as the Bible presents it. Unlike the cyclical pattern of Eastern thought, for us in the West the image of history or chronological time is a line. Now I doubt that most of you grew up in just the same theological environment that I did, but whenever I see a straight line drawn on a piece of paper or on a blackboard, I will in my head draw a perpendicular line at either end. In my mind and psyche time has both a beginning and an end. At the beginning I mentally write CREATION, and at the end of my line I write THE ESCHATON or The End of History.

Surrounding this bounded finite line is the great expanse of unmarked paper or blackboard representing unmarked, unbounded eternity. But there is another perpendicular line which bisects my finite line. It is there somewhere in between the beginning and end, always much nearer the right hand end of the line than the beginning. This perpendicular line differs from the other two because it is in the form of a cross.

If you grew up in the religious tradition that I did, after you have located these three basic marks on the line, you add others. There is one toward the beginning which is labeled "The Call of Abraham," another, "The Exodus," another, "The Reign of David," still another, "Fall of Jerusalem." Sometimes approximate dates are affixed to these intermediate marks. But historical dates are very iffy when you come to relating them to sacred history, so the dates are much less important than the stories that they represent. Once I drew one of these familiar lines and put a tiny mark far to the right and labeled it "me, 1932." Thereby rather grandly putting myself into sacred history. Which is grandiose, really, only if when I put my own name in, I exclude anyone else's. Because it is precisely the Biblical affirmation that all of God's

creatures have a place of significance in sacred history. Didn't Jesus say,

Are not five sparrows sold for two farthings, and not one of them is forgotten before God? But even the very hairs on your head are all numbered. Fear not therefore: ye are of more value than many sparrows.[3]

The words sound to me like those of a mother, gently teasing her much loved child, who has come to her crushed and full of self-doubt.

But back to the time line. What these three primary marks and the secondary marks on the line say to me is something like this: Time is finite. Within the infinite expanse of eternity (and in the Bible eternity is not just lots more time, but a whole different quality of existence), time as we know it on our small planet moves purposely from beginning to end. But from time to time, at critical points in human history, time is invaded in a special way by the eternal.

By now you've caught on that my view of time is not Einstein's view of time or Newton's view of time or even the view of time that most of us have when we set our alarm clocks or consult our daily calendar of events. My view of time has been shaped by a distinctly Biblical view of time, which is outside of scientific or philosophic arguments about the nature of time, but which is actually a very helpful model for someone who wants to write fiction.

Eudora Welty once said that "Southerners do have, they've inherited, a narrative sense of human destiny."[4]. And this "narrative sense of human destiny" is closely related to that time line on the blackboard. Well, of course, that's why we're known as the Bible Belt. We were raised on this book that has a beginning, a middle, and an end, wonderful, richly human characters, and a powerful overall theme.

I want to take a few minutes to address the question of theme in the Biblical narrative, because it is not a matter on which everyone who reads the Bible would agree. Some people see the theme of the Bible in terms of morality. There is, they would maintain, a moral law woven into the fabric of the universe. There is a basic difference between right and wrong. Those who do right, though they may suffer along the way, will eventually be rewarded, and those who do wrong, though they seem temporarily to prosper, will ultimately be punished.

I'm not going to get myself in trouble by telling you that there is no difference between right and wrong and a person who sows rutabagas will end up picking roses. I actually believe there *is* a difference between right and wrong, and observation teaches me that, generally, and in the long run, persons do seem to reap what they sow.

I'm not arguing the premises. I just don't think morality is the basic theme of the Bible. I think the theme of the Bible is closer to what the physicist would call beauty, and by itself, morality is not beautiful enough. Just listen:

And God said: Let there be light. And there was light. And God saw the light, that it was good.... And God saw everything that he had made, and behold, it was very good.

The word *good* here is not a moral quality but an aesthetic one. God saw that what he had made was very beautiful.

And turning to the Gospel:

And suddenly, there was with the angel, a multitude of the heavenly host, praising God and saying, Glory to God in the highest, and on earth peace, good will toward men.

I can't hear those words without hearing the "Gloria" in Mozart's Twelfth Mass, speaking of beauty.

And the beauty of these words tells me what the Bible is all about. The Bible does mention eternity, but only as a background for the real drama which is a story of earth, even more narrowly, a story of humanity's brief appearance on earth. This is also the stuff of fiction — the actions of human beings within the limits of time and space. But the Bible says something more. It says that the posture of the Eternal Creator towards the finite creation is that of good will.

Now, every society, as Joseph Campbell has demonstrated, has its myths by which it finds meaning for life, and those myths have certain similarities. The story of the hero who sets out into a realm of supernatural wonder, meets and conquers fabulous foes, and returns again able to bestow boons on his fellows — this is a story which occurs over and over again in the mythologies and folk and fairy tales of the world.

But even as I look at the paradigm of the universal story of the hero, I flesh it out with Abraham and Sarah and Jacob and Moses, Ruth and David and Jeremiah and Jesus, and throughout see evidence of the good will of the Creator toward perverse and often foolish creatures. As my mother, who never cursed, used to say, "We've made a mell of a hess of things." Reading any day's newspaper is enough to drive a thinking person to despair, and yet for all this, as Gerard Manley Hopkins says:

And for all this, nature is never spent;
There lives the dearest freshness deep down things;
And though the last lights off the black West went
Oh, morning, at the brown brink eastward, springs —
Because the Holy Ghost over the bent
World broods with warm breast and with ah! bright
         wings.

Can you understand why I become uncomfortable when people ask me about the morals of my stories or the values I'm trying to impart? Moral judgment is, first of all, not my prerogative. Of course, I will make moral judgments for myself, and as a parent I will seek to teach my children that which I believe to be right and good and that which I see as evil and wrong. And I will do whatever I can to work for peace and justice, which I believe to be good and right and to combat war and oppression, which I believe with all my heart to be evil. But when it comes to passing judgment I have to tread very carefully. If the Bible is to be believed, when the Creator, whose prerogative moral judgment is, when the Creator becomes the judge it breaks his heart.

So when I write a story for children it is not to make moral judgments, though the story may portray the observed human truth that behavior has consequences. I am seeking, as best as I am able, to tell a story from my own heart and mind — with the hope that it will speak to another heart and mind. I will endeavor to make this story as good as I can

— good in the sense of beautiful. And I define that beauty by the qualities of simplicity, harmony, and brilliance.

Simplicity — I think probably this is the quality I have the least trouble with. E. B. White said somewhere, and I can't for the life of me find out where, that he thought he was ideally suited to writing for children because he didn't have a very large vocabulary. I think we'll all agree that Mr. White had a vocabulary equal to whatever need arose. But I understand, I think, what he was saying. I think I'm ideally suited to write for children because I basically have a simple mind. I don't catch on to things quickly. For me, reading a book like *Infinite in All Directions* is like pulling crabgrass out of the flower bed. Given a choice, I will always prefer the concrete to the abstract. I am forever trying to reduce everything troublesome or mysterious to a story — or at least to simile or metaphor.

So, for example, when my eight-year-old son's best friend is killed during the same period that I must struggle with the fact that I have had cancer and am frighteningly mortal, I turn not to philosophy or theology; I write a story. By writing fiction which must have a beginning, middle, and end, I give shape to what in life seems chaotic and unmanageable. Writing stories is considerably cheaper than psychotherapy and, I tell myself, far more satisfying.

Harmony is a quality I have more difficulty with, certainly if you are to listen to some of my critics. The book that has garnered the most abuse when we think of harmony is *Jacob Have I Loved*, which a great number of critics felt was out of balance. Now as I have confessed before, I often don't know what I'm doing when I write, but in the case of the ending of *Jacob* I was wide awake at the time. I made a deliberate decision to compress Louise's years in school to a very few pages and jump from Rass Island to Truitt Valley with little in between, because I wasn't interested in the academic curriculum of either the University of Maryland or the University of Kentucky. It seemed to me that Louise's higher education had very little to do with

what Jill Paton Walsh calls the "trajectory" of the story.

Let me quote to you Jill's idea of trajectory, which is a marvelous explanation of the difference between story time and clock time:

The trajectory of a book is the route chosen by the author through his material. It is the action of a book, considered not as the movement of paraphrasable events in that book but as the movement of the author's exposition and the reader's experience of it. And a good trajectory is the optimum, the most emotionally loaded flight path across the subject to the projected end.[5]

Every book has its own unique trajectory, although the kind of book, the genre, will lead you to expect a certain kind of trajectory. If you're reading a love story, as Jill says, and the hero is just about to kiss the heroine, you become very annoyed if the author suddenly decides to insert a police chase. Whereas if you're reading what is meant to be a detective story and the author freezes the chase and pans to a tender love scene just when the murderer is about to be apprehended, you may very well skip the romantic scene in order to get back to the chase.

Readers do tend to be sensitive to what they sense does or doesn't belong on the trajectory of a particular story. I remember reading some years ago a quite powerful novel in the middle of which the writer supplied the recipe for a favorite family food. It was a good recipe. I may have even used it for my own family. But as a reader I was jarred. It didn't seem to me to belong on the book's trajectory.

I used to think that children hated descriptions. They only hate descriptions that are stuck in for effect — that don't belong on the trajectory. You could no more have *The Secret Garden* without lengthy descriptions of the garden than you could have *Charlotte's Web* without paying tribute to the changing seasons. Though neither, strictly speaking, furthers the plot, they are on the trajectory. Those descriptions are vital to the harmony of the book.

When you think of harmony, you have to consider every element that has gone into the making of a book. When I was writing *Jacob* I tried to write it in the third person. I do not like writing in first person. It seems to me an arrogant and limiting point of view. But I found to my unhappiness that the book was refusing to be told in any voice other than Louise's. This many years later I can say, "Well, of course. How obvious. Jealousy can only speak in the first person. It can't imagine another point of view." In order to maintain the harmony of the book, the point of view had to be first person singular. Think about the play *Amadeus*. A great deal of its power derives from the voice of Salieri telling the tale.

Brilliance — I once said to Virginia Buckley, my editor, when we were struggling with a passage in one of my books that a suggestion of the copy editor would ruin the rhythm of a particular sentence. "Rhythm," I intoned solemnly, "is everything." And then heard myself add, "but clarity is more." I rewrote the passage under dispute.

One of the stories I tell myself from time to time is the story of the speech I had to write when *The Master Puppeteer* won the National Book Award. Because of time constraints I had to write what became known in the family as "Mother's 500 Deathless Words" in one afternoon and dictate them on the telephone to Virginia that night, so she could give them to the Academy of Arts and Letters the following day.

Now, this was to be my first real venture into the public eye as a writer, and I was to share the stage on this occasion with, among others, Richard Eberhart, Erskine Caldwell, Bruno Bettelheim, Irving Howe, Jacques Barzun, and C. P. Snow.

I was a little nervous. My children could not imagine why it would take anyone eight hours to write 500 words, but when Virginia called, I had to stop frantically revising and dictate what I had — the time had run out. Now, I must confess, as nervous as I was about the 500, I thought I had a sockeroo ending. And with a sockeroo ending, who would worry about the other 495 words?

At Virginia's suggestion I read the whole speech through once and then went back and read it sentence by sentence so she could take it down. When I got to my sockeroo five-word final sentence the second time, there was a long pause at the other end of the line. Finally, a gentle voice said: "It sounds wonderful, Katherine, but what does it *mean?*" Now, whenever I am revising and I come upon a particularly felicitous group of words, I apply what I call "The Sounds Wonderful, But What Does It Mean?" test.

And, of course, the basic test for beauty — simplicity, harmony, and brilliance or clarity — is to read the whole story aloud, preferably at one sitting. Actually, I don't believe that this is a test for children's books only. I'm suspicious of any book that can't be read aloud, though, obviously, there are books that cannot be tackled in one sitting. But there is hardly any exercise more helpful to a children's writer than to hear the whole story aloud. I was very troubled about *Park's Quest* until Jean Little gently bullied me into reading it out loud, and when it worked out loud, I felt it was all right. It would do.

The problem with the book was that it was in the shadow of the powerful legend of Parzifal, and I could only compare my feeble words upon the page with that immortal story. We do this over and over again when we write. We seek to lay hold of a story which exists out there somewhere beyond the ordinary boundaries of space and time and focus it into a specific place and time of our own choosing.

Usually, the particular myth, legend, folk tale, or story behind a book is more or less subconscious. I certainly didn't know as someone later explained to me, that *Gilly Hopkins* was a retelling of Pilgrim's Progress. I had thought it was "The Prodigal Son." But I knew from the very beginning, even before I knew where the story would be set or who its characters would be, that the overriding shape of *Park's Quest*, if not the details of the plot, would be the Parzifal legend as retold by the German romantic poet Wolfram von Eschenbach in the early years of the thirteenth century.

This is the only time I've seen quite so clearly the legend behind the story I'm trying to tell. Certainly the story of Jacob and Esau is background to *Jacob Have I Loved*, but in a less direct way. I wouldn't be surprised if some of you out there know better than I do the stories behind some of my books. As I indicated earlier, we writers are famous for not knowing what we're doing.

But now after nine novels I can see that the overarching theme of them all is the theme that I see in the Bible — the theme of the divine good will. The more common word for good will in the Old Testament is loving kindness. In the New Testament it is called grace. Like the word God, the word grace cannot be abstractly defined. We are always reduced when speaking of it to simile, to metaphor, to once upon a time.

In writing realistic fiction, which is in one sense narrowly confined in space and time, we are still moving in other dimensions. As Penelope Lively said, the writer is involved not simply in the moment of the story as it happens but in the whole time of the story as well as in her own life which may or may not have any direct relation to the story that is being written. Again, this is an image of Biblical time. The story of humankind is going along but we are reminded that it's not the only show in town.

In a statement of Jesus that has almost as many translations as it has words, Jesus says to his disciples: "The kingdom of God is at hand or within you or among you." Now, in Mark the whole quotation reads, "The time is fulfilled, and the kingdom of God is at hand; repent, and believe in the good news." We have a lot of problems with the word repent, because it has been interpreted to mean "Quit your meanness or God's gonna get you." But the word repent doesn't really have to do with moral conduct. It is the Greek word *metanoia* which really is concerned with (in Northrop Frye's phrase) "a change of outlook or spiritual metamorphosis, an enlarged vision of the dimensions of human life." The religious people of Jesus's time and place had been talking for a long time about the "day of the Lord" — the Time when God would interfere with human folly and set things right — the day when the eternal would transform or perhaps, better yet, destroy the temporal.

So I think what Jesus is saying here as he announces his ministry is "This is it. Wake up. Open your eyes and your ears to what's happening, this is the Time you've been waiting and praying for." But even his closest friends had trouble with Jesus' version of the Day of the Lord. None of them could and none of us can quite believe that when the eternal dimension invades the temporal, the evidence is healing and humility.

Well, I can't really believe that this podium is a mass of bouncing energy, either. We're such pitiful creatures. We're so bound by convention and education and prejudice that we cannot allow ourselves to see or believe much of anything. But surely it is our human as well as spiritual duty to stretch our shriveled little receiving apparatus. To repent — to take a new wider vision of the universe. That's what this week has been about, hasn't it? Learning new ways to see and hear and feel the immense beauty of which our lives are a part.

Northrop Frye says "It is the function of literature ... not to run away from the actual, but to see the dimension of the possible in the actual." Which is why a realistic story, limited as it will be by clock time and map space, may be, perhaps must be, set in the larger dimension of myth.

I fell in love with the story of Parzifal before I'd ever really heard it, before I knew what a powerful story of good will it was. I fell in love with it when I heard a speaker at the National Women's Conference to Prevent Nuclear War say "We cannot frighten people into responsibility. People are so frightened now that they have to deny that there is a nuclear threat. I think," she said, "what we must do is to ask the question of Parzifal."

A shiver went through my body. I didn't know what the question of Parzifal was, but I knew I had to find out.

In the legend as Wolfram tells it, Parzifal, the Grail Knight, is brought by enchantment to the castle of the Grail King. The king is suffering from a wound that will not heal, and he will be healed only on the day that the Grail Knight appears and asks the question. The young Parzifal, however, is the prototype of the innocent fool. He has no idea that he is the Grail Knight. When he finds himself in the mysterious castle of the Grail, he's not about to ask any questions because he has been told by those wiser than he that a man who keeps asking questions appears to be even more of a fool than he is. So he does not ask the question. The king is not healed. And Parzifal is thrown out of the castle on his ear. In his subsequent wanderings our innocent fool becomes sadder and, if not wiser, certainly less gullible and increasingly world weary. Try as he will he cannot find his way back to the Grail Castle. He refuses to return to Camelot, convinced that he is no longer worthy to take his seat at the Round Table. Eventually he loses all track of space and time until, finally, he loses his faith as well. Then one day in the forest he comes upon a family of pilgrims. They are amazed to see a knight armed and in armor, for it is Good Friday. They speak to the despairing Parzifal, and he takes heart. Perhaps the One mighty enough to bring the world into being would have the power to bring comfort to his lost and despairing soul.

Parzifal seeks out a hermit who tells him again the gospel story, hears Parzifal's confession and sends him once more upon his quest. At last Parzifal comes a second time to the Grail Castle, and this time he asks the suffering king the question. "Dear Uncle," Parzifal asks, "what aileth thee?" Upon hearing these compassionate words, the king is healed. And so also, is Parzifal himself.

In my once upon a time, Parkington Waddell Broughton the Fifth is also the innocent fool unaware that he is in truth the Grail Knight entrusted with the compassionate question, and so he fails his quest and loses his way for a time in the wilderness. I've already warned you about my view of the universe. I've already explained at great length to you that I believe that there is an eternal mind who created from nothing a universe of beauty and whose posture towards all and everyone is that of loving kindness, grace, good will. Thus, whether or not you have read this particular book, you will suspect that in the world as I know it, even in the darkest wilderness, there are angels; and a knight, no matter how lost and despairing, will always be

given another chance to fulfill his quest.

With Park easing the wheels down over the stoop and Thanh holding on to the footrests, they were able to get the chair off the porch with only a minor jolt.

"Okay?" Thanh asked the old man.

Park turned the chair around and started slowly toward the gate. Once out of the yard, Thanh tried once more to take over the pushing.

"He like fast," she said. "Don't you like fast?"

"No," Park said. "Not tonight. It's dark. We gotta see where we're going."

"Yellow chicken," she said amicably, shrugging an apology to the old man, and then, with Jupe frolicking around her legs, she danced ahead of them down the road. As the path dropped off more steeply, Park had to hold back to keep the chair from racing downhill. In the moonlight he felt as though he were following fairy shadows. He wondered if the old man sensed the enchantment.

By the time they got to the gate, she was standing there, holding it open. "What I do," she said. "I go get water. Take to crow. Get gun. You wait at spring. Okay?"

He was relieved that she didn't expect him to push the chair uphill and down to the far pasture, but — to wait alone with the old man? His heart began to pound faster. He licked his lips. "Okay," he said. "Sure."

Jupe looked at the girl and then at the chair, as though torn. When he realized that she was going and they were staying, he gave a yelp of delight and raced after her.

Now they were truly alone. Park turned the chair so the old man could see the moon, and set the brake. He started to sit down on the grass. It was damp, so he sat on his haunches Thanh-style a few feet from the chair. The afghan had come loose in the trip down the hill. He went over and squatted in front of the chair and began to tuck it close around the old pajamaed leg.

"Haaaa." There was nowhere to run. His heart had stopped, but Park made himself look up into the old face. Even in the shadows, he thought he could see tears. "Haaaa."

"What's the matter?" Park willed the words out of his mouth. "Does something hurt?"

The clawlike left hand came out from under the afghan and reached toward him. Park held himself tightly so as not to flinch, not to retreat. The back of the hand touched Park's cheek, then fell away. With an effort, the old man lifted the hand again. This time it went back and forth several times, cool and baby soft against Park's face. "Haaaa," he repeated. "Haaaa." The hand flopped heavily from Park's cheek to his own chest.

"Yes," said Park, suddenly understanding. "Park. You mean Park. I'm Park, and you're Park. That's what you mean, right?"

His grandfather turned his twisted head slightly, as if to nod, then repeated the stroke of Park's cheek and the touch of his own breast with gentle *haaaa's* each time.

"Yes, we're both Park." Park could understand him! He was, if not making conversation, at least making contact with his grandfather. He wanted to grab the old hands or hug the old body. Suddenly the withered arm was flung out toward the sky.

"HAAAAAA!" the old man sobbed out.

"HAAAAAAA!" The arm fell lifeless to the side of the chair. There was no question now about the tears.

"What is it?" Park was crying too. "What is it? Do you miss him? Is that it?" But the pain in the eyes said more than grief.

"Don't cry, please don't cry." Park hugged the old knees. The sobbing did not lessen.

"What is it?" He stood up and took the wasted face between his hands and held it. His grandfather's tears wet his fingers. The tears were running down his own cheeks, too, catching in his glasses. He let them run. "What's the matter? Please tell me," he begged. And now, looking into the eyes, he saw his mother's eyes and his own eyes, as in a mirror. So that was it.

"You think you killed him," Park said softly. "You think it's your fault."

Between his fingers, he could feel his grandfather's head move forward and back. He was nodding yes.

Park let the face go and put his arms around his grandfather's shoulders and held him tight while they both cried like lost three-year-olds returned at last to their mothers' arms.

"Gone!" Thanh was yelling as she ran down the road, waving his bloodstained T-shirt above her head. "Gone!"

"Gone?" Not their crow. Not dead. Not now. "What happened?"

"Okay!" she cried. "Okay. Fly free!"

She threw him the T-shirt and ran past them into the springhouse. When she came out, it was slowly, carrying in both hands the coconut shell, filled to overflowing with cool, sweet water. "Now," she ordered. "Now. All drink."

Then they took the Holy Grail in their hands and drew away the cloth and drank of the Holy Wine. And it seemed to all who saw them that their faces shone with a light that was not of this world. And they were as one in the company of the Grail.

1. Margenau, New Story of Science pp 79-80

2. New Story, pp. 38-39.

3. Luke 12:7-8.

4. Paris Review Writers at Work 4th Series p. 278

5. 'Lords of Time' Essay in Openhearted Audience, pp 187-8.

BETTY LEVIN AND GREGORY MAGUIRE

Travelers in Time: Synthesis

ONCE UPON A TIME lived Bran son of Febal. An early traveler in time was Bran. A beautiful woman, who appeared to him as he slept outside his stronghold, sang to him and held out a branch of an apple tree. And led him to the Otherworld. He and his men followed her in their coracles to an island with women and gardens, a timeless place without strife or sickness or want of any kind. There they dwelt until some of them felt such pangs of homesickness that they all set off to visit home. The women warned them not to touch the land of their origins, but when they finally neared the shore and viewed the familiar and yet different land, they longed to row onto the beach.

A man called out, asking who they were. Bran answered that he was Bran son of Febal. The man on shore said he knew no such person, although the Voyage of Bran was one of his people's ancient stories.

Then the most homesick of the men leapt from the coracle and splashed ashore. When he touched the ground of his homeland, he dissolved, and where he had stood there was only a small heap of ashes, soon blown away by the wind. Then Bran and his followers rowed away and from that day were seen no more.

The Voyage of Bran, a Celtic legend, shows two or more simultaneous times. It shows time as circular, the serpent swallowing its tail. Bran is a hero in ancient tale about a hero in an ancient tale about ... Here are John Townsend's time slip and slippery time combined.

And so were we led — with apple branch and spellbinding song — across the sea of fact and fancy to spend one week that may be only a few days, but enclosed us all in an eternal moment. Of course we didn't all cross the same sea; some of us crossed no sea at all. But for most of us jet lag was a cruel reminder that Western time is arbitrary and that when we take a quantum leap, even if only from one time zone to another, we are wrapped in strangeness — strangers in a strange land.

"You look down from the aeroplane," said Susan Cooper, "flying over Britain, and you see a patchwork, a map of the past. It is the story of a people, written upon the land; a long dialogue between people and place ... And the story can best be read from a long way away. A long way up. Looking down from the height of three miles or so, you see their earthworks, their hillforts, their standing stones in mysterious circles and avenues, the pattern of their farming ... You see their old ways and their modern roads; the spreading tentacles of their villages and towns. And always, not more than one hundred miles from any part of these islands, you see the other dominant part of the place. The sea."

Or, in Paul Heins' words after his most recent reading of *Unleaving* "the restless, multitudinous seas."

In our time the voyage across the sea may be no less daunting than driving on the M40 or any other high-speed motorway. Think of the scene John Townsend described from Nesbit's *The Story of the Amulet*, Caesar gazing across the Channel, influenced by Edwardian children's report of marvels to come, if only he would cross the water. Nesbit's children were too convinced that they were setting Britain on the right, true course to be troubled about messing with events of the past. This confirmation of history conjoining with fantasy echoes Caesar's own observation: "It was not certain that Britain existed until I came there."

Caesar was only one in a long line of intrepid travelers, as Barbara Harrison spoke of us all on our first morning together.

From the start, as travelers, we pitched tent and pitched in, holding for each other the endless succession of doors in Newnham's corridors of time. Debbie Kirsh, at her first institute, got down on her hands and knees before a word of welcome had been uttered, to fiddle with the fickle microphone and try to coax it back to good behavior. Kathy Fitzgibbons, jet-lagged and bleary-eyed, foreswore a much-needed nap to help Martha Walke separate pages from the *Times Educational Supplement*. Katherine Paterson and Maud Anderson and Maggie Chang stuffed packets along with the steering committee and Jane Langton. Audrey and Ed Briggs collected donations for the buffet supper. Joanna Long negotiated extending the Lady Mitchell hours with the authorities. A CLNE tradition of cooperation rooted itself in this friendly site almost without prompting. It seemed to burst from the participants unbidden, and so very welcome.

After Marilyn Butler's gracious welcome, John Langstaff gathered us together in song. "When people came to the new world," he said, "they lost many things, but not their songs and stories. They brought those and kept them." And at the close of the institute Ashley Bryan proposed an opposite vision when he recited a Langston Hughes poem evoking estrangement from the past: "So long, so far away is Africa ... Subdued and time-lost are the drums ... So long, so far away is Africa's dark face." And at the same time Ashley Bryan confirmed for us the survival of experience through the imagination. "Still got it!" he recited. Not the candy in the store nor the sand house on the beach. But the poem, composed on the kitchen floor. "Still got it!" we repeat after him.

"All institutes are connected," said Barbara Harrison; "all stories are one story."

Introducing the concept of the great flux of time, she proposed one perspective after another: time devouring all things and time sustaining life and time as an immense brevity and the world as a circle. Bruegal's visions of time provided images for each concept. And the book, she told us, movement in narrative through time (and especially fiction about the young), shows myriad unfoldings of the one story.

Susan Cooper reminded us: "We have to tell stories to unriddle the world."

Having traveled in body and unpacked songs and poems to sing and tell, we commenced with Jill Paton Walsh and Paul Heins to look at the imaginary and elastic nature of fiction. When a story moves from one significant moment to the next, said Jill, it skips across the surface of time. Paul spoke of the accordion principle, one quick squeeze of events after another. At the close of their joint lecture Paul concluded, "By now it must be obvious that the nature of narrative time is not to be stated simply." Jill added, "I think the world is so complicated, and some aspects of it, like time itself, so mysterious, that the rational, conscious part of ourselves cannot contain and hold within one steady gaze all that we have perceived."

These views were supported and extended by other speakers. Leon Garfield said he preferred to tell his daughter *The Sleeping Beauty* backwards to increase suspense. Susan Cooper, referring to *Red Shift*, remarked on the power of "sounds and events that echo backwards." Gillian Avery told us that she rejected the first person voice because as a child she always knew that the protagonist would be rescued. And Eleanor Cameron quoted Ursula LeGuin, whose people might "be going to have lived long, long ago."

We reminded ourselves of Barbara Harrison's challenge and promise: "Each of us a traveler in time, single current in the great river of time; participants and witnesses in an ongoing saga that began before we were born and will continue after we are gone."

The idea of each child as the eternal Adam was a way of explaining the eternal present. "The expulsion from Eden was the expulsion into history," said Neil Philip, and if at times during this institute the child may have seemed a very diminished figure in the cosmic effects of time and change, we were glad for this remark. On the stage behind Neil Philip the apple tree in the garden tub took on a clearer meaning. What stands at the beginning of human history in at least one of the cycles of creation myths? The apple tree. And Neil went on to say that "the myth of the fall informs much children's literature."

Peter Dickinson told the story of the leftover rib of Eve, made into a comb — the oldest artifact of the world. Think of the cross-stitched sampler some of us saw when kindly invited into the home of Ann and Anthony Thwaite. Adam and Eve beneath the apple tree. Think of the Conrad Aiken poem: "This is the shape of the leaf, and this of the flower, and this the pale bole of the tree!" The copper beech Clare plants in the yard of the house in Norham Gardens will outlast the aunts and Clare herself. Think of the power of oak, ash, and thorn. And think of the song we sang with John Langstaff: "a rare tree, a rattlin' tree." And the child holds the seed, and the seed holds the child. And there's another image of time.

On our first day we divided into houses for discussion of books on our reading list. We established Bigelow House and Sedney House, and Houses Scotto and Thwaite and Powdermaker. We became Cameron House and Davis and Porter House; we gathered in Houses Watkins and Golodetz and Kruse. We argued over Garner and *Arilla Sun Down*. We added many a book to our personal lists and volubly subtracted a few, too. The books and the themes and the material of our own lives could be vigorously reshuffled and skipped and played on the accordion.

Betty Levin moved backward from contemporary nostalgia factories of our time to views of the past in the early history of America. Crucial to the disparate titles on her list was the movement of their protagonists from a static or fixed state, a self-centered present, to an awareness that enabled them to connect with the past and look to the future — to see with time's eye.

Some of us spoke of time as thief, devourer, of time growing short and of time no longer. Susan Cooper told us that a sense of the continuum is our treasure, although we are sometimes only aware of it when it is gone, when we feel the aching gap. Janni Howker saw that the gap existed in her working-class childhood as exclusion from the course of history.

Helen Cresswell spoke of the lost time of Eden. "The world has gone usual," she said. "Not like the tree when Adam and Eve saw it for the first time." While Annie Dillard may have felt as a child that "if one day I forgot to notice my life ... the blank cave would suck me up entire." Helen Cresswell did not believe in time, and she was certain she would die young.

Speaking of slippery time, John Townsend pointed out that for St. Augustine time did not exist before God created the world, and that for Stephen Hawking "the concept of time has no meaning before the beginning of the universe."

At the opposite end of the brief human span of time stood Jane Langton, who inveighed against the months and years flitting by. "And then, whether we want to our not, we find ourselves having sixtieth birthdays and seventieth and eightieth, and after a while we look around and discover we're dead."

Virginia Hamilton said, "My books are composed of generations." She quoted from her new work: "Gram lost plenty of time, but she could speed it up if she felt like it." But Gregory Maguire quoted Janni Howker's Isaac Campion, who stored up details to keep that day and who in his memory, went on to wonder "whether robbers are the only ones who have the nerve to steal from their own lives. We are receivers of stolen goods." Greg wondered whether he had stolen from the child in Nicaragua when he accepted her gift, the snapshot of herself. And at the opposite end of the brief span of human time stood Sarah Parker, storing up details too, and letting them go, not stealing from her life, but giving. Betty Levin proposed that like those older characters who pass on their gifts to the young in many children's books, the writers bear a similar relation to their readers, handing on the gift.

Penelope Lively has written: "Moments shower away, the days of our lives vanish utterly, more insubstantial than if they had been invented. Fiction can seem more enduring than reality ... and when you and I talk about history we don't mean what actually happened, do we? The cosmic chaos of everywhere, all time? We mean the tidying up of this into books."

Tony Watkins introduced his discussion group's interpretation of *Red Shift* as a palimpsest of violence, and generated argument about that book and others. Beryl Turner observed that *Lord of the Flies* seeps down to children. "Define children," said Therese Bigelow. Diana Paolitto said, "We writers and psychologists both collect story fragments that we reframe for our own purposes." And Ethel Heins quoted Sendak: "We don't remember childhood; we discover it." "We don"t remember childhood," Penelope Lively maintained; "we invent it."

At the close of her lecture Diana Paolitto concluded: "I think that we shall find that the best works of literature are still those where time plays a central animating role that can be read and explored on as many different levels as there are young and old to read them."

Helen Cresswell's view of the world is and was mystical: "We need to feel there is another dimension of time," she said. John Townsend discussed books that explored such a dimension, while Diana Paolitto showed us that children bring their own non-linear time concepts into their reading or listening. Philippa Pearce claimed to be short-sighted and still the child she was, although she is at the same time her parents and grandparents. "There is a great comfortableness in writing of a period just before your own — your parents' or your grandparents'". Agreeing, Ann Schlee spoke of the sense of freedom and pleasure she found in writing about the recent past, her own childhood's time.

David Lowenthal said, "Our childhood saga has the shape of fable." Philippa Pearce said she wanted Tom's present and Hatty's past to be equal, and she pointed out that Tom as

well as Hatty, and the words themselves, have all now gone into the past. "And it's a mystery," she said, "a mystery I respect." David Lowenthal said, "We are enlarged by other places, differences. We need empathy, but we also need to recognize strangeness... Children need to learn how thought leads to action and action to cause and cause to consequence." Penelope Lively spoke of the different ways the past is viewed by historians, biographers, novelists, and children. Children, she said, impose their own present on the past. And Rosemary Sutcliff spoke of the difference between the God's-eye view of history and the man's-eye view. "All of us," she said, "in our particular stretch of history stand too close up to be able to follow the whole pattern, and we never know how the story ends ... That is why children can surely get a truer picture of the past if something that breathes life into the bare bones is given to them over and above the factual side of history." She writes, she said, for the child who writes to tell her: "It makes me feel as though I were there."

Yasouyo Inouye said that when she first read *Tom's Midnight Garden* at the age of thirteen, she didn't finish it, because it made her feel sad. "One year after, I tried again and finished. But the scene of the present-time house where Tom stayed remained in my mind since then. Where is Tom now in 1989? Does he work as a businessman in the city? Does he keep trying to open the door to the garden?"

Time and again we set out to draw a picture of time and again. Time-shapes were drawn, considered, revised, echoed. Time as a line. Time as a circle. Time as a spiral. Time as a globe. Time as a hem of a skirt, looping so an ant can cross. Time as the warp and weft of a handkerchief. Time as a series of linked sausages.

The metaphors continued. "Time," said Helen- Cresswell, "is cold corn to the winds. I don't believe in it." "Time," Neil Philip quoted, "is the moving image of unmoving eternity." A host of novelists and thinkers gave us their metaphors, while at the same time invoking the theories of Newton, Einstein, and Hawking as regularly as the beating of a gong. Somewhere in between the beauty of a scientific theory and the beauty of an apt metaphor lies another beauty: that of our perpetual uncertainty about time. It is one of the things that make us human.

Again and again speakers defined what it meant to be human, an interesting development in a conference on time in literature. Penelope Lively said, "Knowledge of history, of the past, is what dignifies humanity. It's in fact what makes us human, besides language." Peter Dickinson said, "What makes us human isn't anything but the ability to use the word if." Someone else said, "What makes us human is imagination," but we can't remember who said it. What makes us human is thinking about what makes us human.

Eleanor Cameron distinguished between types of time fantasy, defending it strenuously as a sub-genre to be recognized on its own merits. At home with the scientific concepts which can strengthen a time fantasy, Eleanor applauded the psychological tensions in books like *Elidor* and *Earthfasts,* and paid tribute to the power of a nineteenth-century epigram quoted in Jill Paton Walsh's *A Chance Child:*

Dissolving and passing away are the world, the ages, and me.

The ideas Eleanor Cameron articulated were echoed all week long in the discussions held at the Houses. "I part the darkness and I follow slow," quoted Eleanor. And that is what Ethel Heins did in her comprehensive survey of time in picture books. She provided a vigorous visual counterpoint to the observations of Diana Paolitto. She made continual connections with fiction and nonfiction for older children, and quoted Isaac Singer, Eudora Welty, Einstein, St. Augustine, Walter de la Mare, David McCord, Gabriela Mistral, E.S. Hart, Anne Tyler, the Opies, and P.L. Travers, and still attended to what Arnheim credits as the province of the word: "the entire realm of the soul, the imagination, the will."

Shirley Hughes considered her own work and showed slides of the work of artists she admires. She read aloud a book for very young children, which included the two lines:

Some things you can throw away
Some things are nice to keep

another affirmation of the enduring word, to echo and to stand as a prelude to Ashley Bryan's recital: "Still got it! And a reminder of Puck's, "Hold fast! Hold fast all I give you."

All week long the music that transcends time was just about to play. John Langstaff spoke the music of Susan Cooper's poem when he introduced her:

So the shortest day came,
And the year died,
And everywhere down the centuries
Of the snow-white world
Came people singing, dancing,
To drive the dark away.
They lighted candles in the winter trees;
They hung their homes with evergreen;
They burned beseeching fires all night long
To keep the year alive.
And when the new year's sunshine blazed awake
They shouted, revelling.
Through all the frosty ages you can hear them
Echoing, behind us — listen!
All the long echoes sing the same delight
This shortest day,
And promise wakens in the sleeping land.

Susan Cooper mentioned music in relation to *The Dark is Rising.* John Townsend noted that music is a pattern in time as a painting is a pattern in space. Katherine Paterson referred to a multitude of the heavenly host singing, "Glory to God!" "What shall we sing?" asked Madge in *Unleaving.* "The beauty of the world." "What shall we sing?", said Sarah Parker from beyond the grave; "Joy to the World." And with John Lanqstaff at Old Hall, Queen's College, leading us in *Sumer is icumen in* it didn"t matter that summer had been here for some time and was racing on.

Always at Newnham there was a hand to tip milk into our coffee, a face in the window of the porter's lodge, a friendly driver of a minivan, a thoughtful mistress of housekeeping. The hands and the faces belonged to people and they had names.

We are poor passing facts
condemned by such to give
Each figure in the photograph
Its living name,

went the lines from Robert Lowell which Gregory Maguire quoted on Tuesday. But these people were rich facts, eager to be of help, glad to witness our delight at Cambridge, England.

There was Hugh Surridge of Lady Mitchell Hall; Gavin in the college bar; Sharon Flint, the deputy domestic bursar; Lindsey Fraser and her staff at Heffer's, who made us welcome in the shop and were so helpful at the college; Alf, the driver of the minivan to Norwich, who listened patiently to our oohs and ahs over Norman thises and Saxon thats, Gothic and Romans and Georgian others, and then, pointing to an empty field, said, "And do you know who used to live over there?" We didn't know; so he told us - "The Flintstones!"

After all the references to time as a straight line and time as a circle, on our last full day Jean Little commented, "All history all over the world intersects. Rosemary Sutcliff's books are part of our history, not just your history." Jill Paton Walsh replied, "You are not just welcome here, you are entitled here." Then she added, "Someone said, 'The English language is my motherland.'" And Wendy Davis said, "For those of us who visited Lucy Boston, time was so thick there." Jim Davis thanked the English writers. Frances Sedney said, "Once the book is written, it belongs to the readers," which Tony Watkins expanded:

"Once it's published it enters into the history of readership." And Barbara Scotto reminded us that the composition of reading changes with each successive reading. Each of us, children and adults, read differently through time.

> Through all the frosty ages you can hear them
> Echoing behind us — Listen!
> All the long echoes sing the same delight.

In *Past and Present* Thomas Carlyle wrote:

> The past is a dim indubitable fact; the future too is one, only dimmer; nay, probably it is the same fact in new dress and development. For the present holds in it both the whole past and the whole future — as the life-tree Igdrasil, wide-waving, many-toned, has its roots down deep in the Death-kingdoms, among the oldest dead dust of men, and with its boughs reaches always beyond the stars, and in all time and places is one and the same Life-tree.

And Susan Cooper said to us: "Music is after all made of time and carries it down the centuries in a chain of renewal — like the seasons and the turning year, and all other patterns of life, spreading out over the continuum like the widening ripples in a pool. When Jack draws you into music at the end of this institute, and you sing, think of the echo that carries our mystery from the blue end of the spectrum to the red, all through the rainbow of here, out beyond the universe."

To which we add, in Barbara's opening words:

"Let our circle continue."

SPEAKERS AND LEADERS.

GILLIAN AVERY is a noted historian of children's literature, and the author of several children's novels, including *The Warden's Niece the Elephant War* and *A Likely Lad,* winner of the Guardian Award. Her stories for younger readers include *Ellen's Birthday* and *Ellen and the Queen.* Gillian Avery has also written *Victorian People in Life and Literature,* and *Childhood's Pattern: a study of the Heroes and Heroines of Children's Fiction, 1770-1950.* She is now completing a book about the heroes and heroines of American children's books of the nineteenth century.

THERESE BIGELOW is coordinator of children's and young adult services at the Hampton Public Library in Hampton, Virginia. An active member of the Virginia Library Association and the American Library Association, she has served on several committees and is currently serving her second term on the Notable Children's Book committee; she has also been a judge for the Boston Globe/ Horn Book awards. Ms. Bigelow teaches children's literature at Christopher Newport College.

ASHLEY BRYAN, formerly head of the art department at Dartmouth College, is a painter, book illustrator and reteller of African folk tales for children. His books include *Walk Together, Children: Black American Spirituals; Beat the Story-Drum, Pum-Pum,* winner of the Coretta Scott King award; and *Turtle Knows your name,* a 1989 publication. Ashley Bryan has also illustrated John Langstaff's *What a Morning! The Christmas Story in Black Spirituals.* He recently received an honorary doctorate from the Massachusetts College of Art.

MARILYN BUTLER was Fellow and Tutor in English at St. Hugh's College, Oxford, before being appointed to the King Edward VII professorship of English at Cambridge University. Her books include *Jane Austen and the War of Ideas,* and *Romantics, Rebels, and Reactionaries: English Literature and its Background 1760-1830.*

ELEANOR CAMERON is a critic, lecturer, and noted author of children's novels. She is the winner of the National Book Award for *The Court of the Stone Children,* the Boston Globe/Horn Book award for *A Room Made of Windows,* and the Mystery Writers of America Award for *A Spell is Cast.* Among her books cited as notable by the American Library Association are *Julia and the Hand of God* and *To the Green Mountains.* She presented the prestigious Gertrude Clark Whittall Lecture at the Library of Congress. Her critical essays are collected in *The Green and Burning Tree: on the Writing and Enjoyment of Children's Books.*

SUSAN COOPER, born in England and for many years a resident of Massachusetts, is the winner of both the Newbery Medal and the Welsh Tir-nan-Og Award for *The Grey King,* the fourth of five novels in *The Dark is Rising* sequence. The author of several picture book texts, including *The Silver Cow* and *The Selkie Girl,* she is also a successful playwright for the stage and television.

HELEN CRESSWELL is the author of *The Piemakers, The Nightwatchmen The Winter of the Birds, The Secret World of Polly Flint,* and of the five comic novels known as "The Bagthorpe Saga". Several of her books have been cited by the American Library Association as Notable Children's Books, and she has been runner-up for the Carnegie Medal, the Guardian Award, and the Whitbread Award.

ROSEMARY DAVIDSON has recently retired as Editorial Director of Educational and Children's Books at Cambridge University Press, and is currently Chairwoman of the Educational Publishers' Council. She runs the Broughton House Gallery in Cambridge, specializing in contemporary paintings and limited edition prints by artists from the U.K., North America, Australia and Europe.

WENDY DAVIS teaches children's literature in the sixth, seventh and eighth grades in the public schools of Carlisle, Massachusetts, and also has considerable experience teaching English as a second language.

PETER DICKINSON, a former editor and reviewer for *Punch*, is a prolific writer of fiction for both children and adults. His children's books include *The Dancing Bear, The Blue Hawk, The Seventh Raven* and *Tulku*, which won both the Carnegie Medal and the Whitbread Award. Among his novels for adults are *Sleep and his Brother, One foot in the Grave*, and *Tefuga*. His latest children's books are *Merlin Dreams* and *Eva*. Peter Dickinson is also the recipient of the Guardian Award and the Boston Globe/Horn Book Award.

LEON GARFIELD is the author of many historical novels, among them *The Strange Affair of Adelaide Harris, The Confidence Man*, and *The Apprentices*. His *Devil in the Fog* won the first Guardian Award for children's fiction in 1967. With Edward Blishen he wrote *The God Beneath the Sea* which won the Carnegie Medal, and *The Golden Shadow*, and for *John Diamond* (U.S. title *Footsteps*) he received the Whitbread Award. Garfield's most recent book is *The Empty Sleeve*.

CAROLYN GAVETT is production manager of the book division at J.I. Rodale Press in Emmaus, Pennsylvania. Formerly she was the vice president of a commercial design firm in Harrisburg, Pennsylvania.

VIRGINIA GOLODETZ teaches children's literature at Saint Michael's College, Col-

chester, Vermont. On the staff of the Vermont Reading Project, she functions as a "humanities scholar" for children's literature; in addition she is a project director for "Consider the Source," a reading discussion program sponsored by the National Endowment for the Humanities, and the New England Foundation for the Humanities.

VIRGINIA HAMILTON is the celebrated author of both fiction and nonfiction. For *M.C. Higgins The Great* she received three major honors — The Newbery Medal, the National Book Award, and the Boston Globe/Horn Book Award. Virginia Hamilton is also the author of *The Planet of Junior Brown* and *Arilla Sun Down*. For *Sweet Whispers, Brother Rush* and *The People Could Fly: American Black Folktales*, she was given the Coretta Scott King Award. Her most recent books are *Anthony Burns: the Defeat and Triumph of a Fugitive Slave* (for which she was given the Boston Globe/Horn Book Award), *In the Beginning: Creation Stories from Around the World*, and *The Bells of Christmas*.

BARBARA HARRISON is the coeditor of *Innocence and Experience: Essays and Conversations on Children's Literature*; she was the founding director of the Center for The Study of Children's Literature at Simmon's College, and has taught in the public schools of Newton, Massachusetts, and Washington, D.C. She is the author of reviews and essays published in *Commonweal, The Horn Book Magazine*, and *The Quarterly Journal of The Library of Congress* Barbara Harrison was codirector of research for *JFK: In His Own Words*, a television documentary of the life of John Fitzgerald Kennedy, and has recently completed a biography of Kennedy for children.

ETHEL HEINS, lecturer, critic, and reviewer for *The Horn Book Magazine* was adjunct professor of children's literature at the Center for the Study of Children's Literature, Simmons College. Formerly children's librarian at The New York Public Library and the Boston Public Library and school librarian in

Lexington, Massachusetts, she was for ten years the editor of *The Horn Book Magazine.* She has been cited for "Distinguished Achievement" by Douglas College, and received an honorary doctorate from Simmon's College.

PAUL HEINS, critic, lecturer and essayist, is editor of *Crosscurrents of Criticism: Horn Book Essays 1968-1977.* Formerly a teacher of English in the Boston Public Schools and recipient of a Ford Foundation Fellowship for study at Oxford University, he is editor emeritus of *The Horn Book Magazine,* the translator of *Snow White* from the German, and the recipient of an honorary doctorate from Simmons College, where he was adjunct professor of children's literature.

JANNI HOWKER is the author of *The Nature of the Beast,* winner of the Whitbread Award, and *Badger on the Barge,* winner of the International Reading Association Children's Book Award. Her most recent novel is *Isaac Campion*; all three of her books have been ALA notable books.

SHIRLEY HUGHES is the author and illustrator of many books, including *Lucy and Tom's Day, Helpers, Dogger, Up and Up,* and the Alfie books, of which the latest is *The Big Alfie and Annie Rose Storybook.* She is also the illustrator of numerous books by many important writers; in addition she has written two children's novels. Shirley Hughes is a recipient of the Children's Rights Workshop Other award, the Kate Greenaway Medal, and the Eleanor Farjeon Award for her contribution to children's literature.

GINNY MOORE KRUSE is the director of the Cooperative Children's Book Center, University of Wisconsin—Madison, and a regular children's book reviewer on Wisconsin Public Radio. Active in the American Library Association, she has served on the Newbery and the Caldecott Awards Committees as both member and chairperson, as well the Coretta Scott King Book Awards Committee. She is the recipient of several awards for her

contributions to the advancement of children's literature, including the 1988 Chicago Children's Reading Round Table Award. The CCBC, under her direction, is the winner of the 1989 John Phillip Imroth Memorial Award for its contribution to intellectual freedom.

JOHN LANGSTAFF, singer, folklorist, and teacher, has collected songs for children in such books as *Sally go Round the Sun, The Season for Singing, American Christmas Songs and Carols,* and *What a Morning! The Christmas Story in Black Spirituals.* He has also written the texts for numerous picture books, including *The Two Magicians* and the Caldecott Medal winner *A Frog went A-Courting.* Two of his recordings, *Let's Make Music* and *Songs for Singing Children,* have just been reissued. Langstaff is the founder and artistic director of the much loved *Christmas Revels* and of Revels, Inc.

JANE LANGTON, author of books for children and adults, is well known for *The Diamond in the Window, The Swing in the Summerhouse, The Fragile Flag* and the Newbery Honor Book, *The Fledgling.* For adults she has written and illustrated mystery novels, such as *Dark Nantucket Noon, Emily Dickinson is Dead,* and *Murder at the Gardner,* She has taught writing for children at Simmons College and Radcliffe College.

BETTY LEVIN is a sheep farmer, a teacher and a children's novelist, whose work includes *The Keeping Room, A Binding Spell, Put on my Crown, The Ice Bear,* and her latest, *The Trouble with Grammary,* winner of the Judy Lopez Memorial Foundation Award. Having taught at Pine Manor Open College, Simmons College, and Massachusetts Institute of Technology, she is also a former fellow of the Mary I. Bunting Institute of Radcliffe College, and is currently on the faculty of the Radcliffe Seminars. Betty Levin has recently completed a historical novel, *Brother Moose.*

PENELOPE LIVELY, an acclaimed novelist for children and adults, received the Carnegie Medal for *The Ghost of Thomas Kempe* and the Whitbread Award for *A Stitch in Time,* and has written many other books for children. Her novels for adults include *Judgement Day, Treasures of Time,* for which she received the first National Book Award given by the Arts Council of Great Britain, and *Moon Tiger,* winner of the Booker Award. Her latest book for children is *A House Inside Out.*

DAVID LOWENTHAL is the author of *The Past is a Foreign Country,* on the changing perceptions of the past and its impact on conceptions of time and culture. He has taught at Vassar College, Harvard University, the City University of New York, and University College, London. A Fulbright Fellow and a Guggenheim Fellow, Professor Lowenthal is also the author of *George Perkins Marsh: Versatile Vermonter* and *West Indian Societies.*

GREGORY MAGUIRE is the author of several children's books — The *Lightening Time, The Daughter of the Moon, Lights on the Lake, The Dream Stealer,* and most recently *I Feel Like the Morning Star* — and is both author and illustrator of a forthcoming picture book, *Lucas Fishbone.* He is coeditor of *Innocence and Experience: Essays and Conversations on Children's Literature.* Maguire was assistant professor and associate director of the Center for the Study of Children's Literature at Simmons College, and has also taught at Emmanuel College and Lesley College.

DIANA PRITCHARD PAOLITTO, psychologist and lecturer on education in the Program in Counseling and Consulting Psychology, Harvard Graduate School of Education, is joint author of *Promoting Moral Growth: from Piaget to Kohlberg* and has written articles and book reviews in *Contemporary Education, Harvard Education Review,* and *The Education Digest.* As teacher and developmental psychologist she has worked with children of all ages, and has taught graduate students in the Division of Counseling Psychology at Boston College.

KATHERINE PATERSON, the widely acclaimed author of historical novels and contemporary fiction for children, has written *The Sign of the Chrysanthemum, The Master Puppeteer,* and *Of Nightingales That Weep,* as well as *Bridge to Terabithia, Jacob Have I Loved, The Great Gilly Hopkins* and *Park's Quest.* She has been honored with two Newbery Medals, two National Book Awards, and the Lewis Carroll Shelf Award. Ms. Paterson has also translated two picture-book texts from the Japanese — *The Crane Wife* and *The Tongue-cut Sparrow. Gates of Excellence: on Reading and Writing Books for Children* and *The Spying Heart* are two collections of her essays and speeches.

JILL PATON WALSH is the author of two novels for adults, and numerous children's novels, including *Fireweed, A Chance Child, The Emperor's Winding Sheet, A Parcel of Patterns,* and *Gaffer Samson's Luck.* She is the recipient of The Whitbread Award, the Boston/Globe Horn Book Award, and the first annual Smarties prize. Highly admired as a speaker, she gave many lectures at the Simmons College Center for the Study of Children's Literature, where she was adjunct professor of children's literature, and also delivered the prestigious Gertrude Clark Whittall Lecture at the Library of Congress.

PHILIPPA PEARCE, internationally known for her children's books, received the Carnegie Medal for *Tom's Midnight Garden* and the Whitbread Award for *The Battle of Bubble and Squeak.* Her other novels include *A Dog so Small, Minnow on the Say (U.S. title The Minnow leads to Treasure)* and *The Way to Sattin Shore.* She has also written picture book texts, such as *Mrs. Cockle's Cat* and *Emily's own Elephant,* and short story collections including *The Elm Street Lot, What the Neighbors Did* and *Who's Afraid?* Philippa Pearce has also worked as a children's book editor, and as a scriptwriter and producer of children's programs for the BBC.

NEIL PHILIP is a critic, writer, folklorist and reteller of tales. He is the author of *A Fine*

Anger, a critique of the work of Alan Garner, and is also the reteller of such stories as *Guleesh and the King of France's Daughter, Drakestail Visits the King* and Hans Andersen's *The Snow Queen. The Tale of Sir Gawain* is his first full-length novel for children. He is the General Editor of the Penguin Folklore Library. With his wife he owns and directs Albion Press.

BERT PORTER teaches fourth grade in Carlisle, Massachusetts, where he has contributed enormously to furthering the study of children's literature by both children and adults. He has done considerable work on the development of the curriculum, especially in the area of folk and fairy tale.

DOROTHY POWDERMAKER is department head of the Newton North High School Library in Newton, Massachusetts. Previously she worked as a junior high school librarian for the Newton Public Schools. Through the years she has participated in various capacities in children's literature conferences both at Simmons College and at Harvard University.

ANN SCHLEE is the author of several historical novels for children, among them *Guns of Darkness, The Consul's Daughter* and *Ask Me No Questions,* a Boston Globe/Horn Book honor book. *The Vandal*, a novel of the future, won the Guardian Award; her novels for adults include *Rhine Journey, The Proprietor* and *Laing.*

BARBARA SCOTTO teaches fifth grade at the Michael Driscoll School in Brookline, Massachusetts. She is on the 1990 Caldecott Committee, and reviews children's books for *Appraisal* magazine, and general nonfiction for the *Wilson Library Bulletin* She is former editor of *The Book Bag* a quarterly of the Foundation for Children's Books, Inc.

FRANCES SEDNEY, coordinator of children's services at the Harford (Maryland) County Library, is an active member of the American Library Association, serving on administrative and organizational committees;

she has also been on the Newbery Award Committee, and is on the Board of Directors of the Association of Library Services to Children. She has been a lecturer at the Simmons College Center for the Study of Children's Literature and is well known for her enormous commitment to the child and the book.

ROSEMARY SUTCLIFF, recognized worldwide for her novels and retellings, has exerted a significant influence on the development of the children's historical novel; among her more than thirty books are *The Lantern Bearers The Eagle of the Ninth, Warrior Scarlet, Beowulf, The Hound of Ulster, Tristan and Iseult, Blood Feud,* and *Song for a Dark Queen.* Her prestigious awards include the Carnegie Medal, the Lewis Carroll Shelf Award, the Boston Globe/Horn Book Award, and the Children's Rights Workshop Other Award; in addition she was made an officer of the distinguished Order of the British Empire, and is a Fellow of the Royal Society of Literature.

ANN THWAITE is well known in England as a writer of children's books, an anthologist, and as a reviewer. On the adult list she is a distinguished biographer, having written the definitive life of Francis Hodgson Burnett. *Waiting for the Party,* soon to be reissued as a paperback in the U.S.A., a life of Edmund Gosse, and a life shortly to be published of A.A. Milne.

JOHN ROWE TOWNSEND is a critic, a lecturer, and a writer whose many books for children include *Gumble's Yard (Trouble in the Jungle) Noah's Castle, The Visitors, Dan Alone, Downstream,* and *The Fortunate Isles. The Islanders* received the Christopher Award, and *The Intruder,* serialized on television, won both the Boston Globe/Horn Book Award and an Edgar from the Mystery Writers of America. Highly respected for his critical works, *A Sense of Story, A Sounding of Storytellers* and *Written for Children* (shortly to be reissued by Bodley Head in a revised edition) he was also adjunct professor at the Simmons College Center for the Study of Children's Literature. He has delivered the Arbuthnot Honor Lecture, the Anne Carroll Moore Lecture, and the Gertrude Clarke Whittall Lecture at The Library of Congress.

MARTHA WALKE is school librarian in the Barrett School in Arlington, Virginia, and was previously at the Abingdon School in Arlington. She has contributed her immense talents as teacher and librarian to furthering the causes of children's literature.

TONY WATKINS has taught English at a university in Africa, and in schools and colleges in the United Kingdom, where he has spent several years in teacher education. Currently he is teaching in the English Department of the University of Reading, and is in charge of the M.A. program in Children's Literature. He has been a column editor of the Children's Literature Association Quarterly, has contributed articles on children's literature to journals in the United Kingdom and the U.S.A., and following his paper to the International Research Society for Children's Literature in Spain in September 89, (*Reconstructing the Homeland: Loss and Hope in the English Landscape*) now serves on the committee of the I.R.S.C.L.

THE INSTITUTE READING LIST

Recommended Readings
Natalie Babbitt *Tuck Everlasting*
Susan Cooper *The Dark is Rising*
Helen Cresswell *The Secret World of Polly Flint*
Alan Garner *The Stone Book*
Virginia Hamilton *Arilla Sun Down*
Rudyard Kipling *Puck of Pook's Hill*
William Mayne *A Year and a Day*
Ann Schlee *The Vandal*
Alison Uttley, *Traveler in Time*

Narrative Time
Peter Dickinson *Merlin Dreams*
Leon Garfield *Footsteps* (U.K. title: *John Diamond*)
Betty Levin *The Keeping Room*
Katherine Paterson *Jacob Have I Loved*
Jill Paton Walsh *Unleaving*

Memory
James Berry *A Thief in the Village*
Eleanor Cameron *The Court of the Stone Children*
Janni Howker *Isaac Campion*
Penelope Lively *The House in Norham Gardens*
Margaret Mahy *Memory*

Slippery Time
Alan Garner *Red Shift*
Jane Langton *The Diamond in the Window*
Penelope Lively *The Ghost of Thomas Kempe*
Philippa Pearce *Tom's Midnight Garden*
John Rowe Townsend *The Visitors* (U.K. title: *The Xanadu Manuscript*)

Time's Eye (Past and Future)
Lucy M. Boston *The Children of Green Knowe*
Gregory Maguire *I Feel Like the Morning Star*
Jan Mark *The Ennead*
Ruth Park *Playing Beatie Bow*
Rosemary Sutcliff *Warrior Scarlet*

Picture Book Time
Mitsumasa Anno *Anno's Journey*
John Burningham *Come Away from the Water, Shirley*
Virginia Lee Burton *The Little House*
Barbara Cooney *Miss Rumphius*
M.B. Goffstein *My Noah's Ark*
Russell Hoban *The Rain Door*
Arnold Lobel *On the Day Peter Stuyvesant Sailed into Town*
Charles Keeping *Willie's Fire Engine*
Jill Paton Walsh/Mary Rayner *Lost and Found*
Cynthia Rylant *When I was Young in the Mountains*
Maurice Sendak *Where the Wild Things Are*
Brinton Turkle *Thy Friend, Obadiah*
Chris Van Allsburg *The Wreck of the Zephyr*
Brian Wildsmith *Professor Noah's Spaceship*

Also Recommended
Nina Bawden *Carrie's War*
Eleanor Cameron *Beyond Silence*
Robert Cormier *I Am The Cheese*
Penelope Farmer *Charlotte Sometimes*
John Masefield *The Box of Delights*
Alan Garner *The Owl Service*
William Mayne *Earthfasts*
Ivan Southall *Josh*
Madeleine L'Engle *A Wrinkle in Time*
K.M. Peyton *A Pattern of Roses*

Source Books.
Gillian Avery *Childhood's Pattern*
Eleanor Cameron *The Green and Burning Tree*
Barbara Harrison and Gregory Maguire eds. *Innocence and Experience*
Paul Heins, ed. *Crosscurrents of Criticism*
David S. Landes *Revolution in Time*
David Lowenthal *The Past is a Foreign Country*
John Rowe Townsend *Written for Children*

Calendar

SUNDAY, AUGUST 6

5-6	Sherry Reception
6.30	Dinner
8.00	Welcome: Marilyn Butler, Ashley Bryan, John Langstaff, Jill Paton Walsh, John Rowe Townsend

MONDAY, AUGUST 7

9-10	Introduction: Barbara Harrison, John Langstaff
10.30-11.45	Seminar: Narrative Time — Jill Paton Walsh, Paul Heins
1-2	Book discussion groups.
2.15-3.30	Helen Cresswell
4-5	Leon Garfield
8-9	Virginia Hamilton

TUESDAY, AUGUST 8

9-10	The Child's Perception of Time — Diana Paolitto
10.30-11.45	Seminar: Memory — Gregory Maguire
1-2	Book discussion groups
2.15-3.30	Peter Dickinson
4-5	A conversation between Penelope Lively and Betty Levin
8-9	Philippa Pearce

WEDNESDAY, AUGUST 9

9-10	The Past is a Childlike Country — David Lowenthal

10.30-11.45	Seminar: Slippery Time — John Rowe Townsend
1-7.30	Free time/excursions
8-9	Susan Cooper

THURSDAY, AUGUST 10

9-10	The Inimitable Qualities of Time Fantasy — Eleanor Cameron
10.30-11.45	Seminar: Past and Future — Betty Levin
1-2	Book discussion groups
2.15-3.30	Creating and Recreating the Past: Gillian Avery, Janni Howker, Ann Schlee, a panel moderated by Neil Philip
4-5	Shirley Hughes
5-8	Sherry reception in Heffers' Children's Bookshop, supper in Queens' College

FRIDAY, AUGUST 11

9-10	Historical Figures in Contemporary Fiction - Jane Langton
10.30-11.45	Seminar: Picture Book Time — Ethel Heins
2.15-3.30	Rosemary Sutcliff
4-5	Seminar panel: Jill Paton Walsh, Paul Heins, Gregory Maguire, John Rowe Townsend, Betty Levin, Ethel Heins
8-9	Katherine Paterson

SATURDAY, AUGUST 12

9-10	Ashley Bryan, John Langstaff
10.30-11.45	Synthesis — Betty Levin, Gregory Maguire